*An Arkansas
Folklore
Sourcebook*

An Arkansas Folklore Sourcebook

EDITED BY W. K. MCNEIL
AND WILLIAM M. CLEMENTS

THE UNIVERSITY OF ARKANSAS PRESS
FAYETTEVILLE 1992

96   95   94   93   92   5   4   3   2   1

This book was designed by Ellen Beeler using the Goudy typeface.

The paper used in this publication meets the minimum requirements of the
American National Standard for Permanence of Paper for Printed Library Materials
Z39.48-1984. ∞

Library of Congress Cataloging-in-Publication Data

An Arkansas folklore sourcebook / edited by W.K. McNeil and William M. Clements.
    p.   cm.
    Includes bibliographical references and index.
    Discography: p.
    Filmography: p.
    ISBN 1-55728-254-4 (alk. paper)
    1. Folklore—Arkansas.   2. Arkansas—Social life and customs. I. McNeil, W. K.
II. Clements, William M., 1945–
GRI10.A8A75 1992
398'.09767—dc20   92-5544
                                                                              CIP

Contents

Introduction

WILLIAM M. CLEMENTS

In addition to and alongside their participation in the mainstreams of American life, Arkansans from various parts of the state engage in a number of activities that might be considered peculiar by some. They may sing songs that are not among the Top Forty, earn part of their living by wielding a broadax, speak a variety of English that may be incomprehensible to outsiders, tell stories with themes that conflict with late twentieth-century rationalism, and treat their ailments without the benefits of modern medicine—to cite just a few instances of "unofficial" cultural activities practiced by Arkansans.

For example, one of the songs in the repertoire of Almeda Riddle from Heber Springs (Cleburne County) was a ballad she called "The Four Marys." This song, which Harvard English professor Francis James Child, first president of the American Folklore Society, titled "Mary Hamilton" and included as Number 173 in his important anthology, *The English and Scottish Popular Ballads*,[1] probably dates from the early eighteenth century. It's one of several ballads, or narrative folksongs, which are called "criminals' last goodnights." Related in the first person, the ballad presents the bitter history of Mary Hamilton, a member of the royal court of Scotland who has had an illegitimate child by the "highest Stuart of them all." She cast the body of the stillborn infant into the sea and awaits execution for her indiscretion. Almeda Riddle usually began her version of this widely known ballad with a particularly poignant stanza:

> Last night there were four Marys.
> Tonight there'll only be three:
> Mary Beaton and Mary Seaton
> And Mary Carmichael and me.

The content of "The Four Marys," full of circumstantial detail, results from the apparent combination of two historical occurrences. Although Mary Stuart, Queen of Scots, had four ladies-in-waiting named Mary (their last names were Beaton, Seaton, Fleming, and Livingston), none of them appears to have been guilty of any improprieties. However, during the 1560s a French girl in Mary's court did have an affair with the Queen's apothecary. A century and a half later, a Scotswoman named Mary Hamilton in the court of Czar Peter of Russia was involved with an officer named Orloff. "The Four Marys" probably represents a response in song to these separate scandals.[2]

Up until the last generation or so, one of the ways that many rural Arkansans augmented their incomes was by manufacturing crossties to supply the continuing needs of railroads in the state and in other parts of the country. Every mile of railway requires about three thousand crossties. Even with modern preservation techniques, those crossties deteriorate rapidly and must be replaced often—particularly in damp areas such as the northeast Arkansas bottomlands. George "Mann" Alberson of Fair Oaks (Cross County) is an old-time east Arkansas tie-hacker who was producing crossties by hand as late as the 1970s. As a child, Alberson helped his father make crossties, and by the 1930s when he was in his twenties he had become so proficient in this pursuit that he was known as the "walking sawmill." After selecting a tree that was large enough to provide the material for an eight-foot crosstie, Alberson would saw it down using a crosscut saw. He would use the same implement to cut it to the proper length. The process of shaping the round log into a squared-off crosstie required Alberson to use a chopping ax and a broadax. With the chopping ax, he would cut notches in the log ("score-hacking," he called it) every few feet. Then he would "slab off" the material between the notches with the broadax. Since one side of the

FIGURE 1. *George "Mann" Alberson of Fair Oaks (Cross County) uses his broadax to "slab off" material in order to fashion the straight edge of a railroad crosstie.*

blade of this tool is unbeveled, Alberson could produce a relatively even surface between the notches. After he had hewed out four straight sides, Alberson would mark the completed crosstie with an X on the end, his signature on the completed product. Back in the early thirties, he could sell his product to a railroad representative for about fifty cents. Prices had risen to fifteen dollars when he hewed out his last crossties forty years later.[3]

For some students at the University of Arkansas in Fayetteville (Washington County) as well as their counterparts throughout the country, the focus of campus life is the Greek system, the social fraternities and sororities that have developed for some of their activities a distinctive vocabulary that nonfraternity members—"independents"—don't understand. In order to be invited to become a member of one of these organizations, one must participate in "rush," a period during which new students visit fraternity and sorority houses to look them over and, in turn, to be looked over. Fortunate students will be asked to "return"—pay a second visit to a group—and ultimately to "pledge" a Greek organization, while those who are less fortunate—the "culls"—will be "cut" (eliminated from further consideration), receive a "movie ticket," or get a "hatchet job." Potential initiates into a fraternity or sorority—the "pledge class"—spend a probation period called "hell week" during which they may be hazed, or "jacked around," and which may culminate in a preinitiation ceremony known as "silence." Throughout their first semester as fraternity or sorority members, pledges learn the traditions of the group and carry out prescribed responsibilities, such as answering the telephone and "hashing"—serving a meal at the house. Pledges perform their responsibilities on "duty days," though some may try to "skate," or shirk their duties. Among the fraternities active on the Fayetteville campus are the "skis" (Sigma Chis) and the "snakes" (Sigma Nus).

These specialized terms associated with Greek organizations represent only one strain of the often distinctive language of college students. Some of that language may circulate among only certain elements of the academic population such as fraternities and sororities, while other terms are widely known because they deal with matters that concern virtually every student. Though only a Greek might fully appreciate all the terms connected with pledging, any college student might characterize a classmate as someone who "dogs around" (takes his or her academic responsibilities lightly), might be tempted to use "crib notes" for unauthorized assistance on an examination, or might be wary of a professor who is reputed to be "bad news" because he or she frequently "burns" students (grades them stringently). And since most students, Greeks and independents, are interested in the social side of university of life, they are likely to "rally"—have a good time—whenever possible.[4]

Southwest of Magnolia (Columbia County) lies a swamp of evil reputation known as Bear Creek Bottom. Today it is full of quicksand and snakes, but stories about it in the past suggest supernatural associations. A black man who lived near the swamp and knew it well allegedly would never venture into it because he believed that the site was in fact a living entity. Once—so the legend goes—a man disappeared into Bear Creek Bottom. He had three good friends who decided to try to find him. However, they remained so long in the swamp that their acquaintances had given them up for lost as well. Finally, one of them staggered out of Bear Creek Bottom and collapsed on a road. When he was found, he had lost his mind, his body was mangled and covered with splinters, and his hair had turned completely white. He raved over and over that the swamp was alive. Some people thought that his condition was the result of witnessing his companions' dying some particularly horrible death, but others remembered the black man's opinion that Bear Creek Bottom itself was alive and punished those who violated it. The person who related this legend, or belief-oriented prose narrative, to collector Jan Calhoon apparently did not take it very seriously since he dismissed it as just "one story about the swamp." However, one can imagine a group of Boy Scouts around a campfire on a dark night finding the account to be much more believable.[5]

Despite the advances of modern medicine in ridding people of diseases and in making ailments more bearable, many people continue to employ remedies that do not involve physicians and hospitals. This is particularly true for ailments for which the medical establishment has not yet discovered satisfactory cures—the common cold and arthritis, for example—as well as for problems that are regarded more as relatively trivial inconveniences than as serious threats to health. For example, African Americans in such Delta communities as Crossett (Ashley County), Dermott (Drew County), and Eudora (Chicot County) utilize a variety of remedies for colds. One approach to curing a cold involves the external application of heated poultices. A particular kind of cloth—perhaps red flannel—will be soaked in a mixture of tallow, snuff, and turpentine (or kerosene), heated, and then applied to the sufferer's chest. Another external remedy requires the application of heated coal oil to the soles of the feet before going to bed. Other cold remedies require that substances be ingested. For instance, a mixture of red onions, tallow, sugar, and turpentine may be cooked down until it is hard and then it is eaten as if it were candy. Liquid cold medicines include May apple root tea, hot toddies, and a mixture of Black Draught laxative and whiskey. The coughs that accompany or follow a cold may be treated with syrups made from button willow bark and turpentine or from mullein and holly leaves sweetened with sorghum. A fever may respond to a bath in the liquor produced by boiling ragweeds or to a tea made from mullein.[6]

Almeda Riddle's "The Four Marys," the production of crossties by hand, the specialized language of students at the University of Arkansas, the legend of Bear Creek Bottom, and cold remedies of African Americans in the Delta are all examples of Arkansas folklore, the subject of the essays in this volume. But what are the shared elements that allow each of them to be called folklore? How can cultural stuff so varied as a centuries' old song and the very up-to-date speech of college students be subsumed under the same rubric? Answers to such questions are not so simple because defining "folklore" is not simple. Since 1846 when English antiquarian William J. Thoms coined the term "folk-lore" as a "good Saxon compound" to replace the Latinate "popular antiquities" in the English vocabulary,[7] his neologism's meaning has evolved and changed. In fact, folklorists, those who study the kinds of cultural stuff we've just illustrated, have proposed a myriad of different definitions and—unnecessarily, I think—have lamented the lack of exact agreement in those definitions. For example, back in 1949 editors Maria Leach and Jerome Fried put together *Funk & Wagnall's Standard Dictionary of Folklore, Mythology, and Legend,* a reference work that's still fairly useful for some of its definitions. They included a section of definitions of "folk-lore"—twenty-one in all. They probably could have included many more definitions of the term, but they solicited the opinions of only twenty-one contributors.[8] Since then definitions have proliferated with every introductory textbook, general survey, or anthology of readings weighing in with a point of view. Moreover, essayists in professional folklore journals directed at specialized scholars occasionally decide that defining "folklore" merits their attention. The result has been a lot of definitions, and at first glance these attempts at definition might suggest that the study of folklore is founded upon intellectual chaos. However, these definitions are in general agreement and may be synthesized quite straightforwardly: most of them imply that the term "folklore" includes cultural material that is traditional and unofficial as well as the processes by which that cultural material is learned and communicated. This synthetic definition of "folklore" covers the examples we've presented. It also leads into some of the features that commonly characterize folklore: its oral/aural nature, its variability, its tendency to assume patterns and formulas, and the frequent anonymity of its creators.[9]

THE NATURE OF ARKANSAS FOLKLORE

The word "tradition" lies at the heart of most definitions of folklore. For some people, "tradition" suggests that folklore must be quite old. In fact, a key phrase in Thoms's explanation of his newly coined "folk-lore" was that it referred to cultural materials from "the olden time." A rule of thumb used by some folklorists in the past has been that three generations, or about a hundred years, is the minimum age for something to be considered folklore. Therefore, a song such as "The Four Marys," which had been in existence for at least two-and-a-half centuries when Almeda

Riddle was performing it, is clearly traditional. Most contemporary folklorists, though, view tradition less rigidly. They've looked at the etymology of the word (ultimately from the Latin *trans*, across + *dare*, to give) and perceived tradition as a process that involves giving something across something. Once folklorists might have identified the something across which the something was given as time, and we thus have the logic behind the three-generations rule: for something to be traditional it must have been given across three generations in time. But if we identify the something across which the something is given differently—say, as social space, we come up with a more flexible approach to tradition. It becomes a process that may take very little time to accomplish and may—in fact, it usually does—involve people from within the same generation. So a person may tell a joke about a subject taken directly from the headlines such as the Challenger disaster or AIDS or famine in Africa (the stuff of folklore isn't always quaint and pretty) to a friend who then tells it to another friend. Within days the joke has become traditional.

The concept of tradition essentially means that the something that is given across has multiple existences. More than one person knows and perhaps uses it. But what is this something? It may be several kinds of cultural material. It may be a song, such as "The Four Marys." Or it may be a particular way of doing something, such as hewing out a crosstie with a broadax. It may be an idea, such as the theory that a cold may be cured by applying coal oil to the sufferer's feet. Or it may be a part of one of these kinds of cultural material—a line from a story or song (that is, a formula) that is combined with lines from other stories or songs to create a new song, or an episode from a narrative (that is, a motif) that is combined with episodes from other narratives to create a new story.

Most folklorists would agree that folklore is traditional in the sense outlined above, but they wouldn't stop their characterization of folklore there. For many cultural items and processes are traditional without being considered folklore. For example, it's been traditional that sonnets consist of fourteen lines since the poems of Petrarch in the fourteenth century. It's traditional for a Roman Catholic Mass to include a unison recitation of the Nicene Creed, composed in the fourth century. It's been traditional since 1787 that each state in the Union have two senators representing it in the United States Congress. These traditions, important as they may be as part of the cultural fabric of the Western world, are not folklore. That's because they are *official*. We learn about them and practice them within the contexts of the official institutions of our culture: the form of a sonnet derives from academic institutions, the recitation of the Nicene Creed derives from religious institutions, and two-senator representation derives from legal institutions, to cite the examples above.

Folklore, though, achieves its traditionality by being given across social space through unofficial channels in unofficial settings. Most often the unofficial channel through which folklore is given involves oral, face-to-face communication. Almeda Riddle, for instance, learned many of her songs from her parents, who sang them to her when she was growing up in central Arkansas. The narrator of the legend of Bear Creek Bottom learned the story from hearing someone else tell it, not from a written history of Columbia County. Fraternity and sorority members at the University of Arkansas take no courses in which they learn the language of the Greek organizations. Instead, they learn that language from one another, usually in casual conversations. Sometimes the unofficial channels through which folklore is given across social space involve little more than observation and imitation. So Mann Alberson learned to hack out crossties by watching his father and then imitating him. He didn't have to attend vo-tech school to learn this process. Folklore may also be unofficial because of the settings in which it is given across, for folklore is likely to flourish in institutions such as a family, a group of age mates, a coffee klatch, or a group of old men who have substituted a central location in the shopping mall for the courthouse square as a gathering place. Such contexts are more compatible for the transmission of folklore than the classroom or recital hall (though folklore may indeed occur in those contexts when the lecturer or the performer utilizes something he or she has picked up through unofficial channels).

Because folklore circulates through such unofficial channels as oral, face-to-face interactions in such unofficial contexts as family reunions or fraternity parties, it is often subject to considerable variation. A story that is told and retold by a number of storytellers is not frozen into a fixed text as a printed story might be. Even when a folklorist collects a legend or a folktale from an Ozark raconteur and publishes it, the story will probably still be circulating orally. The published text represents just one version or variant of it. Just as a photograph will capture one moment from a basketball game that proceeds in spite of the photograph, the printed text captures one instance in the ongoing process of oral storytelling.

As oral folklore is told and retold or as processes such as tiehacking pass from one person to another, several kinds of changes are likely to occur. A singer, storyteller, or artisan may omit details that his or her source included, may add something to the original, or may make substitutions. Omission may result from something as simple as memory lapse, for even though the memories of many active folklore performers are prodigious, the absence of a fixed, printed text for reference opens up the possibility of forgetting. But sometimes omission reflects something more positive, for leaving out certain details may hone the focus of a story, song, or craft procedure. For instance, many ballad singers have reduced "The Four Marys" to only a few stanzas that present the most intense of the doomed woman's lamentations. Focusing the ballad on this "emotional core" omits most of the story line, but it emphasizes a particularly memorable lyric that verges upon the tragic.[10]

Variation also occurs when a performer or a craftsperson makes additions. Such addition may result from the merging of different stories or songs into one piece. For example, very frequently elements of the familiar teenage parking legend concerning an escaped maniac with a hook who haunts a lovers' lane may become grafted onto almost any account of a spooky place.[11] Or addition may happen because the performer simply has supplementary knowledge to provide. He or she may draw upon past experience to enhance the folklore material, as when a skilled quilter adds an especially artful stitch to a pattern she may have seen. Similarly, someone who knows the history of a locale may augment a story about that place with references and allusions that were unfamiliar to the story's original teller.

Substitution as a process in folklore variation takes place when a performer or artisan deletes something from a source and then adds something else to replace it. For example, one of the most widely encountered migratory legends in the modern world is one which folklorists have called "The Vanishing Hitchhiker." This oral narrative—often localized in Arkansas variants to a stretch of highway between Little Rock and Pine Bluff—recounts how a young man picks up a young woman clad in a prom dress one night on a lonely road. She directs him to stop at a house several miles down the road and lapses into silence. When he arrives at the house and turns to let her out, he finds that she has disappeared from the car. When he inquires at the house, an old woman tells him that her daughter was killed several years previously at the exact spot where he picked up the elusive hitchhiker. She was returning from her prom.[12] This story, which has been reported from throughout the world and which possibly dates from before the turn of the century, has been updated with the substitution of Jesus bearing an apocalyptic message in place of the promgoer. In the early 1980s a story localized on Interstate 40 near Conway (Faulkner County) reported a mysterious bearded hitchhiker who disappeared from people's automobiles after warning them of the imminent end of the world. Sometimes substitution may involve only minor changes, such as when a storyteller relates an event heard in the first person in the third person. A classic example of substitution occurs in the title of a British broadside ballad that in its eighteenth-century original was known as "The Berkshire Tragedy, or The Wittam Miller." In this country, singers have variously retitled this narrative folksong "The Knoxville Girl," "The Lexington Girl," and "The Waco Girl" among others.[13]

Despite the tendency of folklore to vary from one performance to another, this cultural material also exhibits an inclination toward a certain kind of stability. Folklorists refer to this aspect of folklore's nature as formularization—that is, the tendency for folklore to utilize recurrent materials. Formularization may occur on the most basic linguistic level in oral folklore. The language used in ballads that migrated from the England and Scotland of the seventeenth and eighteenth centuries and that are still sung by Ozark performers maintains a certain consistency. For instance, the aristocratic heroine of various ballads is usually described as having "lily-white hands," and her heroic male counterpart rides upon a "milk-white steed."[14] Similarly, *Märchen* (a German term which folklorists sometimes use in place of the more generally familiar "fairy tale") such as those collected by Vance Randolph in the Arkansas Ozarks often begin with the formulaic "One time there was" and conclude with another formula, "And they lived happily ever after."[15] Often ballads begin with what's known as a "come-all-ye" formula, as in the following example:

> Come all my fellow citizens,
> Wherever you may be,
> I'll tell you of an accident
> That happened unto me;
> I know I was a careless lad,
> I know I broke the law,
> So I'll step out to hear them shout
> For me in Arkansas.

This is the opening stanza of an outlaw ballad called "The Arkansas Song" by its singer, Fayetteville's Harrison Burnett.[16]

Not quite so obvious are some of the stylistic and schematic formulas that recur in folklore. The pervasiveness of the number three, which figures in several folk beliefs and customs reported by Vance Randolph from the Arkansas and Missouri Ozarks, is a case in point. For example, many of the procedures advocated by "power doctors," folk medical specialists who emphasize supernaturally based cures, involve the use of the number three: a person who knows a secret charm to stop bleeding may pass it on to only three people; a wart that has been rubbed with a stolen dishrag will disappear in three days; a general cure-all requires the three-fold repetition of the phrase, "Bozz bozzer, mozz mozzer, kozz kozzer"; malaria responds to a concoction made by placing three drops of cat's blood in a jigger of whiskey.[17] Three also provides a basic patterning device in folk narratives. The hero of a *Märchen* may have to overcome three obstacles—perhaps a dragon, a giant, and a witch—in order to achieve his goal. Often the hero is the youngest of three brothers, and he may have to choose from among three royal sisters the one that he wishes to be his princess.[18]

Another example of how basic stylistic patterns shape folklore may be seen in the ways in which some of the student lexicon on the University of Arkansas campus is formed. One of these processes is what linguists call "clipping," which occurs when standard terms are shortened. For example, the verb "to pref" means to attend the final party given by a Greek organization during rush week. Shortened from "preference," use of the verb means that the potential pledge has indicated which fraternity or sorority he or she regards most highly and would most like to be invited to join. Another process of language formation is "blending," the process of uniting clipped portions of two separate words. University of Arkansas students may negatively characterize some of their classmates by using such terms as "crag" ("cranky" plus "hag") or "frip" ("freak" combined with "drip"). Alliteration also underlies the creation of some terminology; Greek pledges' "duty day" is an instance.[19]

At the broadest level formularization occurs in the repeated theme and plot patterns that recur from one folktale or ballad to the next. Among the formulaic plot patterns found in Arkansas folklore is the murdered-girl ballad formula. Several narrative folksongs—some derived from British originals and some apparently indigenous to this country—deal with the slaying of a young woman by her ostensible lover. Representative titles include "Pretty Polly," "Omie Wise," "Down on the Banks of the Ohio," "Down in the Willow Garden," and "The Knoxville Girl." In each of these ballads—some of which deal with actual crimes—the narrative progresses through predictable stages. The action begins with courtship activity. Perhaps the couple takes a walk through the idyllic countryside, or maybe the young woman thinks they are eloping. But something occurs that spoils the situation. The young woman may refuse her lover's proposal of marriage, or he may be eager to get rid of her, especially if she's pregnant and he doesn't want to marry her. In either case, he angrily confronts her, and she begs for mercy. Although he may use a knife or some other weapon to kill her, most likely her ultimate destination will be the waters of a nearby river or pond. Quite frequently the murdered-girl formula ends with the young man's expressing regret for having killed the "one I loved so well."[20]

Or consider the plot pattern of the standard "Jack tale"—a *Märchen* whose hero is typically named Jack. Jack is usually a young man of somewhat limited attainments who sets out to seek his fortune often to help out his poverty-stricken mother. On his journey he does a favor, sometimes quite by accident, for a creature who turns out to have supernatural power. This creature grants Jack certain magical gifts—maybe the ability to become invisible or a cane that will strike an adversary on Jack's command. Jack then encounters the characteristic three obstacles and uses the magical gifts that his supernatural benefactor has granted him. After overcoming these obstacles, Jack may become wealthy or famous. He often marries a princess.[21]

The occurrence of such formularized language, stylistics, and thematic patterning in folklore arises, in part, from the oral, traditional nature of the material. For even though that nature results in variation, it also encourages conservatism. When a new event or situation becomes fodder for ballad singing or storytelling, the performer very likely will plug that event or situation into familiar, established scenarios of development. Doing so will make the new song or story easier to remember and will contribute to its being accepted by the audience that hears it. For example, we would expect that the man who escaped the eerie forces of Bear Creek Bottom to have had his hair turned white by the experience. Such a physical change is so common in tales of supernatural encounters that it has become an expected formula.[22] So even if the originator of the story had omitted that detail, after a few other storytellers had passed the story on, the whitened hair would probably be mentioned.

Folklore's circulation through unofficial channels in unofficial contexts results also in uncertainty about the original sources of ballads, *Märchen*, quilt patterns, medical remedies, or other materials of unofficial culture. In a sense, each performer of a ballad and each quiltmaker is the creator, for he or she—as noted—may add, subtract, or substitute when singing or sewing. The ballad singer may re-create the ballad as she sings in order to suit the particular listening audience, the physical setting where she is singing, or the time allotted to the singing. The quiltmaker chooses the size for the pattern she sews, the color and the texture of the cloth that she will use in the pattern, and the way in which the pattern may be juxtaposed with other patterns in the completed quilt. But the person who first composed the original version of the ballad or who first conceived a particular quilt pattern may have long been forgotten. Therefore, folklore is often anonymous.

Yet anonymity is a product of the unofficial nature of folklore, not a defining feature. Very frequently, a scholar can trace a particular piece of folklore back to its originator. For instance, the sentimental folksong "Put My Little Shoes Away," one of the favorites of Noble Cowden of Cushman (Independence County), was written in 1873 by Samuel M. Mitchell and Charles E. Pratt.[23] But Cowden and hundreds of other traditional singers throughout the country who have learned this song orally are probably not aware of the identity of the composers. And even if they are, Mitchell and Pratt would be just names. Their composition of the song would not be perceived as giving them any special claim to it, nor would it prevent the singer from varying the song—"re-creating" it—each time the singer sang it.[24]

The unofficial nature of folklore has resulted in several important features of this cultural material and process. Most important is the traditional nature of folklore, a characteristic that is so significant that it frequently is a defining feature. But the way in which it circulates—in oral, face-to-face encounters or through observation and imitation—is also basic in determining what constitutes folklore. Such traits as variability, formularization, and anonymity are concomitants of the traditional communicative process. A wide variety of cultural materials has circulated by means of this process. In thinking about folklore in Arkansas, it's probably handiest to consider the various genres—or categories—that are most common throughout the state. Specifically, what kinds of cultural material are most likely to be a part of Arkansas's unofficial culture?

GENRES OF ARKANSAS FOLKLORE

The materials which comprise folklore in Arkansas represent a number of genres. These materials may be grouped into several broad, overlapping categories: conversational genres, performance genres, behavioral genres, and material genres.[25]

Conversational genres include those kinds of folklore that are likely to crop up in the normal, everyday interactions of people who do not necessarily have any particular talent or inclination for performing. All of us utilize folklore whenever we communicate with others, even if our utilization doesn't extend beyond traditional formulas of greeting (for example, "Howdy. Hot enough for you?") and of leave taking (for example, "See you later, alligator"). The most basic conversational genres of folklore are gestures and folk speech.

Two major categories of gestures play important roles in our daily interactions. One of these includes movements called "illustrators," gestures used as complements to verbal communication. We use illustrators when we describe the enormity of the catfish that we hooked but couldn't land, or when we point down the road while giving someone directions. The other important kind of gesture is the "emblem," which communicates on its own without the need for verbal accompaniment. For example, when two Arkansas motorists meet one another on a rural road, they may salute each other by raising their forefingers in greeting without taking their hands from their steering wheels.[26]

Folk speech is the verbal counterpart of gestures. The unofficial languages employed by Arkansans include distinctive pronunciations, vocabularies, and grammatical usages. When a people's language varies from the standard in all three of these ways, it is called "dialect," a term that we most often associate with particular regions in the United States. The dialect of the Ozark Mountain region, for example, includes distinctive pronunciations such as *keer* for *care*, particular vocabulary terms such as "gallynipper" for any flying insect, especially a mosquito, and nonstandard usages such as *holden* for the past tense of "to hold."[27] The term "dialect," though, does not pertain exclusively to regional speech. Any language system that varies in a systematic way from standard patterns of speech in pronunciation, vocabulary, and usage may be termed a dialect. An ethnic dialect has existed among African Americans in Arkansas for generations. Some of its characteristic pronunciation patterns include the substitution of a "v" sound for the medial "th" in a word such as "mother" as well as a dropping of the final "r" sound, the result being "movah" if it were spelled the way it sounds. The dialect of black Arkansans also involves some distinctive vocabulary. Thus, a black college student might refer to another student from his or her hometown as a "homeboy" or a "homegirl." A striking example of distinctive usage in African-American English in Arkansas is the omission of verb tenses when the verb's context clearly indicates the time of action.[28]

When folk speech involves only vocabulary variations, it may be labeled "slang" (usually when it's associated with a particular age group) or "jargon" (the language of an occupation). Arkansas teenagers of the late 1980s and early 1990s may employ such terms as "def" to mean "good," "generic" to mean "cheap," or "That's a fry" to mean that something unexpected has occurred.[29] Examples of jargon include "juggles" (which tiehackers such as Mann Alberson use to mean the material cut from a log during the process of making a crosstie) and "fairy dust" (used by employees at one of the state's most popular pizza chains to mean the mixture of oregano and Parmesan cheese sprinkled on pizzas).[30] One might argue that since going to college is an occupation, the vocabulary of students at the University of Arkansas discussed above constitutes a jargon.

Folk speech may also manifest itself in traditional similes (also called "proverbial comparisons")—phrases such as "mad as a coon in a poke," "as dead as Pompey," "pretty as a bug's ear," and "as scarce as snake's feathers."[31] "Proverbial phrases" are another kind of folk speech. This term refers to traditional descriptions or characterizations, often employing a metaphor or some other poetic device. Examples include Arkansas frontiersmen's claims that particularly delicious food would "make a mule colt kick its mammy" or "make a boy push his daddy in the creek."[32]

A more complex conversational genre of Arkansas folklore is the proverb. Used perhaps to comment upon someone's behavior or to defend one's own actions, proverbs offer traditional responses to recurrent situations in a terse, witty, often poetic format. For example, one may criticize a young woman's fickleness in frequently changing boyfriends by stating, "A rolling stone gathers no moss," instead of by directly scolding her. This proverb—which employs the poetic devices of metaphor and assonance, thus making it especially memorable—allows its user to invoke the wisdom of the ages (that is, all the previous generations that have supposedly used this proverb) instead of merely relying upon his or her own moral authority. But the same proverb might be used defensively by the young woman in question. After all, she might argue, who wants to gather moss anyway? Thus the meaning of a proverb emerges from its conversational context. Those proverbs that have survived in oral tradition for generations—even centuries—are probably those with enough flexibility in meaning to work successfully in a variety of contexts.[33]

Often, orally circulated stories, such as the personal narratives, legends, and oral history treated by George Lankford, enter into ordinary discourse and thus operate as a conversational folklore genre, but stories also fall into the realm of performance genres. Folklore in this broad category is characterized by being used in specialized contexts in which one individual clearly assumes the role of performer and another (or others) becomes the recognized audience for the performance. The most important kinds of folklore performance activity in Arkansas are storytelling and music, though other activities, such as riddling, might also be included. Riddles are questions that often involve the performer's clever manipulation of language and the audience's attempt to decipher the witty puzzle posed by the performer. Riddles are similar to proverbs since they frequently use the poetic device of metaphor, but while the value of a proverb depends on the hearer's ability to interpret the metaphor correctly, the successful riddle presents an obscure metaphor. For example an Ozark riddle goes as follows:

Crooked as a rainbow
Teeth like a cat
Guess a lifetime and can't guess that.

It takes some careful consideration—though perhaps not a lifetime's cogitation—as well as a knowledge of how language may be used figuratively to conclude that this riddle refers to a blackberry bush.[34]

Arkansans tell a variety of stories in addition to the kinds discussed by Lankford. Especially prized by folklorists have been the long wonder tales or *Märchen* collected by Vance Randolph in the Ozarks and by Richard Dorson from African Americans in south Arkansas. More commonly called "fairy tales," these stories usually depict naive heroes setting forth to seek their fortunes in a world populated by magical helpers and supernatural perils. Arkansas versions of such tales, most of which have long histories of being told and retold in Europe, often rationalize the magical and supernatural elements, thus requiring the hero to triumph by his wits and a little luck. One story of this sort which Randolph collected from Lon Jordan of Farmington (Washington County) is entitled "The Magic Cowhide." Our hero Jack is cheated of his inheritance by his two brothers and sets out to seek his fortune with only the hide of a cow.

After trying for a while to sell the cowhide at various houses, Jack gets tired and uses the hide as a covering while he sleeps. He awakes to find the sun shining and some crows pecking on the hide. After capturing one of the birds, he resolves to build a cage for it so that he can teach it to talk. But he hears someone coming and hides. Two robbers pass by discussing the cache of gold they have buried in a neighboring farmer's fireplace. After they have gone, Jack and the crow visit the farmer. Jack tells him that the crow has told him about some buried gold in the fireplace. They find the gold, and Jack and the farmer split it fifty-fifty. Then the farmer offers Jack half of his share for the remarkable talking crow, an offer which Jack eagerly takes. When later confronted by the angry farmer who claims the bird does nothing but squawk, Jack says that in order to understand the language of crows, one must sleep under a magic cowhide for three nights. The farmer offers Jack the rest of the gold if he can borrow Jack's magic cowhide. Jack thus winds up with all the gold and goes off to Little Rock to spend it.[35] Versions of this *Märchen* have been reported from all over North America. It also appears in printed texts and in archival collections in many European countries stretching from Scandinavia to the Iberian Peninsula.[36]

Animal tales also represent an important category of stories told by Arkansans. Dorson encountered several of these during a folklore-collecting trip he made to Pine Bluff (Jefferson County) in the early 1950s. While there he recorded a story from Silas Altheimer entitled "The Quail and the Rabbit," in which the rabbit, typically the victorious trickster figure in African-American animal tales, is fooled by the quail.[37] The pair are foraging for ripe fruits and vegetables when the quail comes upon a patch where peaches, plums, watermelons, and peas grow in abundance. Not wanting to share this bounty with the rabbit, the quail pretends to be injured. When the rabbit expresses concern, the quail claims to have suffered a beating and convinces the rabbit to leave the vicinity before the perpetrator of the beating attacks him. After the rabbit leaves, quail and family enjoy a feast of fruit and vegetables.

Some Arkansans have developed reputations for telling tall tales—stories in which the point seems to be to present the most heightened exaggeration as the sober truth. A good example of this kind of story is one told by J. R. Mote of Sheridan (Grant County). In matter-of-fact style, Mote relates how a hunter came across two deer proceeding carefully through the woods. He realized that one of the deer was blind and was being guided by the other, whose tail it held in its mouth. The hunter shot the guide deer, cut off its tail, and then led the blind deer back to camp where he could kill and butcher it without the inconvenience of hauling it in from the woods.[38]

While *Märchen*, animal tales, and tall tales are still popular among some Arkansas storytellers and their audiences, they may have lost some of the impact they had a few generations ago. But the art of storytelling still flourishes in the pithy, pointed joke. Jokes constitute one of the most important performance genres in the folklore of modern Arkansas. Characteristically, jokes are shorter than the story types we've considered, and they always involve a "punch line," which provides the often ironic point of the joke. Jokes may be very ephemeral since they frequently deal with topics of quite current interest. However, some jokes remain in oral tradition for quite a long period of time. A good joketeller may be just as much of an artist as an effective performer of tall tales since joke performance requires not only a good memory for the details of a narrative, but an ability to time one's delivery, to dramatize action and dialogue, and to gauge audience receptivity to certain kinds of material.

Traditional musical performance involves both singing and playing instruments. As W. K. McNeil points out in his essay on music, the "mountain" heritage that many people equate with folksong represents only a part of the rich heritage of traditional music in Arkansas. Equally as important, for instance, has been the blues, which flourishes in Delta communities in the eastern and southern counties of the state.

Behavioral genres of folklore include beliefs and activities that form a part of people's everyday behavior, but which—unlike the conversational genres—do not rely solely upon verbalization. Traditional games provide a good example of behavioral folklore. Children and adults in Arkansas play a variety of games that they learn in unofficial contexts by watching the play of others and through verbal instructions. This is how most people have learned to play the folk game of washers, for example. Although variations upon its format exist in the state, the most common way in which washers is played involves the digging of two shallow holes about fifteen feet from each other. The players—individuals or two-person teams—position themselves behind or beside one of the holes and pitch washers at the opposite hole. One scores by getting a washer into the hole or by getting one's washer closer to the hole than the opponent's washer.[39]

Often, behavioral folklore such as games incorporates material from conversational and performance genres, but the focus is not just on those genres but on the complex of activity of which those genres are a part.

For instance, a children's game may involve a formulaic chant such as "Red Rover, Red Rover, let Lyn come over,"[40] but the verbalization is only a part of the whole play activity. Similarly, a card game may involve formulaic folk speech (for example, "Who's dealing this trash?" or "Jacks or better; trips to win"), but again folk speech is just one part of the complex of play activity.

Traditional beliefs such as those treated by Byrd Gibbens fall under the heading of behavioral genres. Very frequently, such beliefs are never articulated at all. Instead, they become evident by what a person does or refuses to do. For example, among University of Arkansas students during the 1950s a folk belief was attached to the names written by members of each graduating class in the concrete of Senior Walk. It was considered bad luck to step on the Class of 1900, since every member of that class died a violent death soon after graduation.[41] The student who knew this lore might never relate it to someone else, but he or she might carefully avoid stepping on the tabooed spot in the concrete.

Traditional beliefs are likely to cluster around certain focal points. One of these may be the times in people's lives when they face important changes. Beliefs associated with these transition periods often cohere into rites of passage and express themselves in ceremonies such as the retirement party described by Robert Cochran and Michael Luster. Rites of passage attend births, graduations, weddings, and deaths as well as many other critical points in individuals' life cycles. Another focal point for folk beliefs involves periodically recurring events. These calendar customs include holiday observances stretching from New Year's Day with its black-eyed peas eaten for good luck all the way to the next New Year's Eve.[42] Cochran and Luster's depiction of a gospel quartet's anniversary observance exemplifies calendar customs. Providing a third focal point for traditional beliefs are those aspects of our lives that remain wholly or partially unknown or uncontrollable. Predicting the weather, curing the common cold, ensuring that the fish bite, and foreseeing who a future marital partner may be have all generated a body of behavioral folklore consisting of beliefs about cause-and-effect relationships and activities associated with those beliefs.

The material genres of Arkansas folklore include tangible objects produced according to traditional patterns and processes as well as the activities that produce those objects. Material folklore includes the traditional foodways discussed by Earl Schrock. It may range from the vernacular houses treated by Sarah Brown to art-and-craft objects woven, carved, sewn, or manufactured in some other way by tradition-oriented

Arkansans. The difference between art and craft is none too clear, but most folklorists would draw the line on the basis of function. Roughly, folk art includes objects and processes designed for the purpose of providing aesthetic pleasure, while folk craft is directed toward more prosaic purposes. But frequently the same object may have multiple purposes. A quilt, for example, provides warmth on a nippy January morning, but it is also a thing of beauty, treasured as much for its appearance as for its ability to protect one from the cold.

When considering art and craft as folklore, folklorists may think in terms of patterns, materials, and procedures. Any or all of these may be learned through traditional means—in the case of most material folklore, by watching someone else. Pattern in folk art and craft refers to the recurrent forms that particular types of objects assume. For example, the patterns important for traditional quiltmaking involve the overall shape of the quilt (square or rectangular rather than round), the layered nature of the quilt, and the designs with which these bed coverings are made aesthetically pleasing. Among the traditional designs used by Arkansas quilt makers are those called "Blazing Star," "Ohio Rose," "Log Cabin," "Little House," "Wild Rose," and "Dutch Doll."[43] Another example of the use of traditional patterning by a folk artist occurs in the work of John Arnold, a woodcarver from Monticello (Drew County). Arnold's specialty has been link chains carved out of single pieces of wood. He follows conventional patterns in shaping the various kinds of links that he incorporates into one of his chains—examples include what a folklorist has called "Single Links," "Double Links," "Ball-in-Cage," "Slip Joint," and "Step Design" (figure 2). All but the last are patterns that other carvers of link chains employ, and they represent the use of tradition in Arnold's art.[44]

Folklorists also concern themselves with the material used by folk artists and craftspersons. Perhaps in some golden age folk artisans used only naturally occurring materials that they harvested in the woods or grew on their plots of farmland. So a traditional basketmaker in the Ozarks would utilize weaving materials produced by reducing a native white oak to malleable splints.[45] Or a dollmaker might create dolls from apples or corncobs grown in his or her orchard or garden. However, folklorists realize that the creators of material folklore evolve with the rest of culture and may use materials from other sources. Contemporary basketmakers may import some of their material, and dollmakers may purchase necessary items at a discount store. Good examples of the creation of folk art from modern materials are the pipe man and the muffler man in

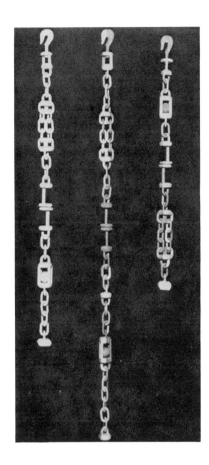

FIGURE 2. *Link Chains carved from single pieces of basswood and cedar by John Arnold of Monticello (Drew County) illustrate recurrent patterns called "Double Links," "Single Links," "Slip Joint," and "Ball-in-Cage." By permission of Arkansas State University. Photo by Diane Gilleland.*

Jonesboro (Craighead County). The former has been produced by converting a length of concrete drainage pipe into a recognizable human head (figure 3). The muffler man's body consists of an automobile muffler, and exhaust pipes form his limbs (figure 4). Both creations serve as eye-catching advertisements for businesses, the pipe man for a concrete pipe manufacturer and the muffler man for an automobile exhaust system service.

Folklorists also have an interest in the methods by which the folk artisan converts material into traditional patterns. Ideally, that conversion should involve the use of hand-operated tools: the quilter's needle, the woodcarver's knife, or the tiehacker's broadax, for example. But again artists and craftspersons have usually kept pace with the times. The quilter may now use a sewing machine for at least a part of the

FIGURE 3. *Jonesboro Concrete Pipe Company, manufacturers of drainage pipes in Craighead County, advertises its wares by using a traditional anthropomorphic pattern.*

FIGURE 4. *Employees at Three Star Muffler Shop in Jonesboro (Craighead County) have used non-traditional materials to create a traditional pattern.*

process of quiltmaking, the woodcarver may employ a jigsaw to produce the rough outlines of the fancy links he will finish into a wooden chain with his knife, and the tiehacker may rely on a chainsaw, if he doesn't surrender the whole crosstie manufacturing process to a sawmill.

These examples of conversational, performance, behavioral, and material genres of folklore in Arkansas do not represent an exhaustive survey. Instead they provide some idea of the scope of the material that folklorists in the state may study. In studying that material, though, folklorists are also studying people—the speakers of dialect, the storytellers, the singers, the players of washers, the quiltmakers. The people who use folklore are the "folk." Who are the folk in Arkansas?

THE FOLK IN ARKANSAS

When William J. Thoms coined the term "folk-lore" in the mid-nineteenth century, he and his contemporaries assumed that the cultural material designated by his neologism was confined largely to peasants, the past-oriented agriculturalists who had not been caught up in the streams of modern progress. The assumption that the people who know, circulate, and utilize folklore—that is, the "folk"—are isolated from contemporary life remains a popular misconception today. For most people the stereotypical representative of the folk in Arkansas would have to be someone from the remotest section of the Ozarks, perhaps an old woman who still lives on the farmstead her ancestors settled before the Civil War. Barely literate, she lacks such amenities as access to the mass media, a telephone, perhaps even electricity and running water. Her house is set far away from major thoroughfares, she grows almost all her own food, and she treats her ailments without the benefits of physicians or hospitals. Only somewhat exaggerated from the popular stereotype, this person has come for many to be the only kind of individual who might legitimately be designated as "folk."

Several of the components that comprise this stereotype emerge from the ways in which folklorists once conceived of the folk and in which many laypersons still conceive of the folk. For one thing, the folk must be isolated—and as uncorrupted by the influences of modern civilization as possible. Also, the folk are past oriented, doing things the way they've been done for generations. Moreover, the folk are self-sufficient, relying on few outside sources for food, shelter, clothing, medical attention, or other necessities.

The examples of Arkansas folklore that we've already noted should make it clear that the stereotype no longer reflects how folklorists in the late twentieth century conceive of the folk. Most certainly there are folk in the Ozarks, and many of them live in old-fashioned ways and practice considerable self-reliance. The stories, songs, beliefs, and other genres that comprise much of their culture provided a rich source of material for collectors such as Vance Randolph and John Quincy Wolf earlier in this century. And they will continue to be a valuable source of information for folklorists well into the next century. However, isolated Ozarkers are not the sole representatives of the folk in Arkansas. The concept of folk has expanded since the days of Thoms and now encompasses virtually anyone.

The only criterion that modern-day folklorists assign to the folk is that for an individual to be so designated, he or she must be involved in folklore. This can lead to a circular definition: the folk are those who have folklore. But that circularity can be overcome when we emphasize that someone becomes a member of the folk when he or she participates in unofficial culture by telling stories, using folk speech, preparing traditional foods, or engaging in any of the other innumerable activities that constitute folklore. Since everyone participates in unofficial culture at some time, everyone therefore is part of the folk. But if folk has become for modern folklorists merely a synonym for people, its meaningfulness has dwindled considerably. Consequently, what folklorists today mean when they speak of the folk is, in most cases, members of "folk groups."

A folk group is at least two people who participate together in unofficial culture. In order for people to constitute any kind of group, they must have some sense of their interrelatedness as well as a degree of stability through time in their relationship. The smallest folk group is the dyad, two people associated perhaps by kinship, marriage, or friendship. A husband and wife, for example, may have pet names for each other or traditional ways of exchanging information while in a crowd (gestures like pointing to the wrist to signify the passage of time or code words that have special meaning only to the spouses). Or they may have standing jokes about experiences they've shared or distinctive ways of referring to some of the other people, such as co-workers or neighbors, with whom they may interact. Other dyads that share folklore may be a parent and child, siblings, a pair of fishing buddies, or a team of bridge players.[46]

Folklorists have become more and more interested in the family as a folk group. Both the nuclear family consisting of parents and children living together under one roof and the extended family, which includes several generations living in different places, enjoy a wealth of folk traditions. Such traditions may be stories about family members. For example, an African-American family in eastern Arkansas shares the tale of a Depression-era ancestor who as a sharecropper's child stood up to the white landowner and prevented his family from being cheated out of their rightful portion of the farm income. Arkansas families also have traditional ways of designating particular family members; for example, a grandmother may be known as "Granny" or "Big Mama" or "Memaw" or "Nana." Family folklore frequently centers upon holiday observances. A family from Strawberry (Lawrence County) uses as an ornament for its Christmas tree a card received from the father when he was hospitalized during the holiday one year. A family from Jonesboro (Craighead County) compensates for a child's December birthday, so near the holiday, by making that date the customary beginning of the Christmas season, a day for decorating the tree and reading the New Testament account of the Nativity. Often particular family members become associated with the preparation of particular holiday foods so that Thanksgiving dinner would be incomplete without Aunt Polly's pecan pie. Of course, families also create their own holidays on members' birthdays and wedding anniversaries and may congregate once a year (usually in the summer) for a family reunion, where many of the family traditions may be displayed.[47]

Clearly one person could be a member of a dyad (or perhaps more than one) as well as of a family folk group. The idea of multiple group membership is central to the modern folklorist's concept of the folk. A wife may share one set of traditions with her husband in their dyadic relationship, another set of traditions with him and her children in the nuclear family of which she is a member, and still another body of folklore with her aunts, uncles, and cousins in the extended family. Furthermore, she will be a member of many other folk groups whose unifying feature may be ethnicity, place of residence, gender, religion, occupation, or shared recreational interest, among others.

The two most prominent ethnic groups in Arkansas are African Americans and those people whose ancestry is primarily Anglo-Saxon. Members of the former group cluster in the Delta areas of eastern Arkansas and in cities throughout the state. The Anglo-Saxons dominate the culture of the Ozarks and contribute significantly to the culture of most of the rest of the state. Most black Arkansans maintain a strong sense of their ethnic identity and may express that identity in conversational genres such as folk speech, performance genres such as blues and gospel music, behavioral genres such as Kwanzaa celebrations and soul food, and material genres such as quilting. People of Anglo-Saxon descent generally do not identify themselves ethnically except to emphasize their distinctiveness from those whom they regard as "racially" different. Such attitudes may be evident in folklore forms such as ethnic and racial jokes.

In addition to these two large ethnically defined groups, Arkansas's population includes a number of other ethnic folk groups. Among these are Native Americans (especially in the northwestern part of the state), Germans (particularly in the rice-growing belt of eastern Arkansas), Chinese (a presence in the Delta), Italians (in communities in opposite corners of the state), Mexicans (primarily in southwestern Arkansas), and recent immigrants to the United States such as Vietnamese and Hmong, who have settled in several Arkansas cities. Arkansans of Italian descent live throughout the state, but several communities have particularly large concentrations of Italians. In Tontitown (Washington County), a sizable Italian contingent exhibits its ethnic folklore to the public at the Tontitown Grape Festival each August. But throughout the year, the community's Italians share an ethnic folklore that includes traditional foodways, religious traditions that exist alongside the official observances of Catholicism, storytelling, and music. A less visible Italian ethnic community flourishes in Little Italy (Perry County), maintaining its ethnic folklore primarily through the food that is prepared and eaten. In southeastern Arkansas, Italians who came to the state to work as sharecroppers on some of the large plantations near Lake Village (Chicot County) preserve an ethnic folk tradition rich in stories about the sufferings and triumphs of their forebears.[48]

A person may also be a member of a folk group by virtue of where he or she lives. People from the same community often share stories about the area's history as well as lore about the best places to fish, pick blackberries, or get a haircut. Gender can also be the primary determinant of a folk group, and women frequently share folklore from which men are excluded. Men also engage in an unofficial culture in which women do not participate. A person's religious group may be a folk group to which he or she belongs. Members of a particular Southern Baptist church, for instance, will not only share the beliefs, worship practices, and polity that are more or less officially prescribed by their denomination, but they will also participate in a body of unofficial lore, including jokes about preachers and knowledge of the food appropriate for a covered-dish supper. Occupation also can be an important factor in folk group deter-mination. Every occupation has its body of unofficial lore that coexists with the knowledge and skills that comprise the primary focus of the job. Factory workers have a distinctive terminology for aspects of their work. They may also have traditional ways of initiating new workers. They may tell stories to one another about the insensitivity of management or the unscrupulousness of the foreign competition that threatens their job security. Another factor that may define a folk group is shared recre-ational interest. Softball players, fishermen, joggers, or gun collectors feel kinship with others who enjoy the same activities and may communicate distinctive folklore with them.

Almost any factor can be the defining feature of a folk group, and as long as people share an unofficial culture as members of a group, they constitute the "folk" in the contemporary folklorist's parlance. Conse-quently, while folklorists still seek out the ballad singer in an isolated Ozark hollow or a granny woman in the Delta who concocts her own herbal remedies, in reality they can find representatives of the folk any-where there are people.

THE STUDY OF ARKANSAS FOLKLORE

Folklorists study unofficial culture. Some of them are trained profession-als with advanced degrees in folklore studies or a related field, such as linguistics, anthropology, history, or literature. Others are amateurs whose interest in Arkansas folklore may be highly serious, but is demon-strated with less scholarly rigor. The contributions of both professionals and amateurs to the study of Arkansas folklore is surveyed in W. K. McNeil's essay.

Some folklorists study folklore for the sake of preserving it. Although folklore as a kind of culture runs no risk of disappearing, particular items and genres may fall victim to the natural processes of culture change. The long Märchen are not as popular as they were several generations ago, for instance. Some folklorists realize the importance of recording the disappearance of Märchen telling, even though they recognize that other performance genres are now more important. Another motivation for folklore study is the desire to make stories, songs, and other aspects of unofficial culture available to a wider audience than would ordinarily encounter them. Folklorists whose interest in the material is inspired by such an attitude generally are most attracted to performance genres.

Other folklorists see unofficial culture as a source of historical, psycho-
logical, or sociological information, that may be preserved with less self-
consciousness in folklore than in the more usually exploited sources of
such data. And some folklorists are interested in the material for its own
sake—because it constitutes an important component of what it means
to be human.

In order for folklorists to investigate any of the genres of Arkansas
folklore among any of the state's folk groups, they must encounter that
folklore in as natural a context as possible. This means that folklorists
must go into the "field."[49] For some folklorists, including Vance Randolph
and John Quincy Wolf, the field has been the Ozarks. Both these
collectors explored the mountainous portions of the state in search
of generations-old traditional material from the predominantly Anglo-
Saxon inhabitants of the region. Randolph was particularly successful in
garnering a wide range of folklore extending from conversational genres
such as folk speech to performance genres such as folktales and folksongs
as well as behavioral genres such as folk beliefs. Wolf focused his energies
more specifically on folksongs, especially the British-derived ballad
heritage.[50]

Randolph's technique was to participate and to observe. He lived in
the Ozarks most of his life and gained the friendship of his neighbors by
joining them in many of their activities. Consequently, he was able to
encounter folklore in its natural contexts—he was on hand when stories
were told or songs were sung. Wolf, though an Ozark native, relied more
on collecting forays in which he sought out talented ballad singers and
requested them to sing for him. Both collectors were scrupulous in following one of the cardinal principles of folklore collecting: accuracy in
the recording of materials. Although Randolph did not always have
access to a mechanical recording device, he took care to write out the
texts of the stories or songs he heard shortly after encountering them and
preserved as best he could the precise ways in which people in the
Ozarks rendered the material.

With the easy availability of inexpensive tape recorders today, folklorists are able to make accurate records of the verbal folklore they
encounter. Folklorists interested in behavioral or material folklore can
rely on photography—both still and motion pictures—to capture the
unofficial culture they encounter. Before setting out to record folklore,
though, the collector should become thoroughly prepared by learning as
much as possible about the folk group and its lore. Such preparation may
involve reading extensively in works of history, cultural geography, and

local color in addition to previously published folklore collections. Before going into the field, the folklorist should have some idea of what he or she is going to encounter. Once there, the folklorist attempts to locate talented folklore performers or individuals who know about the behavioral or material folklore of the group. One can meet these individuals by contacting someone who knows the community well—for instance, a local historian—or by visiting a place where people congregate—perhaps the feed store or shopping mall. When the folklorist has some leads about people to contact, arrangements can be made to interview them or to attend events at which they are going to perform their folklore.

Many amateur folklorists have their best luck collecting folklore from members of groups to which they themselves belong. Their "field" will thus be very close to home. If they're interested in family folklore, they could observe what goes on at the next reunion, making notes throughout the event and then writing a fuller account as soon after it's over as possible. They can approach family members who are noted for their storytelling or for their talents in organizing family get-togethers and interview them formally, getting taped versions of frequently told family legends or a detailed account of the intricacies of staging a fiftieth wedding anniversary.

Before folklorists present folklore in print, they must carefully transcribe their tape-recorded material. This laborious process requires the careful presentation of the folklore material verbatim as it was related— preserving everything that one's source said and adding nothing to it. Folklorists today also try to indicate something about how things were said so that at least a general sense of the source's manipulation of volume, tempo, and voice quality is conveyed. Folklore presented in print should also include a thorough depiction of the context when it was presented, including audience responses.

Print is not the only medium through which folklore materials may be presented. Audio recordings are an important way of getting folk music, for example, to a wider audience. Films and videos capture some of the processes of behavioral and material folklore. Museum exhibitions of folk arts and crafts join demonstrations by artisans as excellent ways of presenting material folklore.

The unofficial culture of Arkansas remains rich and varied. As the essays in this volume demonstrate, folklore in Arkansas continues to be one of the state's most valuable resources—one in which all Arkansans share everyday as they participate in the ongoing processes of unofficial culture.

Folklore Studies in Arkansas

W. K. McNeil

Like all states, Arkansas is rich in folklore and, like most states, has had a large number of people collecting these traditions over a period of several decades. This situation suggests that the recording of folk traditions has been carried out in Arkansas in a carefully planned manner, but that impression is misleading. Much of the collecting has been conducted by people primarily concerned with other matters. Moreover, the collecting has been spotty in several respects. A vast majority of the work has been done in the Ozarks; the varied folk traditions of other parts of the state have rarely been considered. Indeed, it is not unfair to say that much of the folklore collecting in Arkansas has only dealt incidentally with the state, the major concern being with the Ozarks. A further shortcoming of the efforts to date is that they have been generically one-sided. Folksongs, ballads, folk narratives, and beliefs have been emphasized to the virtual exclusion of all other folklore genres; this situation holds for the Ozarks as well as for all other parts of the state. Furthermore, many reporters of Arkansas folk traditions have been highly selective in whom they have gathered lore from. There is nothing wrong with this per se, after all even the most highly planned fieldwork is limited in some way. Any folklorist focuses on a specific group to study. The difficulty is that, with very few exceptions, those who have noted down Arkansas folklore have gravitated toward quaint, colorful, atypical rural dwellers, overlooking the urban residents and the more typical rural citizens. In effect, they have given a distorted image of who the folk are. In their defense, it can honestly be argued that such distortion has been common among students and collectors of folklore throughout the United States.

When one speaks of the study of Arkansas folklore one is primarily speaking of collecting activities, because, with a few notable exceptions, there have been few critical analyses. It is impossible to group the various collectors of Arkansas folklore by theoretical approaches for, in most cases, no specific thesis is involved; the recording has been motivated merely by curiosity, or by some similar nontheoretical reason. These collectors can be placed in six broad, but not rigid, categories: explorers and travelers, journalists and literary figures, local historians, members of the folk community who have published volumes mainly of their own traditions or those they remember hearing, students, and academics. The earliest of these groups, and the only one no longer actively recording Arkansas folklore, are the explorers and travelers. The first of these worthy of more than a mention here is Thomas Nuttall.[1]

Nuttall (1786–1859), was a native of Yorkshire, England, who spent several years as an apprentice in his uncle Jonas Nuttall's printing house in Liverpool. Then, in 1807, at age twenty-one, he went to London and a year later, in 1808, to the United States. His intense interest in botany was the motivating factor behind his move to the New World. Specifically, he sought to find previously unknown and undescribed plants in the interior reaches of North America. Shortly after his arrival he met Benjamin Smith Barton, a noted botanist who was immediately impressed with the young Englishman and hired him. In 1810, in Barton's employ, Nuttall set off on the first of many scientific expeditions that found him traversing much of the North American continent. Eventually he ended up as lecturer in natural science and a curator of the Cambridge Botanical Garden of Harvard, and he also found the time to write four books.

In 1819 Nuttall traveled from the mouth of the Arkansas River to Fort Smith, describing his explorations there in *Journal of Travels into the Arkansas Territory, 1819* (1821). An honest and sharp-eyed reporter, Nuttall missed very little during his stay in Arkansas and commented on much of it. Because his main interest was in botany, much space is taken up with discussions of plants, but his book is valuable also for its numerous mentions of wildlife, minerals, geography, as well as for its several comments about the Indian and white inhabitants. In a manner helpful to today's folklife specialists, Nuttall frequently discussed the total range of traditional life. Thus, he described the people, their houses, customs, amusements, etc., in some detail. Unfortunately, he also sometimes evaluated the people he encountered in ethnocentric terms. For example, note the following extract from his discussion of a settlement along the Arkansas River:

> Such is the evil which may always be anticipated by forcing a town, like a garrison, into being, previous to the existence of necessary supplies. With a little industry, surely every person in possession of slaves might have, at least, a kitchen garden! but these Canadian descendants, so long nurtured amidst savages, have become strangers to civilized comforts and regular industry. They must, however, in time give way to the introduction of more enterprising inhabitants.[2]

Nuttall was particularly interested in the traditions and customs of the various Indians he encountered in his travels and devoted considerable space to such matters. For example, in his comments on the Quapaw Indians he devotes several pages to their traditions and character; later an equal amount of attention is given to the manners and customs of the Cherokees.[3] Nuttall also was one of the first explorers to report information on the origins of place names, although his remarks were in the form of uncritical acceptance of existing legends. Nevertheless, he reported only place name explanations that seemed logical. Thus, he relates that Magazine Mountain received its name because "its peculiar form" reminded early French hunters of a magazine or barn.[4] Although this explanation has been disputed, it is the one still generally accepted.[5]

At the same time Nuttall was traveling through Arkansas, another notable personality was also making his way through the state. Henry Rowe Schoolcraft (1793–1864) was a native of Albany County, New York, who initially earned his living as a glass maker and later became an Indian agent and, eventually, superintendent of Indian Affairs for Michigan. Primarily because of his *Algic Researches* (1839), and subsequent treatises on the Indians, Schoolcraft is known as the father of American anthropology and folklore. Therefore it is hardly surprising that he paid attention to the folk traditions of Arkansas when he made a tour in 1818–19 through the Ozarks of Missouri and Arkansas in search of lead mines. He wrote down impressions of the Arkansas backwoodsmen he encountered in three books, *A View of the Lead Mines of Missouri* (1819), *Journal of a Tour into the Interior of Missouri and Arkansaw* (1821), and *Scenes and Adventures in the Semi-Alpine Regions of the Ozark Mountains of Missouri and Arkansas* (1853). Of these the latter two are the more important for present purposes.

Schoolcraft found Arkansas a most interesting place, because of the scenery and the traditions of the people. He noted several customs, folk beliefs, and aspects of folk life, and concluded that the inhabitants were little more culturally advanced than the Indians who lived among them.

> When the season of hunting arrives, the ordinary labors of a man about the house and cornfield devolve upon the women, whose condition in such a state of society may readily be imagined. The inhabitants, in fact, pursue a similar course of life with the savages, having embraced their love of ease, and their contempt for agricultural pursuits, with their sagacity in the chase, their mode of dressing in skins, their manners, and their hospitality to strangers.[6]

Writing about one day's travel along the banks of the White River, Schoolcraft set down what is probably the first example of folk humor recorded in Arkansas.

> The reins were now resumed, and as we descended the bluff the hunter lavished great encomiums upon the sagacity and faithfulness of his horse, whose pedigree and biography we were now entertained with. In due course of narration, it was shown where the horse had originated, what masters he had been subject to, how he could live in the woods without feed, how long he had been the fortunate owner of him, what "hair-breadth escapes" he had made upon his back, etc., etc. All this was mixed with abundance of the most tedious, trifling, and fatiguing particulars, so that we were heartily glad when he had arrived at the conclusion that he was an animal of uncommon sagacity, strength, activity, and worth. For, as in most other biographies, all these words had been wasted to prove the existence of wisdom where it never was, and to make us admire worth which nobody had ever discovered. The end of this dissertation, that had only been interrupted by the occasional stumbling of the beast itself, (which was in reality a most sorry jade,) brought us to within half-a-mile of their cabins, when they both discharged their rifles to advertise their families of our near approach, and in a few moments we were welcomed by dogs, women, and children, all greasy and glad, to the nailless habitations of our conductors.[7]

In the 1830s two travelers important in this history of Arkansas folklore made extended trips to the state. The first of these, George William Featherstonhaugh (1780–1866), was far less sympathetic to Arkansas than Nuttall, Schoolcraft, or most other writers of travel accounts. British-born Featherstonhaugh was employed by the War Department to make a geological inspection of a portion of the then Western frontier. As part of his job he visited Arkansas in 1834–35. His experiences and observations are recounted in a slim volume, *Excursion Through the Slave States*, whose subtitle, *With Sketches of Popular Manners and Geological Notices* (1844), accurately describes its contents. Featherstonhaugh was both amused by and hypercritical of Arkansans and often dipped his pen in acid while describing them. Even so, there is no reason to doubt the accuracy of his accounts of Arkansas folk, although there is much reason to dispute his interpretations of what he reported. Featherstonhaugh noted some customs and the like, but he is especially valuable for the large number of tall tales he recorded. Indeed, one authority has remarked that the *Excursion,* "though an ill-natured book, contributes substantially to the history of American humor."[8]

In 1838, three years after Featherstonhaugh left Arkansas, another traveler more sympathetically inclined to the natives came to the state. Friedrich Gerstäcker (1816–1872) was a writer of romances and travel books who came to the United States in 1837 and spent the next six years traveling throughout the West. During most of the years 1838–42, he was in Arkansas. Unlike the other travelers mentioned here, he was forced by financial circumstances to develop close relationships with the natives. Lacking a sponsor to fund his travels, Gerstäcker periodically received small remittances from his home in Germany, but these soon proved to be insufficient. Therefore, he turned to farm labor, hunting, and trapping to support his ventures. While this meant much hard work that took away from the time available for writing, it also meant that Gerstäcker became more intimate with the settlers than did most other travelers. This association with the settlers facilitated the collection of information about the traditional culture of the state, data which was noted down in a loosely kept diary. Two years after Gerstäcker left Arkansas, portions of the diary were published as *Streif- und Jagdzüge durch die Vereinigten Staaten Nordamerikas* (*Expeditions and Hunting-Parties in the United States of America*) (1844). This book is now usually known by the title chosen for an 1859 translation of the more lurid sections of the diary, *Wild Sports in the Far West*.

Because of the rather sensationalistic nature of much of the material reported in the translation of Gerstäcker's diary, his accounts were, for some time, considered unreliable. In recent years, though, scholars have confirmed that they are indeed trustworthy. While they are full of useful data, one should still realize that the books should be used with some caution because they occasionally offer folk legend as historical fact. For example, Gerstäcker presents as an actual happening the story of a young couple who spend the night in an abandoned cabin. The husband starts a fire, and during the night he gets up to give their baby a drink and steps upon poisonous snakes attracted by the warmth of the fire. His wife discovers his body the next morning.[9] But, when used with proper caution, Gerstäcker's diary offers much valuable matter about frontier dances, the lives of women, foodways, legends, and, of course, the tall tales, which have been accorded the most attention over the years. It is not inaccurate to maintain that from a folklore standpoint, Gerstäcker's work is the fullest and most worthwhile of all the travel accounts.

It is by no means certain that the travel writers always set down items of folklore because they realized their potential scholarly significance, although that often was the case. Sometimes the travelers were motivated merely by curiosity, because the folk traditions seemed odd or unusual to them. But, whatever their purpose in recording folk material, they left a treasure-trove of valuable data that except for their efforts would have been unrecorded. In other words, either intentionally or unintentionally, they performed a valuable service for later scholars.

It was not until the last decade of the nineteenth century that anyone deliberately set about collecting folklore rather than merely gathering it incidentally while being mainly occupied with other matters. Credit for that accomplishment goes to a woman named Alice French, who was then a highly regarded literary figure but is now almost totally forgotten. French (1850–1934) published local-color novels and short stories under the pen name Octave Thanet, and during the years 1883–1909 she spent much of her time at Clover Bend in northeast Arkansas. In 1892 she published an essay with an all-inclusive title, "Folklore in Arkansas," that is important as an example of the state of knowledge about folklore common at the time.[10] Despite the title the paper deals with only three aspects of folklore: dialect, songs, and beliefs. Thanet presents a survivalistic, nostalgic view of folklore that enjoyed great vogue among collectors of her day. According to these writers, folklore existed only among quaint and curious people who lived in places isolated from the mainstream of civilized humanity. This is, of course, in direct contrast to modern scholarly thinking, which holds that folklore exists everywhere, among all peoples, in all economic and age groups.

Thanet's theoretical biases are more understandable than the numerous erroneous and misleading statements in "Folklore in Arkansas." After all, her view of the folk and folklore was generally in harmony with that of a majority of the most informed folklorists of her day. The same can not honestly be said about her characterization of the Br'er Rabbit tales as legends. Legends are believable narratives that often call for some statement of belief or disbelief, situations that at no time have held for the Br'er Rabbit stories. Furthermore, Thanet's statement that "the whites of this region have no songs" was patently false and clearly indicates that she had a very narrow focus and was not a perceptive collector.[11] Thus, "Folklore in Arkansas" is a paradox in that it is a very bad work whose negative qualities are nonetheless informative.

Bad though Thanet's one folklore publication is, it is a model effort when compared with the work of Fred W. Allsopp. Although the long-time editor of the *Arkansas Gazette* produced several books of some worth to folklorists, he is primarily remembered for his two-volume *Folklore of Romantic Arkansas* (1931).[12] While it, like Thanet's essay, does have its value, the book has many flaws that greatly lessen its importance. Basically, the book is a poorly edited hodgepodge of clippings gathered during Allsopp's years as an editor. There is little or no documentation for most items, and while there is an index it is an inadequate one. Allsopp either didn't know the difference between fakelore and the genuine article or he didn't care. As a result, he mixes pop culture and non-folk materials (such as pseudo-Indian legends) with those materials that definitely have a life in oral tradition without distinguishing between them. Moreover, Allsopp commits the unpardonable sin of putting together a book that is almost unbearably dull in spots.

Having said all this, it must be added that *Folklore of Romantic Arkansas* is essential reading for anyone interested in Arkansas folklore. There is simply no other book that deals with Arkansas folklore as broadly as Allsopp's two volumes. Furthermore, mixed in with the liberal helping of chaff is a considerable amount of wheat. For example, there is much valuable material on place names in volume one,[13] some good narratives in both volumes,[14] and some useful data on superstitions in both volumes.[15]

One viewpoint that has proven irresistible to many writers on Arkansas folklore is the supposed Elizabethan character of many traditions. This idea is very popular with those who think of folklore in survivalistic, nostalgic terms, which, until relatively recent times, was the way most people discussed folklore. When considering "Elizabethan" traits of folklore, many authors have turned to the consideration of Ozark speech and dialect, and there have been disputants arguing both that Ozark English is Elizabethan and that Ozark English is not Elizabethan. Novelist and playwright Charles Morrow Wilson (1905–1977) felt that speech, and other aspects of folklore, were evidence that the Ozarks and Appalachia were both properly characterized as "Elizabethan America."[16] Charles J. Finger (1869–1941), on the other hand, maintained that there was no such thing as an Ozark dialect, an insistence that gained him more attention in certain quarters than his various writings on other aspects of folklore.[17]

No discussion of the journalists and literary figures who worked in the field of Arkansas folklore would be complete without some mention of Otto Ernest Rayburn. Although largely forgotten now, Rayburn (1891–1960) was a very important personality during the first half of the twentieth century. No less of an authority than Vance Randolph said that, during the years 1925–50, "Rayburn did more to arouse popular interest in Ozark folklore than all of the professors put together."[18] A native of Iowa, Rayburn spent much of his youth traveling to places like New York, London, and Paris. This early experience convinced him that he didn't care for city life, so he moved to the small towns of the Arkansas and Missouri Ozarks where he built a reputation as one of the most important writers and speakers on Ozark folkways. His influence was largely due to his several speeches and his magazines *Arcadian Life*, *Arcadian Magazine*, and *Ozark Guide* that he edited throughout the 1930s, 1940s, and 1950s. He did, however, publish a number of books that are valuable reading; the most important of these are *Ozark Country* (1941) and *Forty Years in the Ozarks* (1957). The former volume is part of the American Folkways Series edited by Erskine Caldwell and includes examples of just about every genre of folklore found in the Arkansas Ozarks. The latter is a well-written autobiography that provides considerable insight into the life of a man who had an almost lifelong love of the Ozarks. Rayburn, however, is significant for one other achievement, his *Ozark Folk Encyclopedia*. This mammoth, unpublished work consists of 250 typescript volumes amounting to at least 120,000 pages. This huge body of material was accumulated by Rayburn over a period of nearly 40 years and includes a heterogeneous mass of information on such topics as Ozark folklore, flora and fauna, scenic beauty, tourist attractions, outdoor sports, Indian legends, and Ozark characters. The

Encyclopedia contains many photographs, drawings, leaflets, and news-paper clippings that are pasted in. The work is supplied with an alphabetical index and bibliographical references in every volume. This extraordinary collection is housed in the University of Arkansas, Fayetteville, library.

A few other journalists and literary figures who did some work in Arkansas folklore deserve mention here. Marguerite Lyon, one-time writer for the *Chicago Tribune* and librarian for the School of the Ozarks, Point Lookout, Missouri, produced three books that, while admittedly popular accounts of life in the Ozarks, contain good information. *And Green Grass Grows All Around* (1942) ranges over many topics important to Arkansas, including stories and anecdotes, folk arts and crafts, and beliefs. *Fresh From the Hills* (1945) includes several examples of folk speech, beliefs, and a discussion of traditional cooking. Finally, *Hurrah For Arkansas* (1947) includes, among other topics of interest, legends of buried gold in Arkansas. Joseph Nelson was a native Arkansan who lived in Carroll County and taught at a school on the Arkansas-Missouri border in the early 1940s. In 1949 he wrote *Backwoods Teacher*, a very interesting and most readable account of his life as a rural Arkansas schoolteacher. Although folklore is not Nelson's major concern, he pre-sents much valuable traditional matter including songs, folk speech, cus-toms, anecdotes, and beliefs. Books such as Nelson's are important sources for folklorists because they give the material in the context of its creation.

Ernie Deane, a former journalism professor and a columnist with sev-eral syndicated columns to his credit, produced two popular works that merit attention from anyone interested in Arkansas folklore. His *Ozarks Country* (1975) is a collection of essays from his column of the same name, and it is especially good in its discussions of folk personalities. The book also contains several informative articles on most genres of Ozark folklore. Most important to folklorists is his *Arkansas Place Names* (1986), which is a well-researched compendium of information on place names in the Bear State. Deane roamed widely in his search for data on place names and, unlike some other students of onomastics, doesn't reject folk legends. Indeed, he considers such sources among the most valuable aids in place-name research. Despite the nonscholarly intent of the author, *Arkansas Place Names* is a fine supplement to the more aca-demic, and still unpublished, materials gathered in 1937–46 by Norman W. Caldwell at the College of the Ozarks, Clarksville.

Too often professional historians and folklorists disdain the efforts of local historians, which is unfortunate because there is often much of value in the publications of these largely unheralded writers. It is true that local historians are often inclined to romantic and nostalgic excesses and to intellectual myopia, or to other "violations" of currently accepted academic practice, but these shortcomings are by no means true of all local historians. Moreover, they often have a passion for, and knowledge of, their subjects that many university professors never acquire. But, perhaps, the major reason the work of local historians is often downplayed is that they are rarely professionals in the discipline and are thus perceived as not being serious about the field. Suffice it to say that there are both good and bad local historians just as there are both good and bad professional historians. It is frequently the case that the books and articles produced by these local specialists are important sources for both historians and folklorists. For the latter, the value of local historians' work is increased because local historians often work in areas where few folklorists have done fieldwork.

Most counties in Arkansas, and many communities, have a published history, a majority of them containing some folklore. There is little point in discussing these numerous works in detail nor is there space to do so, but a consideration of some selected books is merited. One local history that contains a wealth of data for folklorists is Earl Berry's *History of Marion County* (1977), which has a chapter titled "Folkways, Folklore, Home Remedies and Superstitions" and another on "Amusements, Entertainment and Recreation." Scattered throughout the book are discussions of gospel singing, singing schools, traditional sayings and metaphors, place names, stories and anecdotes, and other matters of interest to folklorists. What is most interesting about the book is the way in which chapters are constructed. Berry has each informant write a contribution and then sign it. In this way Berry gets around the scholarly trappings that bother many people and still provides the essential data. In other words, the necessary documentation is given in a way that may be more palatable to a popular audience—the ones who usually purchase county histories—than the more traditional academic manner. This method is also appealing to folklorists because these accounts are, in many cases, firsthand descriptions from people who personally experienced many of the events they talk about.

More traditional in approach is Rebecca DeArmond's *Old Times Not Forgotten: A History of Drew County* (1980), a history based on several hundred hours of oral history interviews. Using conventional historical documentation techniques, DeArmond's volume is unusual in that it contains more folklore than most local histories. Nearly all of the book's

several chapters include some traditional lore, but the history is especially well stocked with tall tales, legends, beliefs, folk medical practices,
and information about dances and play-parties. Written in a highly
accessible style, *Old Times Not Forgotten* is positive proof, if any were
needed, of the utility of not only local history but oral history as well to
folklorists.

While the works just mentioned, and some others not cited, are valuable repositories of folklore, their significance pales in comparison with
the work of Silas Claborn Turnbo. Turnbo (1844–1925)[19] was born near
Forsyth, Missouri, but spent his childhood in northern Arkansas. After
serving in the 27th Arkansas Confederate Infantry during the Civil War,
he returned to the Ozarks where he spent over two decades recording
interviews with residents of the Missouri and Arkansas Ozarks about life
in the region. The material he amassed eventually ran to thousands
of manuscript pages that he planned to publish. Unfortunately, the abilities that brought him success in gaining numerous interviews did not
translate into the ability to find a publisher for his *magnum opus*. Consequently, with the exception of two self-published volumes, both titled
Fireside Stories of Early Days in the Ozarks, none of his voluminous material appeared in print during his lifetime. Instead, the valuable cache of
historical data languished in various repositories. Finally, in the late
1980s some of it has been published, and plans are underway to print
major sections of the mammoth manuscript in the Greene County,
Missouri, Public Library.[20]

Turnbo lacked training in historical methodology, a disadvantage
that proved to be a strength. Having had no indoctrination in the proper
way to do research, Turnbo overlooked no source and few details. While
academic historians of his day were studying only major events and
uncommon aspects of life, he sought out minor events and everyday
occurrences as well. He conducted research not only through personal
interviews but also through correspondence with folks who related their
memories of past times. In addition, he visited graveyards and historical
sites, any place that might shed some light on what was typical and commonplace in an earlier day. Thus, he devoted much attention to schools
and school life, a topic that seemed mundane to many. Indeed, it was the
very commonplace nature of much of his data that probably prevented
his manuscript from getting published in his lifetime. Too many of the
things he talked about were likely viewed as matters that happened to
everyone, hence not worthy of publication. But what was considered
commonplace at the turn-of-the-century was anything but commonplace

within a few decades of Turnbo's death, and now Turnbo's manuscripts are considered valuable for the very qualities that earlier made them seem unimportant. Moreover, it is not only the subject matter that gives Turnbo's efforts their value, it is the documentation as well. He always identifies the sources of his information, something not all historians of his era did.

Books produced by members of the folk community include some of the finest, and most useful, folklore publications from Arkansas. One of the best such books is Wayman Hogue's *Back Yonder, An Ozark Chronicle* (1932), without question one of the finest nonfiction books yet written about the Ozarks and Arkansas. Hogue (1870–1965) was born in Van Buren County and later taught school for many years in Arkansas and Missouri before moving to Memphis where he spent the remainder of his life. *Back Yonder* was his first book and resulted when he returned for a long visit to the Ozarks after a forty-year absence. Hogue's autobiography is no detached scholarly tome but a very readable book filled with details about folklore and folk life set in context. Numerous folk tales are scattered throughout the volume, often along with information about the people whom Hogue heard tell them. In addition, dances, play-parties, beliefs, legends, and various other aspects of lore are treated in some detail.

John Quincy Wolf's *Life in the Leatherwoods* (1974) provides a valuable, albeit unintentional, complement to *Back Yonder*. Although not published in book form until the 1970s, Wolf's chapters were originally written for a Batesville newspaper at the same time Hogue was penning his autobiographical account. Both men are knowledgeable, accurate reporters, and, although there is a certain sameness to their books, they provide interesting discussions of life in two Arkansas Ozark communities during the second half of the nineteenth century.

In some respects the most intriguing publications by members of the folk community are three slender volumes by the late Fred High, the first of which, *Forty-Three Years for Uncle Sam* (1949), is his autobiography. High, a long-time mail carrier and postmaster of the now extinct community of High, Arkansas, later produced *Old, Old Folk Songs* (1951), a selection of what he considered the best items from his own large repertoire, and *It Happened in the Ozarks* (1954), a discussion of pioneer life and old ways of doing things. The books are full of information about ballads, folksongs, stories, anecdotes, beliefs, folk speech, and folk arts and crafts, but they are also valuable because High writes in a dialect that seems to be an attempt to reproduce phonetically his own speech.

Some readers may think this attempt is phony, but it is the same way in which High wrote his personal letters and business communication. Thus, although perhaps unintentional, he preserves some old-time examples of folk speech, such as sold for soul, that are rarely heard today.[21] High also provides some very good examples of tales, including several attributed to a locally famous storyteller named Britt. Although High referred to these as "Britt tales," the printer, evidently thinking this was a mistake, changed it to "Bright tales." Each of the three books is hard going because of the spelling and dialect used, but they are very worthwhile reading for anyone interested in Arkansas folklore.

Even more significant is *A Singer and Her Songs* (1971), an edition of fifty-two songs as performed by Greer's Ferry ballad singer Almeda Riddle. This book was put together by folklorist Roger Abrahams from many interviews held over a period of years with Mrs. Riddle. It is important not only for providing both texts and tunes but also for including Almeda's ideas about what makes a song or ballad worth remembering and for her comments about the various sources of her extensive repertoire. Not every aspect of the book is admirable. Abrahams tells nothing about his editorial practices and pays too little attention to potential commercial influences on Mrs. Riddle's singing. Still, as one of the few "folk autobiographies," the volume is very useful. A yet unpublished revised edition, titled *Preserving Even the Scraps*, promises to be even more important because it deals with nonmusical aspects of Almeda's tradition in greater detail.[22]

Equally significant is *The Hell-Bound Train: A Cowboy Songbook* (1973), one hundred songs compiled by Glenn Ohrlin, a traditional singer from Mountain View. A native of Minneapolis, Minnesota, Ohrlin moved to Arkansas in 1954 after spending several years on the rodeo circuit. As a youngster he learned songs from various members of his family and continued picking up numbers during his time as a rodeo cowboy and after his move to Mountain View. Thus, his repertoire consists of material from many parts of the United States, but that fact doesn't make him atypical, because folksingers, in Arkansas or elsewhere, have always performed songs from various other regions. Unlike most folksong collections, *The Hell-Bound Train* contains music for every song, and in addition includes Ohrlin's extensive comments about the selections and a thorough biblio-discography by Harlan Daniel, himself a native of Arkansas. This is one of the few folksong collections that gives proper attention to the influence of mass media on folksong repertoires. Ohrlin provides considerable detail about Sam Hess, Raymond Sanders, and other traditional singers from Mountain View. All of these features make the book a valuable addition not only to Arkansas folksong literature but to American folksong literature as well.

A work similar in intent to *Back Yonder* is James C. Hefley's *Way Back in the Hills* (1985). Indeed, there is some similarity between the authors of the two books and the reasons why they wrote their respective volumes. Hogue returned to his home community after a forty-year absence and decided to write his account of life in the Ozark community where he grew up in the 1870s and 1880s. Hefley was not so long removed from the Newton County of his childhood, but he also lived outside Arkansas, earning his living as a free-lance writer and teacher in Missouri. Reflecting on his youth in a tiny Arkansas community, he too decided to set down his life story. Hefley had the benefit of modern technological inventions that were unavailable to Hogue in the early thirties, and he made use not only of his memory but of tape-recorded interviews with several relatives and friends who shared his experiences growing up on Big Creek. Better written than many such chronicles, *Way Back in the Hills* often verges on romantic excess, but it still is an accurate, but little publicized account of life in one rural Arkansas community.

The most extensive collection of Ozark folklore, much of it from Arkansas, gathered by a person from a folk background—that of Max Hunter—remains unpublished. Hunter's collection is strongest on folksongs (there are over two thousand items), but it also contains numerous proverbs, fiddle tunes, jokes, and miscellaneous materials. A native of Springfield, Missouri, Hunter's exposure to Ozark folksongs came from his own family. A brother sang and played guitar and harmonica, two sisters played piano by "ear," and his mother had an extensive repertoire of ballads. In 1956 Hunter, who is a musician himself, performed several ballads learned from his family at the Ozark Folk Festival in Eureka Springs, Arkansas. Vance Randolph and Mary Celestia Parler heard Max and encouraged him to collect traditional songs, an activity he enjoys and for which he has natural abilities. A patient fieldworker, Hunter has occasionally spent an entire day with an informant just to obtain tapes of songs, a luxury most collectors do not have. Unlike many other ballad hunters, Max maintains contact with singers even after recording their material. Some of the selections Hunter gathered in several years of active seeking of old songs are included on *Ozark Folksongs and Ballads*.[23] Eleven of the fourteen selections on this 1963 album are songs Max acquired from Arkansas singers. Most of Hunter's tapes are in the Springfield-Greene County Library in Springfield, Missouri. This collection includes an index and considerable data about recording sessions and informants. The song materials are more thoroughly indexed than the nonmusical portions of the collection, and there are some aspects of Hunter's fieldwork that scholars may find troubling. One is his insistence on obtaining only "Ozark" material (most pronounced in regard to songs), by which he means those pieces that either originated in or were learned in the mountain region. For example, he erased a tape of "The Maid of Dundee" upon finding out that Almeda Riddle learned part of the song in the Ozarks, another section in California, and yet a third part from an eastern singer. Such an attitude implies that the bearers of Ozark folk traditions are, or have been, totally isolated from outside influences. As with all stereotypes this one is true to an extent but far less so than many people believe.

Another area of selectivity that Hunter shares with most folklore collectors is his emphasis on recording only the traditional items in folk repertoires. This is a problem he recognizes and notes that it would have been better to have recorded a person's total repertoire, not only to gain a better understanding of what each individual knew but also to achieve a greater comprehension of the material that most appealed to them. Even so, Hunter's mammoth collection as it stands is so important that its significance can hardly be overstated.

College students, most of them at the graduate school level, have made a number of folklore collections in Arkansas, primarily in the Ozarks and mainly dealing with ballads and folksongs. Unfortunately, most of these works are unpublished and therefore generally inaccessible. Perhaps the earliest such study of value is Bonita Musgrave's 1929 M.A. thesis at the University of Arkansas, "A Study of the Home and Local Crafts of the Pioneers of Washington County, Arkansas." The slender seventy-seven-page thesis is full of excellent brief descriptions of house building, furniture making, spinning, weaving, dyeing, tanning leather, shoe making, drying fruits and vegetables, and soap making, based on extensive interviews. Musgrave also includes several photographs of craft objects and the like in this study of Arkansas folk life in the years before 1870. In a shorter study Joanne Farb provides one of the few published investigations of southwest Arkansas folklore in "Piecin' and Quiltin': Two Quilters in Southwest Arkansas."[24] This examination of the quilting techniques of two women includes illustrations and discussions of patterns, style variations, and marketing practices.

There are two good published student papers on folk narrative. One of these, William Harris's "The White River Monster of Jackson County,

Arkansas: A Historical Summary of Oral and Popular Growth and Change in a Legend" is accurately described in the title.[25] Harris interviewed twenty-two informants and provides a detailed analysis of their legend texts dealing with a monster reportedly sighted in the White River near Newport, Arkansas, in 1937. In "Ralph E. Hughey: Northwest Arkansas Storyteller" James Grover demonstrates that, contrary to the popular image, bearers of folk traditions are not always elderly and uneducated. His informant, Ralph E. Hughey, is both young and a college graduate. Admittedly, he is no ordinary informant; he uses no slang and speaks in what seems an artificial, stilted manner. Still, there is little reason to doubt the material's authenticity, for Hughey's idiosyncratic style is, as Grover suggests, largely a result of his aesthetic sense and his choice of a future career (he planned to be a lawyer). Grover's article is important as a good collection from a single informant and as one of the few publications dealing with Arkansas memorates (narratives of actual events, even of happenings personally experienced by the narrator).

But, as already noted, most student collections are of ballads and folksongs. Some, like Maude Wright's "Folk Music of Arkansas," which consists of eighteen songs and four fiddle tunes she gathered around her hometown of Hot Springs, have misleading titles. One, John Stilley's "Ozark Mountain Folk Songs," based on a collection made while he was a music professor at the College of the Ozarks, Clarksville, has disappeared. Stilley submitted part of his material as an M.A. thesis to the music department at Northwestern University in 1942, and he planned to publish the entire collection but, apparently, abandoned the project. Northwestern has lost its copy of his thesis, so none of Stilley's material is currently available to researchers.

One of the most significant early student ballad collections is Theodore R. Garrison's "Forty-Five Folk Songs Collected From Searcy County, Arkansas," an M.A. thesis submitted in 1944 to the English department at the University of Arkansas. Garrison, who is now retired from a university teaching position in Illinois, recorded this material from eleven singers in and near his hometown of Marshall. Because he knew most of these people from early childhood, Garrison includes many details that the typical casual fieldworker might not have obtained. He presents forty-seven texts and thirty-two tunes, but the division of selections makes it clear that Garrison shares the bias common to many ballad collectors, including the great nineteenth-century ballad scholar Francis Child. In general, the Child Ballads are the oldest narrative songs in folk tradition, and Child, and most other folklorists, consider variants and versions of the 305 ballads he canonized in his *The English and Scottish Popular Ballads* (1882–1898) the best of the folk ballads. His material is broken down into three categories: "The Child Ballads," "Other Ballads and Songs of Certain or Probable British Origin," and "Ballads and Songs of American or Uncertain Origin."

A number of excellent local ballads and variants are given in Garrison's manuscript. One of the most interesting is an adaptation of Child 200, "When Carnal First Came to Arkansas," which transplants the European story to Searcy County.[26] "Lee Mills," a murderer's good-night ballad, is another number first reported by Garrison. Unfortunately, his notes on the story behind the song are filled with inaccuracies. This thesis has not been published, but Garrison used some of the material in two articles printed in the *Arkansas Historical Quarterly*.[27]

In 1952, Irene Jones Carlisle, a major informant for Vance Randolph when he was collecting material for his *Ozark Folksongs*, earned an M.A. in English from the University of Arkansas with her "Fifty Ballads and Songs from Northwest Arkansas." She gathered this collection from twenty-one informants from Washington, Carroll, and Sebastian counties. Carlisle's manuscript, with tunes for most entries, variants for some titles, notes about informants and individual recording sessions, and a listing of selections under titles given by singers, is the best of the Child-and-other student works. Generally her annotations are good, but the discussions of "Utah Carl," "Jim Blake," "George Allen," and "Behind the Great Wall," for example, indicate that Carlisle is unaware of potential mass media influences on the traditional life of these songs. Each of the above songs, and others in Carlisle's thesis, have frequently appeared on commercial recordings.

Among student ballad collectors only Dianne Dugaw avoids the Child-and-other prejudice inherited from the early twentieth-century ballad hunters. Under the title "Ozark Folksongs" her collection was submitted in 1973 as an M.A. thesis in music at the University of Colorado. Dugaw met the Ward family, her principal informants, through a college friend whose grandparents and relatives lived in the Ozarks. Over a period of several years Dugaw made many trips to Searcy County and developed a friendship with the people she eventually recorded.

Dugaw presents texts in the order in which they were collected rather than according to categories based on the aesthetics of folklorists. Although she sought old songs, she was not especially concerned with finding Child ballads or memory culture. Her chief interest was the living folksong tradition of the area. She encountered only a few persons who performed the oldest ballads, and two of these were reluctant informants. My own fieldwork indicates that Dugaw's experience is typical and suggests that collectors who have concerned themselves mainly with Child ballads are guilty of distorting the picture of Arkansas folksinging. While such songs are known, they are far less common than most folksong collectors imply.

Dugaw also breaks precedent in giving attention to mass media influences. She acknowledges the role commercial recordings have played in maintaining folksongs. Thus, her headnotes contain liberal references to hillbilly 78s. True, she does miss some, such as "Jewel On Earth," which she fails to identify as Roy Acuff's "Precious Jewel" rewrite of "Hills of Roan County," but in calling attention to mass media recordings, Dugaw differs from most previous folksong collectors.

Among the other positive features of Dugaw's thesis are the considerable description of informants, the extensive analysis of both the music and texts, the inclusion of all types of numbers in a singer's repertoire, and perceptive remarks concerning the collection. These aspects make this an important study that anyone interested in Arkansas, or Ozark, folksong should be familiar with. In 1983 Dugaw published a revised version of her thesis, and she promises to contribute even further to the field because she is presently engaged in an intensive study of one of her main informants.[28]

Like the other groups mentioned here, most of the academics involved in the study of Arkansas folklore have been primarily interested in folksongs and ballads, but they have also produced a sizeable body of work on nonmusical lore. Earliest of these academics was Joseph William Carr, a professor at the University of Arkansas, who published five articles on northwest Arkansas folk speech early in the twentieth century.[29] He includes approximately twenty-two hundred entries, with some duplication, in the various papers, taking his examples from fieldwork and from publications such as Marion Hughes's *Three Years in Arkansaw*. Carr's methodology is understandably dated, but his articles are nonetheless valuable documents. Basically he lists words in alphabetical order with comments on pronunciation, peculiarities of grammar and syntax, and the like. Unfortunately, he says nothing about his informants—how often they used the words, the contexts in which the words were used, and the methods by which words were obtained. Still, Carr's work is more accessible to the general reader than the much more esoteric publications of the Arkansas Language Survey, begun by Gary N. Underwood at the University of Arkansas in 1970. Anyone wishing to read about modern dialect studies in Arkansas should consult three of the least technical publications in the field, two essays by Underwood and an article by his one-time associate, Bethany K. Dumas. In his essays, "Razorback Slang" and "Some Characteristics of Slang Used at the University of Arkansas at Fayetteville," Underwood discusses material collected from 1970 to 1972. He contends that the unusual mixture of rural and urban slang results from students from rural backgrounds coming to a university environment. Dumas's "The Morphology of Newton County, Arkansas: An Exercise in Studying Ozark Dialect" is based on information obtained from a questionnaire answered by twenty carefully selected informants living in Newton County. Dumas concludes that the Ben Hur-Moore area where most of these people live is an important relic area, i.e., a geographic section noted for retaining traditional terms.

Folk games is a topic that has received relatively little attention among folklorists nationally and, of course, in Arkansas as well. A few academics have, however, given the subject some consideration. Among these are Paul G. Brewster, an Indiana native who taught for a time at Henderson College in Arkadelphia and is one of the few American folklorists to earn an international reputation as a game scholar.[30] In common with most students of folk games, Brewster has been mainly concerned with children's games; his major work in this genre is *American Nonsinging Games* (1953). This book contains detailed descriptions of one hundred and fifty children's games, most of them known in the Midwest, fifteen from Arkansas. Brewster does not rely solely on adult informants supplying memory culture as many other game collectors have done, but his book is not ideal. Documentation is poor, no informants are named, and little is said about collecting methods—when, or specifically where, the information was obtained. Possibly many of these items were not personally recorded by Brewster but by some of his students. Whatever the situation, the inadequate documentation makes the book less useful than it otherwise would be.

A better job of documentation is provided by Robert Cochran in his article "The Interlude of Game: A Study of Washers."[31] Cochran's essay is a model study of a folk game and is based on a series of interviews, letters, and published references. He traces the history and geographic distribution of the game, and his full description includes rules, illustrations of the play area, and social aspects of the event. Cochran's essay is one of the few folk game studies that deals with material traditional among adults. "The Interlude of Game" is a masterful article that demonstrates not only what a specific game is but also says much about why it is popular and persists in tradition.

Although academics have paid little attention to Arkansas folk games, the genre has still received more attention than folk art and material culture. Two worthwhile exceptions to this general trend are Frank Reuter's "John Arnold's Link Chains: A Study in Folk Art" and Diane Tebbetts's "Earl Ott: Fishing on the Arkansas." In the former paper Reuter, a one-time professor at the University of Arkansas at Monticello now residing in Berryville, provides an insightful study of the work of a Monticello folk artist. By example, Reuter demonstrates the value of recording an informant's aesthetic opinions. Not only do these views reveal much about John Arnold's carvings and how and why they are created, but they also indicate that a person can make an object that is beautiful and pleasurable to someone not sharing the same aesthetic ideas. Thus, while John Arnold is apparently unconcerned with elitist aesthetic concepts, his carvings are often pleasing to elitist audiences. In a very perceptive essay Tebbetts treats the traditional aspects of fishing on the Arkansas River as practiced by one individual—her father. Tebbetts makes her points without getting overly technical or esoteric; in so doing, she provides an informative essay that is useful both to scholars and a more general reading audience.[32]

One of the foremost American scholars in folk religion is William M. Clements, currently at Arkansas State University, Jonesboro. Some of his publications have dealt with the genre as found in Arkansas. In "The Rhetoric of the Radio Professor" he analyzes sermons delivered by Pentecostal evangelists in Craighead and Poinsett counties, and his "Conversion and Communitas" is an important discussion of conversion rituals and social structures of Baptist and Pentecostal sects of northeastern Arkansas. In these essays and elsewhere, Clements demonstrates the validity of the folklorist's approach to the study of traditional dogma. In many instances, and especially in the literalist, fundamentalist churches, religious belief is largely shaped by folk belief.[33]

The one area of nonmusical lore that has been most often studied in Arkansas is folk narrative. One major book, *Negro Tales from Pine Bluff, Arkansas, and Calvin, Michigan* (1958) is the only sizeable collection of Afro-American lore published from Arkansas. Richard Dorson, the book's editor, gathered all of the Pine Bluff texts in just eight days. Some of this same material was later used in Dorson's *American Negro Folktales* (1967). Another important work, James Masterson's *Tall Tales of Arkansaw* (1942), is one of the best books ever written on Arkansas folklore, but it does not, as some have claimed, cover the entire field. Masterson is very specific in limiting the volume to Arkansas humor.[34] In twenty-one chapters Masterson expertly discusses "every report or rumor of 'Arkansaw' that I have seen in print" and several humorous reports that circulate primarily orally.[35] His is the first book to print unexpurgated the famous "Change the Name of Arkansas" speech, and it contains the most thorough treatment to date of "The Arkansas Traveler." It also includes, among other items, numerous tall tales about Davy Crockett and extensive, richly detailed notes.

One other folk narrative publication that merits mention is my own *Ghost Stories from the American South* (1985). Although the book is aimed at a popular audience and deals with texts from throughout the South (defined as the states that belonged to the Confederacy during the Civil War), several entries are from Arkansas. Unlike most books on Southern ghost legends, all but one of the texts is presented in the words of the folk narrators rather than in literary "improvements." It is, to my knowledge, the only volume in print dealing with folk legends of the entire South. Therein lies one of the book's problems, for no individual in recent times has done extensive fieldwork collecting ghost legends in every Southern state. Consequently, it was necessary to rely on the cooperation of collectors in other states, and several contributed a large number of texts. Unfortunately, though, in some states ghost stories were not a subject that had occupied a significant number of collectors; as a result there is a geographic imbalance. There is at least one other major problem, namely, an unevenness in the quality of textual material. Some collectors are simply more thorough than others; most included a great deal of accompanying data, but others provided none at all. Overall, the quality of the texts shared with me was quite high.

Most of the other academics involved in the study and collection of Arkansas folklore are known primarily for their work on folksong and have confined their attention to the Ozarks. Many, like Clement L. Benson and George E. Hastings, both professors at the University of Arkansas, published little or nothing. Benson obtained a few songs through his students, and Hastings even gathered some ballads himself, but Hastings' only publication dealt with a number recorded by Charles Finger.[36] In several respects the most significant of the academics is Mary Celestia Parler. Her importance is due to the roughly three decades she spent teaching folklore classes at the University of Arkansas, during which time she instructed more students in folklore than anyone else in Arkansas. Although her academic training was in English, Parler became interested in folklore after moving to Arkansas in the 1940s. In addition to teaching, she, along with her future husband, Vance Randolph, and several others, established the Arkansas Folklore Society. From 1950 until its demise in 1960, she was the editor of *Arkansas Folklore*, the Society's journal. Parler gathered numerous folksongs, as well as other types of folklore, from her students. To date, this material is largely unpublished, but it is catalogued and available for use by qualified researchers.

Whereas Parler published relatively little, the same cannot be said for her husband, Vance Randolph. The Pittsburg, Kansas, native is the most famous personality in the history of Arkansas folklore studies but was an academic only by marriage. True, he had a graduate degree in psychology and toyed with the idea of getting a Ph.D. in anthropology, but the closest he came to holding a university position was when he helped his wife grade papers from her classes. He was, however, an excellent fieldworker and prolific writer. An annotated list of his publications, mostly on folklore, fills a small book.[37] Although he dealt with most genres, Randolph's magnum opus is his four-volume *Ozark Folksongs* (1946–1950).[38] Only one published collection of American folksongs, that of Frank C. Brown of North Carolina, is larger than Randolph's. Brown had numerous students and the North Carolina Folklore Society to rely on for contributions, whereas Randolph did all of the collecting himself, except for a few songs contributed by friends and acquaintances. Unlike most folklore collectors Randolph operated without financial aid and with minimal encouragement. Indeed, merely by collecting folklore he found himself in a predicament that few folklorists have had to endure. Certain groups in the Ozarks of the 1930s found the old songs and traditions contemptible and best forgotten, and they deeply resented Randolph's work. In ways both subtle and unsubtle they expressed their dissatisfaction.[39] Such a situation contrasts strongly with the generous, favorable publicity accorded Frank C. Brown for his collecting endeavors in North Carolina.

Ozark Folksongs differs from virtually all other important American folksong volumes in that it stems not from an interest in folksong per se, but from the love and understanding of a region and its people. In a sense all of Randolph's books can be seen as a single study, an ethnography of the Ozarks. His two early surveys, *The Ozarks* (1931) and *Ozark Mountain Folks* (1932), give the background for the numerous texts. No other American collection boasts such thorough descriptions of the setting in which the song tradition thrives. *Ozark Folksongs* is also notable for the inclusion of tunes for about half of its 1,635 texts. It is still far from common practice to include melody transcriptions with texts, and prior to 1950 such inclusion was the exception rather than the rule. By including variants for a majority of entries, Randolph followed a line of thinking common among folksong specialists today but a rarity in the 1940s. Perhaps most remarkable of all, especially considering the exalted position of Child among early twentieth-century collectors, is that Randolph saw value in recording everything sung by the folk. Therefore, he is one of the few collectors to intentionally include then-current hill-billy songs and numbers such as "Frankie and Johnny" with evident pop song influences. His lead in this respect was followed by too few later collectors. Finally, Randolph must be lauded for recording folklore from young people as well as from the elderly, the informants typically sought out by collectors.

While *Ozark Folksongs* is important, its significance does not mean it is a flawless work. There is too little information about informants and specific recording sessions, about attitudes of singers towards the songs, about the frequency of performance, about reasons why the songs were remembered. Furthermore, songs are arranged according to text consider-ations rather than according to singers, giving the impression that the songs exist by themselves rather than because they are kept alive in tradi-tion by those who sing them. But, as I have noted elsewhere, "these short-comings appear in most other American folksong collections, a majority of which lack many of the redeeming qualities of Randolph's work."[40]

One of the largest recent collections of Arkansas folksongs by an aca-demic is that of John Quincy Wolf. Like the collections of Hunter and Randolph, Wolf's contains only materials from the Ozarks. but his col-lection is even more narrowly defined. Only songs from the Arkansas portion of the mountain chain are found in this collection. A native of Batesville, Wolf taught for many years at Southwestern University in Memphis but returned frequently to the southern Ozarks of northern Arkansas to collect traditional songs. He was most active in the 1950s, but he began recording Ozark singers in the late 1940s and continued to do so until shortly before his death in 1972. Wolf was largely responsible for bringing Arkansas singers Almeda Riddle and country-western singer-songwriter James Morris, better known as Jimmie Driftwood, to national attention. Although Wolf collected folk music in Mississippi and Tennessee, the Ozark material is the most extensive part of his collection. Wolf's tapes were re-recorded in 1977 because some were extremely brittle. Material from the entire collection is being prepared for publication by Wolf's widow, Bess.

In 1976 I came to work as the first and, to date, only folklorist employed at the Ozark Folk Center in Mountain View, and have since been actively collecting in the same general region where Wolf worked. My tapes are indexed and available at the Ozark Folk Center Archive. Several of the texts have been published in a column titled "Ozark Folksongs" that appears in *The Ozarks Mountaineer*, a regional magazine published in Branson, Missouri, and in a two-volume *Southern Folk Ballads* (1987–88). The column was intended mainly to give the Ozark Folk Center some free publicity and also to turn up potential informants. It has most of the weaknesses typical of such efforts but does have several important qualities. These include attention to living folksinging traditions, consideration of mass media influences, data about informants and collecting sessions, and annotations of individual songs. However, musical transcriptions are not provided for any of the pieces, a flaw that is corrected in the two books, which, of course, include more than items from my own collection. These volumes, which depend to a great extent on the generosity of other collectors scattered throughout the South, have the same basic shortcomings found in *Ghost Stories from the American South*.

This survey points out that Arkansas folklore studies are only in their infancy. Much collecting has been done, but few people have gone beyond the gathering of data to tell what the material recorded means. One who has is Janet Lynn Allured in her Ph.D. dissertation at the University of Arkansas, "Families, Food and Folklore: Women's Culture in the Post-Bellum Ozarks" (1988). In this 260-page work, Allured uses oral history, cookbooks, and folklore sources to explore women's culture throughout the Missouri and Arkansas Ozarks, arguing that "the culture of Ozark women was dynamic and creative as it evolved to meet the changing needs of the family and the community."[41] There is an even greater need for work that is more expansive geographically, culturally, and ethnically. The rich folk traditions of the Arkansas Delta are barely known, the treasures that await folklorists in the southwestern part of the state have rarely been mined, and the same can be said for every part of the state except the Ozarks. Even the Ozarks, which have been regarded as a mecca for anyone interested in folklore, have been inadequately studied. Vance Randolph's *The Ozarks* and *Ozark Mountain Folks* are outdated attempts to cover the folk life of the entire region, and no one in the sixty years since those pioneering efforts were published has attempted such a comprehensive volume. Instead, authors have concentrated on specific genres, as I did in my *Ozark Mountain Humor* (1989).

There are two volumes that seemingly provide a sorely needed over-all view of Arkansas folklore, but, for different reasons, both fall short of that goal. Nancy McDonough's *Garden Sass: A Catalog of Arkansas Folkways* (1975) was promoted by its publisher as a complete account of Arkansas folkways. This is but one example why one should not take publishers' claims too seriously. *Garden Sass* is better written than the *Foxfire* books on which it is clearly modeled, but it has many of the same faults found in those highly successful volumes. It is a romantic, survival-istic, and nostalgic presentation of folklore that fails to give much atten-tion to the widely traveled nature of oral traditions. Thus, McDonough often presents items as if they were unique to Arkansas when in fact they are known in many corners of the globe. To McDonough's credit she does pay some attention to material culture, a topic that usually gets short shrift in publications on Arkansas folklore. My own *The Charm Is Broken: Readings in Arkansas and Missouri Folklore* (1984) is, as the sub-title indicates, "a representative selection of what has been written on Arkansas and Missouri folklore."[42] Because this book is designed for stu-dents, both good and bad examples are included. Obviously, though, its contents are shaped by what has been previously done on the topic, meaning it is imbalanced in the same ways past studies have been.

No area of Arkansas folklore holds greater promise, and has received less attention, than the traditions of ethnic groups. Beginning with Thanet in the 1890s, there have been a few examinations of Afro-American lore in Arkansas, but, with a few other exceptions, folklore studies in Arkansas have been confined to investigations of WASP lore. One of the exceptions is Deirdre LaPin, Louis Guida, and Lois Patillo's *Hogs in the Bottom: Family Folklore in Arkansas* (1982), an examination of folk traditions in seven families in central and southeastern Arkansas. This most readable book includes among its seven families those of Italian, German, and Afro-American descent. Also deserving of mention here is Ruth Polk Patterson's *The Seed of Sally Good'n: A Black Family of Arkansas 1833–1953* (1985). Patterson's emphasis is on history, not folk-lore, but she does include one chapter titled "African Survivals and Scottish Airs," which is primarily devoted to folklore in this account of her family.

For many people folklore means folksongs and perhaps folktales, an attitude that is in part due to the fact that most folklorists have focused on these genres. Those who have worked in Arkansas folklore are no more guilty of this overemphasis than are American folklorists in gen-eral. As the preceding discussion indicates, students of Arkansas folklore are beginning to cast a wider net than in the past. It is to be hoped that this positive trend will continue to the point that sometime in the not-too-distant future, it will be possible to speak of Arkansas folklore studies that cover all genres, geographic sections of the state, and cultural groups equally well.

Singing and Playing Music in Arkansas

W. K. McNeil

"What is folklore?" Ask many people and they will likely say "Barbara Allen," "John Henry," or "On Top of Old Smokey." Such an answer conveys the popular notion that folklore is basically folksongs, a claim that is much too narrow. Folksongs are, of course, properly designated as folklore, but they certainly do not constitute the entire spectrum of folk tradition. In the United States they are one of the most often collected and studied aspects of folklore and also one of the most suitable for public performance, meaning they have been more publicized than most other genres of folklore. In various so-called folk festivals folksongs have been performed by singers ranging from the most traditional to the most revivalistic. This is a type of exposure that is rarely, if ever, accorded such genres as proverbs, riddles, beliefs, gestures, and legends. Given all this attention it is hardly surprising that popular concepts of folklore and folksong are distorted.

There is further confusion about folksongs because the term is used in two ways by folklorists. First, it is a generic term referring to all songs passed on in folk tradition; second, it is used as a means of distinguishing between lyric and narrative songs. Ballad is the term applied to folksongs that tell a story, while folksong is the designation reserved for those songs that do not present a narrative. Most collectors have focused on ballads but have also generally included many folksongs in their collectanea. This brings up the question of how much narrative a song needs to become a ballad. Often the decision is easily made, for a song such as the following evidently doesn't present a connected narrative; instead, it merely suggests a story but never goes beyond the hint.

Oh, I wish I was a little bird,
I'd fly through the top of a tree,
I'd fly and sing a sad little song,
I can't stay here by myself.

I can't stay here by myself,
I can't stay here by myself,
I'd fly and sing a sad little song,
I can't stay here by myself.

Once I had plenty money,
My friends all around me would stand.
Now my pockets are empty
And I have not a friend in the land.

Farewell, farewell corn whiskey,
Farewell peach brandy too.
You've robbed my pockets of silver
And I have no use for you.

Oh, I wish I was a little fish,
I'd swim to the bottom of the sea.
I'd swim and sing a sad little song,
I can't stay here by myself.

Oh, I can't stay here by myself,
I can't stay here by myself.
I'd swim and sing a sad little song,
I can't stay here by myself.[1]

In the case of some other songs the decision concerning whether a song is a ballad or a folksong is not so clear-cut. Consider, for example, the following texts ("No Sir! No Sir!" "Texas Cowboy," and "Fare Thee Well"), all of which are traditional in Arkansas.

Tell me one thing, tell me truly,
Tell me why you scorn me so,
Tell me why, when asked a question
You will always answer no.

No sir, no sir, no sir!
No sir, no sir, no sir, No!

My father was a Spanish merchant,
And before he went to sea,
He told me to be sure and answer
No to all you said to me.

If when walking in the garden
Plucking flowers all wet with dew,
Tell me, will you be offended
If I walk and talk with you?

If when walking in the garden
I should ask you to be mine,
And should tell you that I love you,
Would you then my heart decline?[2]

It's raining and it's hailing, the moon gives no light,
My horses can't travel this dark road tonight.
Go put up your horses and feed them on hay,
Come in and set beside me, and talk while you stay.
My horses aint hungry, they won't eat your hay,
I travel through Texas and feed on the way.

Your parents aint willing, they say I'm too poor,
They say I aint worthy to enter your door,
They say that I love you, I guess that's all true,
But to say that we'll marry, that never will do.

I courted a fair maiden at the age of sixteen,
She's the flower of Franklin, a rose of Maydeen.
Your parents aint willing and mine are the same,
So go to your record and blot out my name.

Goodbye to the white house and the green meadows too,
Farewell my little darling, I bid you adieu.
The roads is long and rocky, the sea is wide and deep,
I think of you, dear darling, ten thousand times a week.[3]

O fare thee well my pretty little miss
O fare thee well,
A while I'm goin' away ten thousand miles,
Ten thousand miles from here.

And who will shoe your pretty little feet
And who will glove your hand
And who will kiss your ruby red lips
While I'm in a furrin land?

My papa will shoe my pretty little feet.
My mama will glove my hand
No body will kiss my ruby red lips
While you're in a furrin land.

And who will comb your yellow, yellow hair
With a new made tuckin' comb
And who will love you pretty little babe
Till I'm a-comin' home?

And have you seen those lonesome doves
That fly from pine to pine
A-mournin' for their own true love
Just as I've mourned for mine.

I'll love you till the sea runs dry
And the rock lie in the sun.
I'll love you till the day I die
And then our love is done.[4]

Most folksong specialists would probably not classify the first song as a ballad, but the other two are often so categorized. Yet, seemingly, the first piece has as much of a story as either of the others. That being the case, why would it not be called a ballad? The answer is that most folksong authorities have followed the lead of the eighteenth-century poet William Shenstone (1714–1763), who referred to ballads as those songs in which action predominates over sentiment.[5] In actual practice, though, classification often proves to be arbitrary, with some editors categorizing versions of "Texas Cowboy" (which is more widely known as "Wagoner's Lad") as a ballad while others present it as a folksong.[6]

There are three categories of traditional balladry found in Arkansas: Child ballads, broadside ballads, and native-American ballads. Child ballads are not songs for or about children, nor do they have any particular connection with children's lore. They are so called because they are among the three hundred and five ballads included by Francis James Child (1825–1896) in his ten-volume work, *The English and Scottish Popular Ballads* (1882–98). Child, a Harvard professor, combed hundreds of manuscripts and printed sources to produce what he considered the best of the English and Scottish popular ballads. In his first published volume in 1882, he claimed to have gathered "every valuable copy of every known ballad," a statement that now seems naive and, perhaps, even arrogant.[7] Certainly, it was a premature claim, for soon after the publication of Child's magnum opus, ballad collecting in America really got under way. His proclamation is more understandable when one knows Child's view of traditional ballad singing. He did make some attempts to unearth examples of the ballads from oral tradition, but he was convinced that, for all practical purposes, folk balladry was extinct. Thus, in compiling his selection of English and Scottish popular ballads, Child was performing cultural archaeology, "excavating" the best items from a tradition that he believed dead. Shortly after the publication of his final volume, folksong collectors began to prove Child wrong by seeking out and recording variants and versions of his three hundred and five songs from folksingers. In many cases these collectors carried their search to absurd extremes and ignored everything else in their search for the gems canonized by Child. This antiquarian attitude was enunciated as recently as 1956 when a noted collector proclaimed that "the genuine ballad is only one type of folksong. Your 'ballad' is not a true folk ballad unless it is closely kin to one of the 305—no more, no less!—in professor Child's great collection."[8] Generally, though, most collectors no longer subscribe to such a narrow view.

Broadside ballads are songs originally printed on one side of a sheet of paper and sold for a small fee. Many of these ballads found in Anglo-American tradition are classified in G. Malcolm Laws's *American Balladry from British Broadsides* (1957). Generally, broadsides are of more recent vintage than Child ballads. The latter date from roughly 1500 to 1750, while most broadsides date from 1650 to 1900, although there are exceptions on both sides of the line. The lyrics of Child ballads and broadsides are frequently compared to tabloids, for, like them, both kinds of ballads often deal with sensational subjects—robberies, murders, and the like being among their most common, albeit not their only, themes. But examples are better than discussions; so, for purposes of illustration, two ballad texts are given here, the first a Child ballad and the second a broadside ballad. In the first ballad, "The Merry Golden Tree" (a version of Child 286 "The Sweet Trinity" or "The Golden Vanity") a cabin boy finds out too late that the ship's captain is not an honorable person.

There was a little ship and she sailed on the sea,
She went by the name of the *Merry Golden Tree*,
As she sailed on the lowlands lonesome low,
As she sailed on the lonesome sea.

She sailed to the west and she sailed to the east,
And there she espied the *Turkey Shovelee*,
As she sailed on the lowlands lonesome low,
As she sailed on the lonesome sea.

A little cappin' boy he run upon the deck,
Saying captain, oh captain, what will you give me
If I sink her in the lowlands lonesome low,   ·
If I sink her in the lonesome sea?

I will give you money and I will give you fee,
And I have a lovely daughter I'll marry unto thee,
If you'll sink her in the lowlands lonesome low,
If you'll sink her in the lonesome sea.

He had a little auger all made for the use,
He bored nine holes in her little hull at once,
And he sunk her in the lowlands lonesome low,
And he sunk her in the lonesome sea.

The boy bent his breast and away swum he,
He swum till he reached the *Merry Golden Tree*,
As she sailed on the lowlands lonesome low,
As she sailed on the lonesome sea.

Oh captain, oh captain, will you let me on board?
If you don't, you have broken your word,
For I've sunk her in the lowlands lonesome low,
For I've sunk her in the lonesome sea.

I'll neither give you money and I'll neither give you fee,
I'll not be as kind as I said I would be,
But I'll leave you in the lowlands lonesome low,
But I'll leave you in the lonesome sea.

If it weren't for the love I have for your men
I would do the same unto you as I did unto them,
I would sink you in the lowlands lonesome low,
I would sink you in the lonesome sea.

He fell upon his knees and down sunk he,
He bid farewell to the *Merry Golden Tree,*
For she left him in the lowlands lonesome low,
She left him in the lonesome sea.[9]

The second ballad, "The Broken-hearted Boy," is an American version of a broadside known under various titles including "The Girl I left
Behind," "My Parents Treated Me Tenderly," "The Maid I Left Behind,"
and "The Girl I Left on New River," among others. There are two ballads known as "The Girl I Left Behind"—not be confused with "The
Girl I Left Behind Me"—which are both of British broadside origin and
telling similar stories. In one, the narrator promises to be faithful to his
sweetheart before he leaves her to travel to a distant city where he finds
another girl. After marrying his new lover he is haunted by thoughts of
his parents and his girl, who have died of broken hearts. In the other ballad, which is more common in America, it is the girl left behind who is
unfaithful and marries another. Sometimes the narrator refuses the hand
of his new acquaintance before learning of his girl's unfaithfulness.
Usually he is so disheartened by the news that he resolves to spend the
rest of his life in gambling or drinking or both, but in a Scottish text
titled "All Frolicking I'll Give Over," the narrator marries after learning
that his former sweetheart is already wed. In the present text no real
unfaithfulness is detailed, although the protagonist notes "ladies treated
me fine," and his sweetheart presumably died from a broken heart. Thus,
it has elements of both ballads but seems closest to the second.

There was a wealthy farmer
        In Texas near Austin did dwell.
He had a beautiful daughter,
        The one I love so well;
She was so young and beautiful,
        Brown eyes and curly hair,
There is no other in Texas
        With her I can compare.

I went to see this pretty fair maiden;
        I asked her if she would be mine.
She hung her head in deep study,
        Like wishing to decline.
Says I, "The question is left with you;
        Go answer if you can.
But, Love, if I don't suit you,
        Go choose you another man."

She raised her head while smiling,
        Saying, "Love, I'm bound to say 'yes.'
You seem so honest and truthful,
        And you'll prove so, I guess.
But if you'll promise to marry me,
        I'll marry no other man;
So here is my heart, come and take it."
        She gave me her right hand.

I asked her if she'd wait awhile
        Till I could go away,
Till I could go and raise a stake;
        I would return some day.
She hung her head in deep sorrow
        And looked most scornfully;
We kissed, shook hands, and parted,
        I left her to mourn for me.

So now, my kind friends, I must leave you;
        I am inclined to go.
And sure and well he mounted
        And drilled to Old Mexico.
It's when I get there, if not suited,
        I'll drill to some foreign land;
But I never can forget the farmer's girl
        That gave me her right hand.

I stayed six months in Old Mexico,
        And when I changed my mind
I drilled up into old Kansas
        Where ladies treated me fine.
It was there I found the country,
        Fine houses, and fine land;
But I never can forget the farmer's girl
        That gave me her right hand.

I went to Kansas City
        One evening bright and fair.
I stopped off into a post office;
        The mail was arriving there.
I received a letter from Texas
        Which I was glad to see;
I thought it was from the farmer's girl
        That said she would marry me.
The post office being crowded,
        I stepped off to one side

To read this letter from Texas,
>   Which was written both long and wide;
And on it I found my mother's name,
>   And this is what she said,
"The farmer's girl you love so well,
>   I'm sorry to say, she is dead."

This filled my heart with deep sorrow;
>   I knew not what to do.
While folding up this letter,
>   I knew those words were true.
I'm going back to old Texas
>   To live a bachelor's life,
For the farmer's girl I love so well
>   She never can be my wife.

While on my way to old Texas,
>   I stopped in El Paso town;
Got in with a bunch of gay cowboys
>   To ramble the city around.
To drive away all sorrow
>   I taken a glass of wine;
But the love I had for the farmer's girl,
>   She never would leave my mind.[10]

The third type of folk balladry found in Arkansas is the native-American ballad. These ballads are not called "native American" because they have anything to do with American Indians but because they originate in America. Most of these date from 1850 to the present, although the oldest such ballad still sung in Arkansas, "The Rattlesnake Song" (more commonly known as "Springfield Mountain"), is generally thought to date from 1761 when a Timothy Myrick died in Farmington, Connecticut, from a snakebite.[11] This particular ballad is found in both serious and comic versions, although comic versions, such as the following, are more popular in Arkansas:

Oh, Johnny dear, don't you go
Down in the meadow for to mow,
Ra tinga ling day ra tinga ling day
Ra tinga ling linga tinga ling day.

Oh, Molly dear, don't you know
Father's meadow and it must be mowed

Ra tinga ling day ra tinga ling day
Ra tinga ling linga tinga linga day.

He hadn't mowed around the field,
Rattlesnake bit him on the heel,
Ra tinga ling day ra tinga ling day
Tinga ling linga tinga ling day.

They carried him home to Molly dear
Don't you know she felt right queer
Ra tinga ling day ra tinga ling day
Ra tinga ling linga tinga ling day.

Come all my friends and warning take
Never get bit by a rattler snake.
Ra tinga ling day ra tinga ling day
Ra tinga ling linga tinga ling day.

If you do I'm telling you,
Lot of trouble you'll get into.
Ra tinga ling day ra tinga ling day
Ra tinga ling linga tinga ling day.[12]

Like Child ballads and broadsides, native-American ballads deal largely with scandals and tragedies, although themes of American history and developments are also found. The most commonly encountered native-American ballads in Arkansas are those included in G. Malcolm Laws' *Native American Balladry*, a study and classification system first published in 1950 and revised in 1964. A number of native-American ballads very popular with Arkansas folk singers are not found in Laws' classification system, primarily those known to have originated in the popular music industry. Pieces like "The Fatal Wedding," "Little Rosewood Casket," and "The Letter Edged in Black" are omitted on such grounds. Also missing are ballads that are confined to a fairly small area in a region. Thus, songs like the following ballad about Lee Mills, who was hanged in Cleburne County in 1898, do not appear in Laws. It has undeniably entered folk tradition, but its popularity is confined to the county in which the crime occurred and to the few immediately surrounding counties.

Lee Mills is what I call my name;
        Was once without a murder's stain.
You have heard the story told
        Of how I came to be so bold.

'Twas on one bright, sunshiny day
  When Will Hardin led me astray;
He caused me to commit a crime,
  And now I am condemned to die.

Many a night I've lain awake,
  Praying to God for pity's sake.
He has pardoned all my sins at last
  And has forgive me of my past.

My dear old mother's prayed for me.
  Her smiling face I'd love to see;
But death, cold death, has come at last,
  And took these troubles from her breast.

Dear rowdy boys, here as I stand,
  The sheriff with his ropes and my outstretched hands,
You shall hear my experienced words,
  Pray don't let one pass you by unheard.

Now here's the scaffold I do see,
  It was prepared alone for me;
And I must stand upon it soon,
  There to meet my fatal doom.

Now, little girl, we two must part,
  To see your tears it breaks my heart,
I would not hate so bad to die,
  If it was not leaving you here to weep and cry.[13]

The ballad about Lee Mills is what folklorists refer to as a "goodnight" song because it was reportedly written by a criminal who sang it shortly before his execution. That such attributions are mostly apocryphal has not deterred such legends. Indeed, "goodnight" ballads are quite common among broadsides and native-American ballads. There are also many less tragic songs common in traditional Arkansas balladry; for example, many Child ballads, such as "The Farmer's Curst Wife" (Child 278), and broadsides and native-American ballads, like "Father Grumble," "Devilish Mary," and "The Young Man Who Wouldn't Hoe Corn," are humorous in intent.[14]

Traditional ballads—whether Child, broadsides, or native American—all have distinctive characteristics. All three types generally concentrate on a single episode. Typical is the following version of "The Dying Brakeman," which focuses on a tragedy in which the motorman of a mine train is unable to stop the cars in time to prevent them from running over his brakeman:

> See that true and trembling brakeman,
> As he falls between the cars!
> Not a moment's warning has he;
> From those freight cars he is hurled.
>
> See those car wheels passing o'er him,
> O'er his mangled body and head;
> See his sister bending o'er him,
> Crying, "Brother, are you dead?"
>
> "Dying, sister, yes, I'm dying;
> Going to join that other shore;
> For our father and our mother
> I shall never see no more.
>
> "Sister, when you see our brother,
> These few words I send to him;
> Never, never venture braking;
> If he does, his life will end."[15]

Narratives in ballads are advanced primarily by means of dialogue, but most alternate stanzas of dialogue with stanzas of action, with a bit of description mingled in. Typical is the following version of "Young Hunting" (Child 68), which is called "Loving Henry":

> Who is that? Who is that coming down the road?
>   Is it William Hall?
> No, that is Henry, my own true love
>   Who's been gone from home so long.
>
> "Get down, get down, Loving Henry," said she,
>   "And stay all night with me.
> The best of wine you'll have to drink
>   For your good company."
>
> "I won't get down, for I can't get down
>   And stay all night with you
> I'm going to that green valley
>   Where I stayed all night last night."
>
> She reached over the fence so long
>   And give him kisses three;

And in her hand she held a penny knife,
        And she wounded him full deep.

"Ride on, ride on, Loving Henry," said she,
        "Beneath the setting sun,
See if there's ary a doctor in old Scott County
        Can cure your bleeding wound."

I won't ride on, for I can't ride on
        Beneath the setting sun;
For there's nary a doctor in old Scott County
        Can cure my bleeding wound.

She rose up at the break of day;
        Three close housemaids she called,
Saying, "Here's a dead man in my hall;
        I wished he was away."

Some took him by his long, yellow hair;
        Some took him by his feet;
And they took him to a far off well,
        Full fifty furlow deep.

Up flew a little sweet sparrow
        Out of the wood so green,
Saying, "Fare you well, Lord Loving Henry;
        You'll never no more be seen."

I wish I had my bow all bent,
        My arrow and my string;
I'd soar a shaft through your little breast,
        And you ne'er no more would sing.[16]

The narrative approach in Child ballads is impersonal with little or no intrusion of the narrator's point of view. Even where the singer may be sympathetic with the protagonist's plight, that view is not explicitly stated. The same, to a lesser extent, can be said for both broadsides and native-American ballads. Like modern journalism, ballads focus on the climax of an action and its result, giving the happenings in as straightforward, objective a manner as possible. The description of a murder in "Loving Henry" given above is a perfect example of the impersonality of the Child ballads.

Child ballads typically contain all of the preceding characteristics that are also often present in broadsides and native-American ballads. These qualities can be considered primary characteristics while some other features found in many Child ballads, and in other types of ballads, are not essential. Many songs begin *in medias res*, that is, in the middle of the story. A perfect example of this feature is a version of "The House Carpenter's Wife" (Child 243) collected in Cushman, Arkansas. It begins not with a detailed description of the scene but, rather, with the two principal figures greeting each other in the following manner:

> "Well met, well met, well met," said he,
> "Well met, well met," said she.[17]

The background is pieced together by the listener as the ballad progresses. Such a characteristic may reflect loss during the process of transmission and is indicative of the tendency of ballads to retain only details that are absolutely essential.

Another characteristic often found in ballads is called leaping and lingering. This refers to the tendency to treat individual scenes in detail and then shift the narrative to another scene with little or no transition. Various kinds of repetition are also common; at least five different types occur regularly. These include plain repetition in which words, phrases, or stanzas are simply repeated. There is also the climax of relatives in which songs consist largely and sometimes entirely of references to various members of one's family. A third type of ballad repetition is incremental repetition in which the story is advanced by repeating nearly the same lines with minor changes that advance, or increment, the narrative. The beginning of this version of "Edward" (Child 13) exemplifies this technique:

> What blood? What blood on the p'int of your knife?
> Dear son, come tell to me.
> It's the blood of my old Guinea sow
> That ate the corn for me, me, me,
> That ate the corn for me.
>
> What blood? What blood on the p'int of your knife?
> Dear son, come tell to me.
> It's the blood of my oldest brother
> That fought the battle with me, me, me,
> That fought the battle with me.[18]

Other types of ballad repetition include speech and action in which one stanza has a person instructed to perform an action that is carried out in the next stanza. Finally, in some ballads a stanza is repeated, the repetition serving as a means of transition.

Many of these secondary characteristics occur not only in Child ballads but also are often found in both broadsides and native-American ballads. Broadsides, however, differ from Child ballads in that they frequently use the "come all ye" opening stanza and are often narrated in the first person. Native-American ballads are much more likely than the others to include a moral at the ending, although in the United States older ballads have occasionally been altered to include comments of a moralizing nature. All three types of ballads generally have a short narrative, simple action, chronologically arranged scenes, a limited number of characters (usually two, rarely more than four), and typically have no action after the climax.

Although most students of balladry and folksong have emphasized textual matters, the musical half of the songs is also important. The music of the older Child ballads is in a style that, apparently, dates from the Renaissance and the Middle Ages. Most of the tunes are restricted to five or six tones rather than the seven tone scale used in more recent music. Many of the tunes are modal; in other words, they do not fit into the major and minor scales in common use today and thus sometimes sound incomplete. Some singers of Child ballads, particularly elderly ones, use an ornate, embellished style of singing in which they dwell upon or minimize a tone, i.e., a musical sound, or tones. These ornamentations are akin to the "grace notes" of classical music and are facilitated because most of the older Child ballads are sung unaccompanied. Of course, the music of many of the Child ballads performed in Arkansas is, like that of the broadsides and native-American songs, more modern sounding. For example, a version of "The House Carpenter's Wife" as performed by Noble Cowden from Cushman, Arkansas, has a melody line that sounds very "blue." The broadsides and native-American ballads are almost always based on a seven-tone scale and are major or minor rather than modal. Usually they are cast in 2/4, 3/4, 4/4, or 6/8 time, the standard meters that developed during the eighteenth and nineteenth centuries.

The two genres of folksongs and ballads are utilized in several styles of traditional music found in Arkansas and elsewhere, and it is worthwhile to briefly discuss those forms. Earliest of these, and the least documented, is ragtime, a type of syncopated music that arose in the 1890s and faded by 1920. When most people think of ragtime they think of an instrumental music, even though, as John Hasse points out in his book

Ragtime: Its History, Composers, and Music, instrumental rags are one of only four main types of ragtime.[19] The style reached its highest musical development as an instrumental form, its greatest names were primarily concerned with the style as an instrumental music, and the instrumentals have generally stood the test of time better than other forms of the music. For these reasons, when modern writers think of ragtime it is usually as an instrumental form, more specifically as a piano music. "Rags" provide a syncopated melody set against a regular march-style bass; they consist of a number of self-contained sections, generally of sixteen measures each, that are often repeated. Thus, a typical structure would be AA BB A CC DD, each letter representing a separate section with its own melody, rhythm, and harmony. As already mentioned, this music has been inadequately researched with most attention being given to the "classic" composers of ragtime (Scott Joplin, James Scott, and Joseph Lamb). These men, however, were not folk musicians, albeit the genre of music within which they worked was derived from traditional sources. Thus, one can say little about ragtime in Arkansas beyond the statement that it was very popular here during the period 1897–1917 as it was in other parts of the United States. The distinctive features of folk ragtime as practiced in Arkansas must await further research.

About a later musical style, the blues, there is much more information. Blues, like ragtime, is not unknown among whites, but it is generally associated with an Afro-American tradition. Most likely the style originated in the early twentieth century. At least that is the best guess currently possible, and one that many scholars agree with. For example, John W. Work said that it was "safe to consider the blues a twentieth century product, making their appearance about 1900." He then referred to various reports of the form, the earliest being in 1902.[20] Ballad collector Dorothy Scarborough quoted black musician W. C. Handy in 1917 as saying that "about twenty years ago the desire was all for coon songs. Now the tendency is toward blues."[21] Howard W. Odum and Guy B. Johnson, sociologists and collectors of black folksongs, placed the origin of the blues in the early twentieth century. Discussing the topic in the 1970s, Johnson said that none of the singers he collected from in the 1920s had learned blues from an older family member.[22]

Such overwhelming evidence for an early twentieth-century genesis of the blues seems irrefutable, but, even so, one should be cautious about reaching such a conclusion for several reasons. One is that Afro-American secular music was generally ignored in the nineteenth century.

Most of the black writers of the time who might have shed light on the subject "were aspiring toward white middle-class status and were understandably uninterested in seriously considering black folk material, which might, in their own and in white eyes, reflect an inferior culture."[23] Religious black folksong was considered respectable, but was known to the general public in bastardized, nontraditional forms, such as the performances by the Fisk Jubilee Singers. Many of the early collectors of black folksong were men like William Eleazar Barton and James Miller McKim, ministers who were primarily concerned with presenting a certain picture of Afro-Americans, one that they thought could best be shown through sacred songs. Certainly, a secular music like the blues would not have fitted with the image they wanted to present, but, even if it did, the very fact of their being ministers probably resulted in conscious censorship on the part of their informants. Possibly the general bearing of some white collectors also enhanced the attitude of black censorship. While other possible reasons why the blues might have gone unreported in nineteenth-century America might be enumerated, the point is already made that there is some justification for at least remaining open to the possibility that the blues form may predate the twentieth century.

Certainly the "blues," referring to a state of mind, was known in the nineteenth century. In her diary entry for December 14, 1862, Charlotte Forten, a young Northern-born black woman who had come to South Carolina to teach slaves, commented about her return from church, "Nearly everybody was looking gay and happy; and yet I came home with the blues."[24] That Forten used the term in her diary suggests that the phrase had some degree of currency in her day and probably predates 1862 by several years. Some of the lyrics used by bluesmen predate the twentieth century and are occasionally reported in nineteenth-century writings. For example, Lafcadio Hearn, who is known primarily for his works on Japanese folklore, noted the lyrics of songs performed by roustabouts in 1876 on the levee waterfront of Cincinnati, Ohio. Among their songs was one called "Limber Jim" that contained the following verse:

Nigger an' a white man playing seven-up
White man played an' ace; an' nigger feared to take it up,
White man played ace an' nigger played a nine,
White man died, an' nigger went blind.[25]

Over fifty years later, in 1927, North Carolina blues singer Julius Daniels recorded in Atlanta, Georgia, the following lines:

Nigger an' a white man playin' seven-up this mornin',
Nigger an' a white man playin' seven-up this mornin'
Nigger an' a white man playin' seven-up
Well nigger win the money but he scared to pick it up,
This mornin' that too soon for me.[26]

Nevertheless, any suggestion that the blues is anything other than a twentieth-century phenomenon is pure speculation. The earliest known printed blues is in a 1904 ragtime composition by St. Louis musicians James Chapman and Leroy Smith. This number, "One o' Them Things," is a three-part ragtime tune of which the first section is a twelve-bar blues. Later compositions in the blues idiom are Hart Wand's "Dallas Blues," Arthur Seal's "Baby Seals' Blues," and W. C. Handy's "Memphis Blues" (all 1912), but while these derived in varying degrees from folk tradition, they were all like the Chapman-Smith work, i.e., essentially nonfolk. The same can be said about the blues craze started in 1920 when Mamie Smith, a young black singer from Cincinnati, recorded "Crazy Blues." The success of this record suddenly made blues singers very desirable artists sought out by major companies. At first women artists, slick songs, and stylish accompaniments were sought out, but later more traditional artists were able to make records.

That some down-home blues artists made commercial recordings has led to an unfortunate tendency on the part of some writers to equate the recorded tradition with the folk tradition. For several reasons, anyone taking this viewpoint would arrive at an inaccurate picture of folk blues in Arkansas or elsewhere, the most important being that most folk musicians simply did not make records. During the years 1926–36, when major record companies were actively seeking down-home blues artists, many of the sides were cut by field-recording units set up in various towns throughout the South. These sessions were produced by A&R (artists and repertoire) men, most of whom had limited contact in black communities and thus often relied on local "scouts" to supply them with talent. Such a situation meant that sometimes even a phenomenal traditional blues artist was overlooked. There were, of course, also those blues musicians who, for various reasons, would have nothing to do with the making of records.

Throughout much of Arkansas and Mississippi another form of mass media—the radio—was as influential as records in shaping folk blues. Indeed, station KFFA in Helena and its King Biscuit Time program made Arkansas famous for blues. Beginning in 1941, under the sponsorship of Interstate Grocer Company, the program ran for over thirty-five years, and for much of that time live music was featured. A particularly significant performer associated with the show was Aleck Miller (1899–1965) who was known as Sonny Boy Williamson. A native of Mississippi Williamson was a regular member of the show from 1941 to 1947 and returned to the program shortly before his death in May 1965. Although proficient on drums and guitar, Williamson is remembered primarily for his harmonica playing and his singing. As blues researcher Louis Guida discovered "the legacy of Sonny Boy Williamson and King Biscuit Time served as one kind of litmus test when considering the two regional traditions . . . in Arkansas blues."[27] In the Delta those influences are particularly strong not only on traditional repertoires but also on styles. There traditional blues are, much like Williamson's music, chordal, whereas in southwestern Arkansas a more spare, single-note–based sound is heard. Ultimately, though, Williamson's greatest importance is that he shaped "a milieu of blues possibility. Things happened around him."[28]

That Williamson and King Biscuit Time are significant and worthy of recognition here is indisputable, but their importance should not be overemphasized. Folk blues musicians, like all traditional artists, live in the same world all of us inhabit (despite what some writers would have everyone believe) and are influenced by various mass media. Thus, the records of such commercially active musicians as Aaron "T-Bone" Walker, Sam "Lightnin' " Hopkins, Charlie Christian, Earl "Fatha" Hines, Howling Wolf, and B. B. King, among others, have had considerable impact on folk blues performers in Arkansas. On the other hand, to assert that traditional blues in this state, or elsewhere, were wholly shaped by commercial artists would be going too far. Arkansas blues musicians also belong to a local tradition that has also helped shape their music. Because traditional blues in Arkansas is a virtually unstudied field, it is hard to discuss in great detail the varied influences that have affected these performers. Suffice it to say that folk blues artists have been influenced by other traditional musicians, most of whom achieved fame only in a local sense.

The traditional music form that has the largest body of participating musicians and the greatest listening audience of all styles of folk music found in Arkansas is gospel music. Like blues, it reached its present form in the twentieth century, although its origins are traceable to various earlier forms of music. Gospel music, in both its black and white forms, reflects aspects of the personal religious experience of Protestant evangelical groups. Texts generally concern conditions or rewards of an earthly nature, as opposed to those of a heavenly nature or those pertaining to an afterlife. While such songs were heard in religious revivals of the 1850s, they are primarily associated with urban revivalism of the period 1865–1900. Songwriter Philip Paul Bliss was the first to use the term "gospel song" in referring to this specific body of song. His *Gospel Songs* (1874) and *Gospel Hymns and Sacred Songs* (1875), the latter compiled with Ira David Sankey, earned him this honor.

Unlike most previous forms of religious music, gospel music bore a strong relationship to secular music, many of the early melodies being borrowed from marches or songs of the theater or parlor. Gospel songs became a major force in American religious music primarily due to revivals led by such evangelists as Dwight L. Moody, Samuel Porter Jones, and William Ashley "Billy" Sunday, men who employed their own professional musicians. Among the latter, Charles McCallom Alexander and Homer Rodeheaver were particularly important, for they brought a new kind of informality to revival services. Jokes and entertaining banter were a prominent part of the revivals they were associated with. Rodeheaver, in particular, also inclined toward the use of lighter, optimistic, semi-sacred music, such as Charles H. Gabriel's "Brighten the Corner Where You Are."

When speaking about white gospel music today one is discussing a twentieth-century phenomenon. Basically it represents a merging of urban gospel hymnody with the tradition of shapenote hymnody that flourished throughout the rural South since the mid-nineteenth century. This merger coincided with a strong revival movement among Southern fundamentalists and the rise of several recently established Pentecostal sects. The songs of this tradition were relatively simple and were written in an easily learned seven-shape notation that was taught at numerous singing schools throughout the South. The popularity and distribution of these highly rhythmic and harmonically uncomplicated songs were largely dependent on singing conventions and commercial publishing houses. Traveling quartets, or singing schoolteachers, promoting their latest collection, would put on a Sunday afternoon singing or conduct a singing school of several days' duration. This means of popularizing songs became the principal musical activity in many rural communities. By this means the newer gospel songs often replaced the older songs of the shapenote tradition, meaning that it was not the repertoire that was traditional in gospel music but, rather, the singing style.

No more specific date can be given for the origin of white gospel music than the early twentieth century, and it is equally impossible to ascertain the date of genesis for black gospel music. Several writers have held that composer Thomas A. Dorsey should be cited as the "Father of Gospel" and as the inventor of gospel music, and that black gospel can be dated from 1921, the date of Dorsey's first religious compositions. This claim, however, is the product of faulty logic. Styles and genres of music are not born or invented overnight by one individual; instead, they evolve slowly, organically, and often eclectically. What Dorsey did was notate and compose, and help codify and disseminate music that must have been extant at the time. In a sense he was a collector of folk music, for he relied on traditional themes, rhythms, styles, and affective devices for inspiration.

But if one sets the date of black gospel's genesis prior to 1921, at what point should that date be set? It owes something to spirituals and work songs of the nineteenth century, but its basic form does not belong to that era. Charles Albert Tindley (1851–1933), composer of "Stand By Me" and more than fifty other songs, was actively writing religious songs by 1901. Because he used some of the elements now associated with black gospel, he is sometimes categorized as a gospel writer and by others as pre-gospel. If he is accepted as the former, then black gospel music must be said to date from 1901. But, if one insists that the music could not predate its basic performance style, then black gospel developed more recently. The basic performance style originated about 1907 in Memphis. In that year the founders of the Sanctified Pentecostal Church of God in Christ returned from a revival in Los Angeles and established their own highly emotional service that included suitably emotional, frequently improvised music.

While the exact origins of gospel music, white or black, are impossible to chart except in the most superficial way, the same cannot honestly be said about performance styles. The two are, of course, related but also quite distinct. Generally, white gospel has drawn on the close harmony of barbershop quartet singing, on country guitar playing, and commonly features nasal intonation, although in the past two decades, it has inclined more towards urban crooning techniques employed by commercial singers. White gospel also has considerable rhythmic drive and emotional intensity but little of the frenzied technique employed in black gospel. In most respects white gospel is more sedate and less passionate than the form practiced in Afro-American communities. Black gospel is characterized by the basic traits of the Afro-American musical tradition: call and response patterns, blues tonality, swing, individualism of expression, and is usually, though not necessarily, characterized by vocal embellishment or ornamentation, something folklorists and ethnomusicologists refer to as melismatic singing. Also, improvisation is frequently resorted to, and there is a tendency toward lively tempos. Accompaniment is generally of a percussive and rhythmic nature, hand-clapping, piano, and organ being the most commonly used instruments, although drums, tambourines, guitars, horns, and woodwinds are also used.

Another and even more vaguely defined form of traditional music found in Arkansas is what, for want of a better term, is called country. The word covers a vast variety of music ranging from the most traditional to the most commercial, but most people today use it to refer to a form of mass-distributed popular music primarily associated with musicians active in Nashville, Tennessee. That wasn't always the case; at one time, country music was traditional not only in its repertoire but in its style and instrumentation. Most authorities date the beginning of country music from the early 1920s when supposedly the first commercial recordings occurred, and, although like other types of music discussed here, country obviously preceded the first commercial recordings, the early 1920s is a convenient starting point. As far as is now known the earliest commercial country recordings were made by Henry Gilliland, a fiddler from Altus, Oklahoma, and Alexander Campbell "Eck" Robertson, a fiddler born in Delaney, Arkansas, who moved away when he was three to Texas. In June 1922 Gilliland and Robertson recorded "Sallie Gooden" and "Arkansas Traveler" and, as is often said, the rest is history. The first recording stars of country music—Henry Whitter, Fiddlin' John Carson, Uncle Dave Macon, The Skillet Lickers, and others—made their way to the studios at a slightly later date. It was a few years later before any Arkansas country musicians were able to make records. Apparently the first to achieve this distinction was a group of five musicians from Searcy, Arkansas, who recorded under the name Pope's Arkansas Mountaineers. Composed of fiddler John Chism, his son Wallace on guitar, J. W. "Joe" McKinney on banjo, John Sparrow on guitar, and Lee Finis Cameron "Tip" McKinney as featured vocalist, the group cut eight sides for the Victor Talking Machine Company in Memphis, February 6, 1928.

For their first selection Pope's Arkansas Mountaineers recorded

"George Washington," a minstrel show song rewritten by "Tip" McKinney. Their other numbers were mostly renditions of traditional fiddle tunes and included "Cotton-Eyed Joe," "Get Along Home Miss Cindy," "Birmingham," "Hog Eye," and "Jaw Bone." Two other sides, both comic sermons featuring "Tip" talking while John Chism accompanied him on the fiddle, were never released. Although the 78s waxed by this band sold well throughout the South, they had only one recording session. Soon other Arkansas artists, such as Reaves White County Ramblers, Dr. Smith's Champion Horse-Hair Pullers, The Arkansas Barefoot Boys, and Luke Highnight's Ozark Strutters (technically not from the Ozarks, but from Hot Springs), followed Pope's band into the recording studios. Although these artists and others produced some excellent music, none had any great commercial success. It was only with the rise to fame of Marshall's Elton Britt and Patsy Montana from Hot Springs in the 1930s that any Arkansas country musicians became national stars.

The country artists mentioned thus far indicate much about the nature of Arkansas country music prior to World War II. Most performers were men who came from a Protestant, rural background, and they were generally members of a string band rather than solo musicians. The music relied heavily on fiddles, banjos, and guitars for accompaniment. Performances often, but by no means always, occurred at dances. The musicians' performing style was in what, for want of a better term, can be called the "objective" manner of performing. In other words, these musicians maintained a consistent tempo, level of intensity, and timbre throughout a song. To this extent they were indistinguishable from white folk musicians in Arkansas. There was another relationship between these country musicians and folk musicians, namely, the repertoire, which was heavily laced with material common in the repertoires of folksingers. As the music progressed, most country musicians in Arkansas and elsewhere relied more on original material, much of which was still couched in traditional style. Some of these newer songs actually entered folk repertoires. For example, "My Ozark Mountain Home," which was written in the early 1930s by George Edgin from Ozark, has turned up in the list of songs recorded by several folksingers and can actually be heard on a commercially released LP by the Williams Family of Roland, Arkansas. Gradually, though, country music has grown away from folk music. First to go was the traditional repertoire, which plays an ever smaller role in modern country music. Gradually, too, instrumentation changed so that the only connection this music now has with folk music is in the style of singing, and it seems to be slowly moving away from the traditional manner to a more mass oriented, less rural, approach to singing. Such a development is probably to be expected from a form of music that has become increasingly commercial.

One type of country music that has frequently been called traditional, or even folk, and has sometimes been erroneously labeled ancient, is known as bluegrass. This name, which comes from the name of Bill Monroe's band, The Bluegrass Boys, was first applied to the music in 1957, being used then to distinguish it from other forms of country-western music that were perceived as being less traditional. Because the name comes from his band, Monroe is generally credited as "The Father of Bluegrass," and there is no denying that he is one of *the* most important performers in the history of bluegrass. Nevertheless, he did not invent the form any more than Thomas Dorsey invented black gospel or W. C. Handy invented blues. There is some validity to the contention that bluegrass is more akin to folk music than is contemporary country. Bluegrass repertoires tend to be similar to that of older country music (it relies heavily on material created between 1925 and 1955), and some bluegrass musicians even perform traditional folksongs, ballads, and tunes. Moreover, vocal delivery is essentially that typically found among Anglo-American folksingers. Despite these similarities, it is best to think of bluegrass, and country also, in terms of its influence on traditional music rather than in terms of the influence of folk music on bluegrass.

So, what exactly is bluegrass? Basically, it is a professional, commercial music primarily intended for exhibition rather than, as was true of much traditional country music, intended to accompany dancing. It is an ensemble music with performance conventions demanding a high degree of integration. It is played at a higher pitch and tempo than most other country music, frequently featuring a lead vocal that is so high-pitched it is strident. This style of singing has often been referred to by bluegrass enthusiasts as "the high lonesome sound." Harmony singing is an important dimension of bluegrass singing, but there is a tendency toward vocal polyphony. In other words, the combination of two or more voices in such a way that they have beauty individually and together. Typically, bluegrass bands have from four to seven musicians performing on acoustic instruments, usually fiddles, five-string banjo, mandolin, guitar, Dobro, and string bass. Generally, the guitar and string bass have rhythmic roles while the other instruments play leads and provide rhythmic and melodic background for vocalists. The banjo is played in a distinctive manner that is erroneously labeled "Scruggs style" after Earl Scruggs, the banjo player in Monroe's 1945 band, who popularized this method of playing. Basically, the style consists of picking the strings in a three-finger syncopated roll rather than striking down on the strings as in the older frailing style.

Most research on folk music in Arkansas has focused on songs and tunes with very little notice being given to instrumentation. The same statement can be made about American folklore studies in general. This is primarily because the bulk of work has been in the area of balladry, specifically those ballads in the British tradition, and, until relatively recent times, these ballads were generally sung unaccompanied. Even so, instruments have been utilized in Arkansas folk music from the time of the state's first settlement, not only to accompany singing but to provide music for dancing or just for listening. The main instruments used by folk musicians in Arkansas are the fiddle, banjo, guitar, and hammered and mountain dulcimer, although some more obscure instruments such as the picking bow are occasionally used by both white and black performers. Traditionally, the most important of these instruments in white communities was the fiddle, although it has in recent times been supplanted to a degree by the guitar.

No one knows exactly where or when the first fiddles were made, but it seems certain that the instrument was derived from such predecessors as the rebec, lira da braccio, and the Renaissance fiddle. The earliest known examples of the instrument known today as the fiddle are from Italy in the 1550s, the most famous early makers being the Amati family from Cremona. About 1650 the instrument made its way to the New World and came to Arkansas when the first European settlers moved into the region in the late eighteenth and early nineteenth century. Despite being a difficult instrument to master, the fiddle became very popular for a variety of reasons. It was a relatively small instrument that was easy to transport, and it had considerable volume so it could easily be heard even in rather crowded rooms filled with large numbers of dancers. The latter virtue is significant because until relatively recent times, the primary activity of folk fiddling was to accompany dancing. Only in the twentieth century, mainly in the past fifty years, has this fact changed significantly with the development of bluegrass and "Texas style" fiddling. Both are mainly exhibition rather than dance fiddle styles; "Texas" fiddling (consisting of putting as many notes as possible in a tune, thereby often obscuring the melody) is the style that today usually wins fiddle contests in Arkansas and elsewhere in the United States.

This seems to be the place to discuss the difference between a fiddle and a violin. They are the same instrument, but the difference is in how they are played and adjusted. The violin has an extremely high arch to avoid double stops, triple stops, and the like whereas the fiddler deliberately uses such techniques. There are also standard conventional tunings and bowing techniques. Actually, in recent years Arkansas fiddlers have shied away from using as many nonstandard tunings as they once did, although "cross tuning" (tuning to a chord rather than the standard G D A E tuning, going from the lowest to the highest string) is still practiced.

Traditionally the second most important instrument used in Arkansas folk music is the banjo. Thought to be of African origin, the earliest accounts of the instrument are from the mid-seventeenth century in the West Indies where it is referred to as a *banza* or a *strum strum*.[29] It is mentioned in Thomas Jefferson's *Notes on the State of Virginia* (1784) where it is called a *banjar*.[30] The instrument was largely popularized in the nineteenth century by blackface minstrels who claimed to be presenting an authentic picture of Negro life on southern plantations. They popularized the clawhammer, drop, thumb, knocking style of playing beginning in the 1840s. A later style developed about 1900 has come to be called the "Scruggs style" after its most famous exponent, Earl Scruggs. Most Arkansas folk musicians prior to the 1920s used the banjo as a backup to the fiddle; as a melody lead instrument it was uncommonly used. That situation has now changed considerably.

When most people today think of folk music, the guitar is often the instrument that first comes to mind, but it is actually a relatively recent arrival. Although known earlier, guitars did not become widely popular in Arkansas and in the South in general until about 1900, but the instrument made great changes in the music when it did become popular. The guitar made it possible to think of a song as a series of chord progressions rather than as merely a series of melody notes. Musicians could thus strum or finger pick proper chords instead of playing each melody note. Many traditional musicians played guitar with a plectrum or pick, but several also chose to sound the instrument's strings with the fingers of the right hand. The origins of this style are unknown, but it is generally assumed that many guitarists were five-string banjo players first and that finger picking was merely an adaptation of one or another of the finger styles used in playing the banjo. Finger picking facilitated the simultaneous playing of chords and melody lines, something that is extremely difficult, but not impossible, with a pick.

Two basic styles of finger picking are popular with Arkansas traditional musicians. The first is called the Carter style after Maybelle

Carter, the commercial country musician who was the best-known exponent of this technique, and consists of a melody line being picked by the thumb of the right hand while the index finger of the right hand brushes across the strings to sound a harmonic accompaniment. This technique effectively limits the melody line to the bass strings of the guitar. A second style, called the Travis style after Merle Travis, the technique's best-known practitioner, consists of the thumb of the right hand playing a rhythmic series of bass notes while the fingers of the right hand remain free to pick out a melody line.

All of the above mentioned instruments are found in both black and white communities. Dulcimers, both hammered and mountain, however, are commonly used only by white musicians. Although they share a name taken from the Latin word *dulce* and the Greek word *melos* which mean, together, "sweet song" or "sweet tune," the two instruments are not otherwise related. The older of the two is the hammered dulcimer, which is an ancestor of the piano and is possibly several thousand years old. Until recent times it was far more popular in Arkansas than the mountain dulcimer, although neither instrument was as commonplace as, for example, the fiddle or banjo. Many people think of the hammered dulcimer as primarily a German-American instrument, and it was certainly known in such communities, but it was also found among musicians of other ethnic backgrounds.

Of all the instruments considered here, the mountain dulcimer is the one whose history is least well documented. Despite some claims to the contrary, it is most likely *not* an American invention; certainly much of its shape and form is derived from various European instruments such as the Norwegian *langeleik,* the Swedish *hummle,* and the German *scheitholt.* The most direct immediate ancestor is the Pennsylvania German zither, the earliest examples of which date only from the 1790s.[31] As far as is now known, the first American maker of a mountain dulcimer was a Virginia craftsman who was active in 1832. Not long after that the instrument found its way to Arkansas, for one is described in the inventory of the estate of a man who died in the community of Marcella in 1858.[32] For most of its history the mountain dulcimer has remained strictly an instrument used by folk musicians, but recently a few commercial country musicians have utilized the instrument on recordings, so perhaps it will soon penetrate other types of music as well.

The mountain dulcimer is also unlike most of the other instruments mentioned here in that until very recent times it was not mass produced. They were made by individual craftsmen, often, but not always, by someone building it for his own personal use. Since the 1960s, however, this situation has changed drastically so that now there are several dulcimer "factories" scattered around the United States. One of the earliest, and largest, is the Dulcimer Shoppe located in Mountain View, although it was originally started in Forrest City in the late 1960s. Even in these "factories" much of the work is done by hand, so one should not think these places are producing dulcimers in the same way cars are built in Detroit.

Two other instruments occasionally used by Arkansas folk musicians merit mention. The autoharp is significant because it is the only instrument used by traditional Arkansas musicians that is an American invention. It was patented in 1883 by Charles F. Zimmerman, a German immigrant, who had devised a new system of musical notation. Not satisfied that any existing instrument was sufficient to demonstrate his musical notation system, he invented his own. He came up with the autoharp, which is basically an automatic zither. Less common is the picking bow, an instrument found, albeit rarely, among both black and white musicians in Arkansas and other parts of the South. It is not known exactly how old this simple instrument is, but there is a drawing in the southwestern French cave *Les Trois Freres* that has been carbon dated at about 15,000 B.C. that depicts a man using this instrument. There is no truth to the legend that the picking bow was the result of a hunter suddenly being inspired to use his bow as a musical instrument. It seems that the picking bow is derived from a larger, and even older, instrument, called the ground zither.

Folksingers, whether they are performing ballads or folksongs, present their material in a specific manner. Arkansas folksingers, no matter their ethnic or racial background, generally perform in the "objective" style already discussed in the remarks about country music. They remain in a sense detached from the lyrics and rarely resort to intrusions that detract from the song. A routine stanza of a ballad is given equal attention with a stanza containing the dramatic climax. No sudden diminuendo (lowering of volume) or crescendo (increasing volume), such as the art or popular singer employs to spotlight important points in a song, is used. The text is of major importance; all else is secondary.

While in many respects white and black singers present their songs in a similar manner, their method of presentation is not exactly the same. Afro-American singers have a greater tendency to improvise where white singers tend to try and reproduce the song exactly as they heard it.

Blacks lean less toward narrative songs than do their white counterparts, although, of course, ballads are known and performed by black singers. But even ballads performed by black folksingers are often less organized along narrative lines. Afro-American singers are more likely to inject syncopation and other rhythmic features into their singing than are whites. Many of these traits are found in African folk singing and possibly represent a form of cultural survival.

Two further matters remain to be considered: who is a folk musician and singer? What function do these people fill in their community? To provide a succinct answer to these questions is difficult because many different types of people become folk singers and musicians and they fulfill a broad number of functions. Despite certain popular stereotypes, such people are not always rural, isolated illiterates who have no knowledge of, or contact with, urban civilization. Undoubtedly, some such persons have become folk singers and musicians, but their number is indeed small. Most of those who pass traditional lore of any kind on are intelligent and very knowledgeable about the world in which all of us live. While many folk performers may lack extensive formal education, such matters have no bearing on their status as traditional musicians or on their abilities.

Evidently one of the major functions any folk musician or singer performs is that of providing entertainment, but he or she often fills other roles as well. For example, a ballad singer may be perceived by members of his or her community as preserving a portion of local history. Thus, when Almeda Riddle sang "Broken Down Brakeman" about a turn-of-the-century wreck in central Arkansas it was entertainment for her audience, but it was also a presentation of a piece of local history that is not recorded in most books. Certain songs may be seen as reinforcements of community moral codes, the song "Lee Mills" cited earlier being one example. One of the points of the lyric is that crime does not pay. Often the words to songs express some similar "moral" point of view; this is particularly true of native-American ballads, but even a lyric song may occasionally reinforce some generally accepted local code. Of course, musicians and singers are not always viewed positively by their local communities. The very fact that they perform music may cast them in the role of an outsider or an undesirable. For example, in some places fiddlers were considered somewhat nefarious or misguided because they played "the Devil's box," i.e., the fiddle. Many musicians subscribed to the same idea, and upon "getting religion" fiddlers often gave up their music. Likewise, in black communities blues musicians were thought by some to be playing the "Devil's music" and were, to those of that frame of mind, poor role models. Discussion of such matters could continue almost indefinitely, but the comments above amply make the point that folk musicians and singers, like other members of a traditional community, fill varied roles.

Talking Truth in Arkansas

GEORGE E. LANKFORD

As far back as our records will take us, the people of Arkansas have loved a good lie. *We Always Lie to Strangers*, proclaimed the title of one of Vance Randolph's many wonderful books on the narrative traditions of the Ozarks.[1] The proclamation is falsely modest, though, because Arkansans also love to lie to each other, too. It's just more fun to lie to strangers, because they may not know the game and in their innocence allow the narrator an opportunity to reach new heights of outrageously eloquent mendacity.

The tall tale, or "windy," is not restricted to Arkansas, of course. It is popular many places around the world, and it seems to be characteristic of Euro-Americans throughout our history. Americans who have the ability to tell outstanding exaggerations have long been recognized as gifted, and no one has ever gotten their skill confused with the moral problem of lying. At least as far back as the Arkansas frontier period, the art of playing with the truth has been nationally recognized as a little better developed in Arkansas than in other places. "Pete Whetstone" was one of the darlings of the national literary craze called "Southwestern Humor," and he was the invention of the personal experiences and literary pen of

C. F. M. Noland, a Virginian who early became enamored of the windy style of the Ozark frontier.[2] In the second half of the nineteenth century, the "Arkansas Traveler" graced many an American parlor wall and was on the lips of an American people who very much liked the sharp-tongued humor of a frontier squatter who knew the art and always lied to strangers.[3]

Playing with the truth is always alluring, and it is not difficult to see why that should be especially true in America. The novelties of the New World left Europeans astonished from the beginning of their awareness of them; everything—the riches of Mexico, the societies of Florida, the rich soil, the rattlesnakes, the forests—was full of wonder. And who could say which accounts were true and which embellished? The Europeans arrived here, generation after generation, not very clear about what was reality and what was fantasy in this New World. Some of the "truths" they had in their heads were told with a straight face, but those same versions of reality would now be recognized as some of our favorite lies. How hot does it get? "It gets sooo hot here that . . ." We have the biggest bears, the best dogs, the worst droughts, the prettiest hills, the richest soil, and so on. And who can say whether it be true or not? In Arkansas—and in America in general—anything can happen. As many an Arkansas raconteur has commented to his appreciative audience, "It's God's truth," and only the twinkle tells them he's playing. That vision of limitless possibilities has been enshrined in the American tradition of the tall tale, and the extraordinary collections of Vance Randolph in this century have given the Ozarks a widespread image as a region in which the American windy tradition still lives, even in this day of electronic entertainments. Those who wish to feast on the riches of that tradition cannot do better than to read the publications of Randolph.[4]

Telling "lies" is a pleasant way of playing with the truth, a play which nonetheless has a serious side. Recognition that the story we're listening to is a tall tale, after all, depends upon our being able to know—or at least have a hunch—where the line between truth and falsehood lies. Tall tales are "tall" only because we decide they are lies; as long as we have been successfully deceived by the narrator into thinking we are hearing a serious attempt at the truth, then we think we are listening to something other than a tall tale. Folklorists prefer to call that something a "legend."

In recent times, "legend" and one of its subcategories, "myth," have become in popular usage synonymous with "untruth," but the ancient and more respectable meaning is just the opposite. To tell a narrative that purports to describe a real event is to tell a *legend*, and if the topic concerns cosmic reality, then the story may use gods or other cosmic forces to tell about ultimate truth and be called a *myth*. Legends abound in Arkansas, as they do in all areas among all people, because one of the enterprises basic to our humanity is the need to define the line between truth and illusion. It used to be thought that an essential characteristic of a legend is that it be believed by the person who tells it, but we have come to see that that is not necessarily the case. It is enough for a narrator to be interested in the belief at the heart of the story.[5] If the legend offers some evidence to support a particular belief about reality, then the teller may be sharing it precisely because he does not believe it—because he is perplexed about it. "Lord, I believe; help my unbelief" is the central dynamic of the legend. Consider the experience of Beulah Morain when she pursued a legend.

The Belled Buzzard

by Beulah M. Morain[6]

I pulled my car to the side of the gravel road to look at my road map. We had just passed a small crossroads settlement in rural northwest Arkansas. No highway or county road signs were visible among the trees.

"Why don't you go back there and see if anyone can give you directions?" my sister-in-law asked.

"Sure seems logical to me," my husband observed.

Feeling a little irritated, I put the car in reverse without saying a word. Gravel clattered and dust blew up in front of the tires. I pulled my car onto the drive of the general store and got out just in time to hear a curious exchange between an old woman and a young man.

"Don't bell the buzzard, Tommie," the old lady chided.

"But grandma, Dad is being so unreasonable," the boy pleaded.

"Unreasonable or not, he is your father. You can catch more flies with honey than vinegar. Just remember that."

"Yes, Grandma," the scowling teenager acknowledged. He sat balancing his slender body on the wide porch rail as he stared back at the screen door he had just slammed.

His grandmother sat in a high-backed wooden rocker on the shaded end of a wide plank porch. She continued to sew colorful quilt blocks together with tiny stitches, as I approached.

"Could I help you?" she asked.

"I've been out looking for antiques and Depression glass," I explained. "I seemed to have lost my way back to the highway. I just overheard you use an expression that I've only heard a few times before. 'Don't bell the buzzard.' Is it strictly an Arkansas expression?" I inquired.

"Well, I reckon it is. I haven't traveled, so I can't say for sure. The first time I heard it, it was from my father. I'll tell you about it if you care to sit for a spell.

"I'm Hattie Mason." She introduced herself with a smile. "This young man is my grandson, Tommie. My son tends this store now, but my husband started it almost sixty years ago."

"Then you've been here for a good while?" I asked.

"Yes, I was born over in Boone County, near Harrison, in 1895." She laid aside her sewing and pushed her glasses up higher on the bridge of her nose. "My grandparents came from Tennessee around 1840 when my father was just a boy like Tommie. As my grandfather told it, the Panic of 1837 drained settlers from most of the southern and eastern states. They were searching for a place to make a new start in life. The land was cheap and abundant here in Arkansas, the new state to the west." She paused and her face became thoughtful as she recalled this bit of history.

"Yes, I see how that would be an incentive for a family wanting to relocate," I agreed.

"The group of new settlers my grandparents were with chose a river bottom area. The soil was rich along that river. Father told me a lot of stories about his boyhood there.

"One bank of the river was bordered for several miles with high sandstone bluffs. They were topped with scrub oak and other assorted timber. These bluffs protected this community from the cold north winds and sudden weather changes. They were also the home and breeding grounds for thousands of buzzards.

"On the level side of the river the homes were built. The land was opened for cultivation and the people engaged in fruit raising. Hog raising, however, became the main source of income for this new community," she remembered.

"One summer, hog cholera broke out among the pigs; a lot of them died. The buzzards descended from the stony bluffs to feast on the carcasses. In time, the buzzards carried the disease from this community to others in the area.

"The farmers were aware that unless something positive were done to check the spread of cholera, their hogs would be wiped out. They called a town meeting to discuss this serious problem and to agree upon a solution."

"How terrible! What did they decide?" I asked.

"There was an unwritten law that these birds shouldn't be killed. They served a useful purpose to the farmers. They were scavengers who helped the environment by eating the decayed flesh of fallen animals.

"It was decided that they would capture one of these big birds and fasten a sheep bell on it. This, they hoped, would cause the buzzards to leave the area, halt the spread of disease, and restore the economy of the community."

"Did it work?" I wanted to know.

"In time, one of the buzzards was trapped and belled as planned. His return to the flock created a great commotion among the birds. Within a few days great flocks of the buzzards disappeared from the timber. Only the buzzard with the bell remained near the settlement, but soon he too took flight."

"If the story ended right there it would be a happy ending," I commented. "I have a feeling there is more yet."

Hattie Mason shifted in her chair and continued: "At the end of the summer, a typhoid epidemic spread through the community. About the same time the buzzard reappeared. The tinkle of his bell could be heard above the housetops.

"He came and went from time to time. Always his appearance was followed by some new calamity. Each return of the buzzard would arouse feelings of anxiety. His presence had become an ill-omen associated with some new misfortune.

"One day in early fall, the buzzard made a new appearance. Instead of soaring to the timber, as he usually did, he perched atop the chimney on a young man's house. He roosted there all night.

"The man's little daughter, a few months old, died before morning of typhoid fever. The community mourned their loss and started to prepare for the funeral." Mattie's voice trembled as she paused to brush tears away.

"When the funeral procession started to move toward the little cemetery, the great bird floated just above the lead wagon. It circled over the grave during the burial. The small sheep bells tolled all the while. When the mound of earth was rounded up over the body, the bird swung higher in the air and disappeared. Long after the bird was out of sight the mournful notes could still be heard.

"The people believed that this repulsive bird was possessed by an evil spirit. Many people still believe he roams the skies over northwest Arkansas. Any report of a belled buzzard casts a spell of gloom over the inhabitants."

"Then 'Don't bell the buzzard' is an expression heard only in this area of the Ozarks. I'd gather it means 'Don't trade one evil for another one' to those who have heard the legend of the belled buzzard," I said.

A blast from the car horn reminded me that I was delaying others in our party. "Thank you so much. I'll come back another day to visit. I certainly appreciate what you've told me."

I reached for my small green notebook as I climbed into the back seat of the car. "Someone else can take their turn of driving. I've got some important notes to make before I forget the legend of the belled buzzard."[7]

Enshrined in this legend are two important beliefs: that buzzards can cause disease and death, and that buzzards are thinking creatures able to enter into personal relations with humans and to focus their death powers at will. If you do not believe these two propositions, then you will reject the whole story as a description of reality and classify it, perhaps, as a tall tale. If you already believe them, then the account will seem plausible. If, however, you have no strong beliefs either way, then this legend become a source of serious thought, because it offers what may be significant evidence on the issue—the narrator is claiming an experiential proof of the buzzard's role in disease.

Such legends—*belief legends*, they are sometimes redundantly called—are told everywhere in Arkansas, in the cities as well as in the hills, and by everyone, not just the isolated Ozarker. Even more, the *same* legends are told in many different places, and they are always perfectly adapted to the location, reflecting the local terrain, people, and events. These legends are united by the fact that they deal with the same beliefs and the same sort of happenings, even though the details are all different. Most of us have had the experience of saying, "I've heard about that, but it happened back in my hometown, not here!" When that experience happens, it usually means that we have bumped into a different localization of what is called a "migratory legend," a legend which has apparently been widely diffused but which has gone through adaptation in its many locations. Here is Melissa Calley's account of a famous (on state television, at any rate) phenomenon in Arkansas.

GHOST LIGHTS

by Melissa Calley[8]

About four miles from Gurdon, Arkansas, is a railroad crossing known as Sandy Crossing. Sandy Crossing is locally famous because of the light that can be seen there, and has been seen by many people on many occasions. I have never seen the light myself, but, having heard about it since I was a child, I always accepted it as true and thought it was a local occurrence. However, similar light stories at different places have been discussed by Vance Randolph and John Roberts.

The most popular explanation of the "light" at Gurdon is that it is a man looking for his head. In my interview with Roland Calley, of Gurdon, he told me:

> There's been different tales told about it. There was one, uh, the main one that everybody wants to agree on, is, uh, it was a man got run over at that crossing there one time, and it cut his head off. The train cut his head off. And, uh, they found him but they never did find the head. Well, of course they buried the man, but, said, every so often that his ghost comes back looking for that head, and that's the ghost that's carrying a lantern. And that's the light that you see down there, is the lantern that ghost is carrying.[9]

A similar account of a light in Missouri is given by John W. Roberts. Among other origins, the light is said to be 1) a miner looking for his daughter, with his lantern as the light; 2) a man looking for his wife, also with a lantern; and 3) a miner who was attacked by robbers, and, because he wouldn't give them his money, they chopped his head off, and he is looking for his head, though it does not specify a lantern.[10] In the case of the light at Sandy Crossing and in the first two accounts above, the light is a man with a lantern, and all of the versions it is a man looking for something or someone. All of these explanations serve to give the lights a human origin and make an exciting story. They also give the lights a purpose for being there.

Vance Randolph has recorded stories about "Indian lights" in north-eastern Oklahoma, which he has seen, that are supposed to be either the spirit of a murdered Osage chief or of a Quapaw maiden who drowned herself when her warrior was killed. This light can be seen at any given time after dark.[11] The stories of the Indians may be a localized explanation, since Indians have lived in Oklahoma for so long, just as the miner is localized to Missouri and the railroad worker is localized to Gurdon. People explain the lights with something they can understand. There is a "light" story near Stamps, Arkansas, that is almost identical to the one at Gurdon, also set on the railroad tracks. I don't know the basis for that story, but there really was a man decapitated at Sandy Crossing by a train, according to Mrs. Mildred Welch of Gurdon. She couldn't remember the year or many of the details, but she told me that the family of the man got very upset by the perpetuation of the story because they thought it was exploitative.[12] It may be that this account is a secondary legend which supports the primary one.

The settings of these lights are similar as well. The "Indian lights" Randolph referred to are seen on ". . . a lonesome stretch of country road . . ." He also mentioned the "scrubby oak trees at the road-side . . ."[13] Roberts' "spook light" is seen on a "dark country road."[14] Calley describes the Sandy Crossing area as:

> It's, uh, the crossing is in a kind of a curve in the road; it's an old county road. It's only been blacktopped in the last, oh, ten years, I guess. And it was, it's been a pretty dangerous crossing; it was not marked or anything, and they's been several people killed at that crossing. Trains hit 'em and things like that. . . . You can see it (the light) from the crossing. See it down the track. And it's pretty far off down there, but there's been very few people that was crazy enough to try to walk down there and see what it was. Uh, that area right in there is, uh, is a heavily wooded area; it's swamps, and railroad trussels, things like that in there, and I imagine there's probably about any kind of animal there, that there is around here—is in that area in there because there's not any, very little hunting goes on in there. . . .[15]

All of these lights are near country roads in presumably wooded areas with few people living near by, giving them a more lonesome setting. The lights also appear near water or some place that would allow the light to be explained as coming from a vehicle. Randolph, Roberts, and Calley all mentioned swamps, springs, or rivers nearby, so the lights could be explained as swamp gas. Randolph's "Indian lights" have been explained as lights from cars on a highway or airport beacons.[16] Roberts' "spook light" has been explained as cars on nearby roads and town streetlights.[17] The Sandy Crossing light has been explained as lights from cars, though there are few other roads close to the tracks, and as train lights, though the trains never show up.

I also thought it interesting that Roberts refers to his "spook light" as a parking legend. Although there is no place to park except on the tracks themselves, the Sandy Crossing light is most popular with teenagers, especially the younger ones. My twelve-year-old sister has asked me several times to take her and her friends out to the light. I have driven by at night and seen three or four cars parked in the ditch back up the road with their passengers out talking to each other. The police go out by there a lot on weekends to make sure no one gets hurt. The light is especially popular at Halloween, and anyone who goes out there is liable to get pelted with something. I don't think, as Roberts suggests, that the story is told to scare the girls into the boys' arms. People are so used to it I don't think it would work.

I think that the light, the "spook light," and the "Indian lights" are just different versions of the same migratory legend. I don't know what causes the lights, and since I've never seen one myself I don't think I'm qualified to guess. Whatever they are, I do believe people have seen them, and I think the ghost stories are a way of making them a legitimate local feature and giving them a more exciting explanation. My interview with Calley seems to hint at this. The interview began with a general description of the crossing, and he introduced the ghost story itself with: "There's been different tales told about it. There was one, uh, the main one that everybody, that everybody wants to agree on . . ." and he ended it with: ". . . but now whether it is or not, I don't know. That's all I've heard." I thought it was significant, and probably true, that he said that it is the story everyone wants to agree on. After all, who wants to hear about swamp gas or headlights when they could hear about a man forever haunting the place of his death in search of his head?

The phenomenon in question here is an unexplained light at night. The explanation offered by this complex of legends is that ghosts are involved. The motivation for the ghost to produce a light is the variable belief, and it ranges from a decapitated man looking for his presumably unburied head to a ghost looking for a person.[18] The major belief, of course, is that the dead are spirits that can exist in the normal plane of existence and affect human life. This is an idea that seems incapable of proof or disproof, since the human race has not resolved it throughout its history, and thus it is a perennial and universal belief question. Legends of the Gurdon light thus immediately connect us to a vast body of legendry—encounters with the dead. Arkansans participate strongly in this world of speculation, as can be seen by the many state contributions in McNeil's collection of Southern ghost legends.[19] The beliefs, however, are not peculiar to Arkansans, for they are widely found and long antedate the settlement of Arkansas. For example, the belief that a soul cannot rest until the proper burial has been accomplished is at least as old as the ancient Greeks.

Arkansans speculate about other reasons for ghostly activity, however, and the legends are many. Penney Wood did a brief study of some of those reasons as she pondered some legends she heard in Marion County.

WHAT IF?

by Penney Wood[20]

"Do ghosts really exist?" This question has been posed many times by many different types of people, yet no definite answer has been found. Perhaps this is not the proper question to be asking. It seems more appropriate to ask, "Why do ghost stories persist?" Ozark families have passed on tales and legends relating to the supernatural for many centuries. Why is there such a fascination with this phenomenon, and to what types of events are these sightings related?

After interviewing W. Earl Wood and collecting a number of supernatural tales from him, and upon reading Vance Randolph's Ozark Magic and Folklore, I venture to say ghostly tales persist because of the allure and mystery connected to them, as well as their connection to the unexplainable.

Ghosts and apparitions appear in a variety of places for a variety of reasons. One of the most common undertones of ghostly sightings lies in the belief that ghosts often return to avenge their death, if foul play was involved, or they return to relay information to the living so their souls may rest in peace. Those ghosts returning to avenge their deaths most often return to the site at which they were killed and continue to appear there until someone solves the mystery of their death or the killer is caught and justice rendered.

One tale Mr. Wood related to me involved his brother-in-law, Audie Reed, who saw a "ball of fire" in the house where his (Audie's) Aunt Martha was shot and later died. Audie was spending the night in the house and "setting over the table, where she was sitting when she got shot (laugh), he said, was a big ball of fire. That big ball of fire sat at that table all night long." Mr. Wood made it clear that his brother-in-law, and even he himself, saw a connection between the "ball of fire" and the shooting of Audie's Aunt Martha. The ball of fire was apparently Aunt Martha returning to avenge her shooting.[21]

Vance Randolph also relates to us a number of instances in which ghosts or spirits return to avenge their death or to uncover truths. Randolph's work contains tales such as the headless spectre who haunts the scene of his decapitation, the Oak Grove schoolhouse haunted by a man hanged there, and the house haunted by the ghost of a peddler killed there.[22] These ghostly tales, and a number of others, find their basis in unsolved murders and unavenged deaths.

Death is a common factor in a number of ghostly sightings, but even more common is a connection to lost money or lost gold. Life in the Ozarks has always been difficult; money and resources have never been plentiful, and people have always been fascinated with the idea of finding lost mines and hidden gold in the Ozark hills. This thought is alluring to the poor Ozarkians, and as a result, a number of gold legends evolved, and many of these stories contain ghostly guardians who protect the hidden money and often lead people to it.

Mr. Wood relayed a number of these ghostly guardian legends while being interviewed. His accounts ranged from a hidden cave that runs beneath his property where several wagon loads of gold "might" be hidden, to numerous sightings of "jack-o-my-lanterns" which lead to buried money and treasure. Two of the most intriguing sightings went as follows:

> Daddy (Earl Wood's father Robert) told about a house where they stayed . . . I guess it was northern Missouri or somewhere up there. Every night at midnight the front door would open and close, and the back door would open and close, and a horse would whinny as it went through the house. It was a crazy sound, as it went through the house. They said they dug up money under the door step, some people did, that bought the place. The horse never did go through the house no more.[23]

The second sighting refers to a headless horseman:

> About midnight at night, (pause) or so, he'd (Earl Wood's aunt's boy-
> friend) meet a black horse with a guy riding it dressed in black, and the
> guy didn't have any head.[24] He met him and tried to talk to him, and
> the guy would just go right on, he said. One night he tried to talk to
> him, and he took his gun along; he was going to shoot him. He said he
> met him that night; he went purposely to meet him. It was that kind of a
> night. He met him, he said, about halfway down the stretch where he
> always met him, and said he tried to talk to him, and he didn't say any-
> thing, so he whipped the old gun out and said, "If you're trying to scare
> me, you ain't scaring me." He said the guy didn't say a word, and he
> said, "I snapped the barrel all the way around, and it wouldn't go off."
> The man went ahead. He said, "I figured right then that it wasn't some
> guy trying to scare me. I took it (the gun) home and every shell shot."
> The gun wouldn't go off, so he knew it was real. They said they found
> $75,000 in that area. They dug it out of a fence post and never saw the
> ghost again.

As can be seen, these sightings involve a lost treasure and often the
discovery of it by "someone"; no one usually knows the founder personally. Randolph, too, relays such incidents in his work. He states,
"There are many tales about ghosts who speak to people, telling them
to dig at such-and-such a place to find a buried treasure. The ghost is
usually that of some fellow who died without being able to tell anybody
where his treasure was concealed, and who cannot rest quietly until
someone gets the money and enjoys it."[25]

So far two reasons have been stated to legitimize ghostly sightings,
avenging one's death and finding lost treasures. A third basis for the
sighting exists, and it refers back to the idea that warning signs are
issued by God or some other supernatural being to warn man of his
sins or errors and to get him back on the right track, or to warn him of
some potential danger.

> They went to bed one night, and Aud (uh) said (uh) this guy come in
> the door, said they had the door fastened and locked, didn't know how
> he came in. He just come in. Said he came up and was walking around
> the bed. . . . And Aud said he went around and around and stood and
> looked at them. Walked right up to them and looked at them for I don't
> know how long, hour or more. . . . Just laid there like he was asleep. . . .
> He looked till he kind of got tired of looking and went back out the door.
> . . . He said "We give him about five minutes and went through that
> door," and said "it was fastened. Don't know how he fastened it

back inside." . . . They went to Rex and Gladys' with their clothes off and told 'em they had to get in the house, there was a man over there trying to kill 'em. Not long after that a man did try to kill Hoover. . . . (Hoover was the man with Audie in the house.)

Wood seemed to accept this incident as a sign of the future attempt on Hoover Friend's life. He felt very comfortable making a connection between the two incidents.

Randolph also relates an incident of warning in his book. A woman near Pineville, Missouri, was flattened by a violent blow and was warned to "Be good to my children," for she had been unkind to her stepchildren.[26] Ghost legends carry with them an air of mystique. One can not prove or disprove the legitimacy of the stories, for he can not prove or disprove the existence of ghosts and spirits. The excitement of the unknown and the unexplainable generates enough interest to keep the tales alive and keeps the listener thinking, "What if? What if ghosts really exist? Does that mean that there really is a buried treasure, or that a person was really murdered in that spot?" Whether ghosts exist or not, the stories are great to tell to children around the fireplace and are great to pass on through the generations. But, what if? . . .

Earl Wood never stated whether or not he actually believed the tales he told. He constantly said, "they said," or "he said." He did tell of a few strange instances he was involved in, but he never confessed to believing in ghosts or supernatural beings, yet he continues to tell the tales and contributes to keeping the tales alive for centuries to come.

Here are ghosts of various forms and motivations. The ghostly light is again here, but this time it appears to be connected to the lack of justice concerning the murder rather than to the lack of the complete burial. The underlying belief here is also ancient—that a death requires a death, and especially the death of the murderer. It is interesting that this complex belief is read out of a ball of light hanging over a table; the interpretation certainly bears witness to their concern over the unsolved death of the aunt.

Both of these beliefs about the presence of the dead—an unburied body and an unsolved crime—are historical, and they are rooted in the location of the death. Ghosts may also choose to appear to warn the living about the future, either events or behavior which must be avoided.[27] The sequence of events in Wood's last legend shows that the interpretation of the ghostly experience as a warning was arrived at only later, after

Hoover had suffered an attempt on his life. If it was a warning, it was too obscure to have been of much use.

Ghosts can be fairly explicit, however. One anonymous informant who refused to be recorded nonetheless told Norma Barber about her experience in trying to find buried money.

> She said that when she was about fifteen years old, her family rented a house from a man who told her that the former owner of the land had buried money on the place, and he told her where it was buried. She went to the place where the money was hidden, and she dug a hole about three feet deep. She said that she hit a large rock, and that she quit digging for the day. She said that she was really tired that night, because she had really worked hard digging for that money. She said that during the night she saw the man who supposedly buried the money. He was standing at the foot of her bed, and he said, "Leave it alone, just leave it alone!" She said that she was so scared that she would not look under that rock. She said that she went back to the site and filled the hole with dirt. She said that the next man who rented that house became wealthy shortly after living there. She believes that there was a treasure and that the other man found it. She said that she thought that it was under the rock, and that she was very close to finding it. She said she did not know if she really saw a ghost, or if she was so tired that she dreamed it, but it scared her so badly that she would not, or could not, keep looking for the money.[28]

The woman expressed some doubt as to whether she "really saw a ghost," but she radically altered her behavior because of it. Later on she raised the cost of the experience, for the ghostly warning did not simply deprive her of the search for the buried money; she lost "a treasure," a sum which was validated by the later owner's becoming "wealthy."

Her story connected a ghost with a treasure, a connection which Wood found as a major theme in ghost legendry. In the two legends she presented, the legend of a ghostly horse that walks through the house in the night and the headless horseman legend, there is no visible connection between the apparition and treasure. Yet in each case the finding of buried money is added to the narrative, as if it were a natural part of an unspoken larger belief. In collecting legends from some black Arkansans, Lorrie Jenkins found some of the missing connections.

BLACK GHOST AND TREASURE LEGENDS

by Lorrie Jenkins[29]

Ghosts appear in several different forms: an animal, a sound, a person, a group, or an unusual occurrence. When a ghost legend is connected to treasure legends, the ghost usually appears either to protect a treasure or to reveal it, and the treasure is frequently offered as proof of the existence of the ghost (but sometimes the ghostly experience is used to validate the existence of the treasure). The ghost legends compiled in this paper were collected from persons living in or close to the Ozarks. Although some of the tellers do believe in the legend that they tell, they are uncomfortable with telling the ghost legend.

The first three ghost and treasure legends were told by Adolph Jenkins, who grew up in Roland, Arkansas, during the 1920s and '30s. He lived in a cabin, a renovated stable, and a CC camp before working for the railroad and owning his own home in Newport. His three legends are told in detail with a strong belief in the ghost's existence. He uses a legend about a pot of gold that his grandfather found and buried to explain why he saw the ghost.

> Well, what I was saying about the horse was there was some money buried up there (on a hill near where he lived). And when someone gets close to it . . . when someone buried money back in them days, they would carry someone with them and have them dig the hole for them and put the money in. And then they would ask them, "Will you watch that money for me?" Then they would tell them that they would watch the money. So they would kill them and throw them in the hole. And they would watch the money for them. They would come in the form of a horse or a dog to scare people off. At that time (the) money was still up there. And no one has found it.[30]

Mr. Jenkins told another ghost legend about an Indian woman who found gold in her yard. This legend seems to follow along the lines of the buried Indian treasure legends, in which the Indians return to the Ozarks to retrieve some buried gold coinage from former Indian land. Yet the legend has a slight supernatural flavor to it. He indicated that he has always been taught that something happened when one is dealing with buried money.

There was an old house from where we went to school. There was a pot of gold buried in that house. And this old lady (she) dug holes around that house. And she dug it up and left there one night. And you can see the leg spots where she had pulled it up and left. And no one ever heard from her again . . . she was an Indian. . . . There were three leg prints (in the last hole). One of the boys found a five dollar gold piece that she had dropped.

In this legend he used the three leg prints to indicate that there was something a little unusual about her sudden departure. The leg prints along with the lost coin and the location serve to authenticate the story.

Another ghost legend about Indians was told by Roland Calley, a white logging contractor from Gurdon. His legend is about (or from) his black employee, Phillip Allen. Notice how this legend carries the traditional belief that Indians buried money in the Ozarks.

Well, this black guy that works for me, we've been friends for a long time; he was telling me one time about some (treasure) being buried down behind an old church when he was a kid way down in the country there. They had heard about it for years, money being buried down there. But it was haunted; no one would go around it. When he was a teenager, he and two of his brothers decided that they would go out there and dig it up. So they went down there; it was marked. . . . And it was a real pretty day. One of his brothers was down in the hole about twelve feet. He and the other one was up on top. Just about the time he hit something solid down there, it clouded up real fast and went to thundering and lightning. So they threw a rope down there so the other one could come up, because they were afraid that it was going to rain and fill that hole full of water. Before the other one could get out they heard a racket, and they looked up and saw a whole gang of Indians on horses coming through the woods down there just a-whooping and a-hollering and a-waving fire sticks and a-everything else. And (he) said that they got scared and took off. Well, the one that was down in the well, he didn't know what was going on. He was still climbing out. When he got out, he saw what it was, he took off running too. They were all scream-ing, hollering and scared to death. And them Indians just a-riding on, just a-whooping and a-hollering. It was about three or four miles to the house, and they ran all the way. They went in the house up there. . . .[31]

Roland Calley went on to explain that the boys were so frightened that they locked themselves up in the house and would not tell their mother what was going on until they were sure that they were safe. When the boys' mother told them that it had been pretty all day, the boys decided never to try that again. Calley said that he tried to get

Allen to take him to that place, but Allen refused to go and offered directions.

Adolph Jenkins told another ghost and treasure legend that explains the impoverished desperation in which the Depression had left already poverty-stricken blacks. Whenever someone heard that there was some money buried in a certain place, they looked for it. Some people would go back after the money after being frightened away by a ghost the first time.

> I remember my father telling me when he went to hunt some money with two fellows. He said that one of them knew where the money was. So they got out there and went digging for the money. And they said that they must have been getting close to the money, (said) they looked up and said here come a big ole ball of fire down in the hole. So they jumped out and went off. So they decided to go back the next night and dig some more. And so one of them went back that same night and dug it up, and no one knows what happened to him. So they don't know how much it was.

He also explained in his interview that families shared with their neighbors when they could. This is a characteristic of the Ozark people. It was not unusual for people to graze their animals together and kill what they needed for their families. He mentioned that when he was growing up there were not any laws against this. The simple point is that people shared what they could when times were hard, but when times got harder, it was everyone for his own family.

Another story about someone going back after the money after a supernatural event was told by Lizzie Jenkins, from Rosston, Arkansas. She recalls this event which happened when she was about eighteen years old.

> It was a Mr. White and he had lived around Rosston for a long time. And he had heard that money was buried near a graveyard near the Weaver place. . . . And he and several men—about five—had dug a half of a day and had come in to get warm. . . . He came to our house and sat down and talked to my daddy. And he told him that his grand-parents had told him (White) about money being buried at that place. And when they dug, they struck something and they assumed that it was metal. And he said that it dropped, and he said that someone had a greedy mind. He believed that because his grandparents taught him that if he went to find money and someone with him had an ulterior motive, then they would not be able to get to the money, because it would drop every time. When he left . . . he cautioned his workers that if they had

*anything else on their minds other than being fair they would not get to
the money at all. When they finished, he came back later and said that
he was going to dig alone. And whether he got it I don't know. But his
wife said that he was the one with the ulterior motive.*

*She believes that he got the money because he got a new car soon
afterward.*

*In conclusion, ghost and treasure legends, like any other legends
from the Ozarks, depict the time, history, and Ozark culture of the
people who pass them on. In other words, one can understand what
were the great issues of the time the legends were told. In these legends
the great need was money for the family or person who digs for the
money. Mrs. Jenkins grew up with a background similar to her father-
in-law, although the time was about twenty years later. This simply
shows how hard it was for the black family in the Ozarks to move up
and change their lifestyle.*

Lorrie Jenkins found an explicit recognition of the chilling belief
that the ghost of a man murdered and buried with a treasure will remain
to guard it, a belief usually associated with pirate legends. She also found
the connection of Indians with buried treasure in Arkansas. The presence of native Americans is possibly a local development, since the very
assertion of wealth in the region seems implausible, but reference to the
many immigrant native Americans who have lived there adds a bit more
historical respectability. In one narrative, the treasure is guarded by
Indians who are themselves ghosts.

As is characteristic of so much treasure legendry everywhere, the
treasure either is not found (frequently for supernatural reasons) or is
presumed to be found by someone else. The common ground is that the
narrator and his friends did not get the treasure, which is thus perenni-
ally a goal but never a victory. Jenkins astutely connects this theme of
treasure legends with the hope generated by the poverty-stricken. That
interpretation gains force when we consider that the same treasure
theme has been attached to the common Ozarks Civil War legend of the
Jayhawkers, possibly one of the few Arkansas legends unique to the
region.[32]

Death, wealth, Indians, Jayhawkers, justice—all are the themes of
beliefs that are subtly debated in the legends we tell, and there are many
more. As has often been observed, we tell legends to examine and
reconfirm our beliefs about reality, but especially about those portions of
reality that concern us personally. There has been a lot of study of the

modern "urban legend" that focuses on the aspects of technological, urbanized life that worry us.[33] Arkansas participates in those concerns, as we would expect, whether they are reflected in the contamination of our fast foods or in the deadly snakes in our department store merchandise. The much-studied "adolescent legends" are found throughout Arkansas, as is to be expected wherever there are teenagers with their complex concerns—group acceptance, sexual behavior, dangers in their world (demented slashers in parking areas, tragic pranks), and so on.

For several years, each Halloween in Independence County has been marked by a flurry of legends about the operation of devil worshipers in the county, complete with intentions of human sacrifice. The ancient concerns about evil that once were expressed in legends about the Prince of Darkness now seem to be focused on concerns about evil cults, a very contemporary worry that is independent of belief in the Devil himself. Theologically related to this concern about the power of evil is the hope for divine providence, a belief that is frequently expressed in the legends that are told to interpret major disasters, such as floods or tornadoes.[34]

In all of these fascinating areas of legendry, Arkansans, like everyone else, talk about the possibilities of life. The beliefs under discussion are the ones that directly influence the way we live our lives, and the problem is always how to distinguish the true from the false, the real from the unreal. If we take the legend as expressing a correct belief, then there is a certain grim satisfaction that accompanies its telling. If we decide the belief is false, then we fall into skeptical "hmmfs" or even ridicule. But if we determine that the storyteller knew all along that he was lying, then the best response is laughter in pleasure at having been fooled, if only for a moment, by a tall tale. No matter where we end up in listening to our traditional oral narratives, one way or another we're trying to talk truth.

Front porch of the Standlee house in Nashville, Arkansas. Photo by author.

Folk Architecture in Arkansas

Sarah Brown

By studying Arkansas folk architecture, we can better understand who Arkansans were and are as a people and, perhaps, can better answer significant questions about how individuals initiate and come to grips with change. Why look at buildings, or any artifact, for an answer? Academic disciplines, such as history, sociology, and cultural geography, have divided life into discrete spheres of reality. Life, or culture, exists as a totality. People go about their daily routines encountering other people and other things—clothes, furniture, cars, etc. These things reflect values and aspirations, and they improve or diminish the quality of life. Some people put into writing their thoughts and beliefs, but most, throughout history, have not. Moreover, what people write about their worlds is always biased and may reflect what is wished for, instead of what is. Buildings are relatively permanent in the collection of things. They are generally place-specific and are often among the few historical records of many people. Studying architecture will aid us in piecing together the totality that is culture. This, then, is the grand goal of those who study buildings, but it is not a simple task. The following essay is an attempt to survey what has been written about architecture in Arkansas and to unravel the threads of what is a very intricate tapestry.

Focusing on folk houses, the essay demonstrates some of the complexities of the subject and constitutes a minimal base from which future studies may be made.

When folk architecture is studied in classrooms across the nation, few references are made to Arkansas buildings. This fact is due not to a lack of folk buildings nor to an absence of significant research topics in the state, but instead to a lack of scholarly writing about the state's architecture. Most of the available studies use inventories of buildings to determine the relative presence of architectural types and to delineate cultural regions.[1] This approach was initiated in 1936 by cultural geographer Fred B. Kniffen in "Louisiana House Types."[2] Since the publication of this seminal work, Kniffen and other scholars have shown the connection between the diffusion of culture and the occurrence of traditional building practices for almost all of the eastern United States.[3] Using these studies for reference, folk-building practices found in Arkansas may be traced to cultural source areas, that is, to areas of origin.[4]

Also, the state may be divided into regions or subregions of traditional culture. Two subregions, Upland and Lowland South, coexist generally with the state's two major physiographic regions (figure 1; figures begin on page 125). The Ozark and Ouachita mountains are considered Upland South, while the Mississippi Delta and the Gulf Coastal Plain are Lowland South. Within each subregion is a characteristic collection of building forms. For example, the I house (a two-story structure, two or three rooms wide and one room deep) was the typical middle- and upper-class house of the Upland South (figures 2 and 3). The one- and two-story Georgian-plan house (composed of a central hallway flanked by two rooms on both sides) became the typical middle- and upper-class house of the Lowland South (figures 4, 5, and 14). Georgian-plan houses are rarely found outside the Mississippi Delta and the Gulf Coastal Plain in Arkansas. Although the I house is found throughout the state, the lack of Georgian-plan houses in the Ozark and Ouachita mountains makes the I house the most prominent of larger house types in Upland areas.

Most studies of folk buildings in Arkansas represent British-American culture that diffused from the three major East Coast regions—the South, New England, and the Mid-Atlantic (figure 6). These studies of East Coast diffusion do not consider the presence or influence in Arkansas of French-Colonial building traditions. While none of the state's existing structures were built during the French-Colonial period, immigration from Louisiana after the Louisiana Purchase brought French-Colonial and African-Caribbean influences. Studies of African-

American influences upon Arkansas architecture have yet to be conducted, and only a single study contains information about the homestead of a black family.[5]

Houses are considered the most significant architectural form by many scholars.[6] They are studied both as single entities and as part of an ensemble of structures in the cultural landscape. Prior to the technological advances allowing for the development of modern cities, town residences shared with rural residences many of the same production and maintenance responsibilities. As a result, town residences, or "urban farmsteads," consisted of lots crowded with a variety of structures, such as kitchens, smokehouses, spring houses, chicken coops, hog pens, and privies. With the introduction of modern sewage and refrigeration systems, such outbuildings were given different functions or were destroyed.[7] One structure, however, that has not disappeared on either rural or urban steads, due to the continued occurrences of tornadoes, is the storm cellar.[8]

The most obvious difference between rural residences and urban ones is the presence on rural homesteads of large outbuildings associated with the production of crops and livestock for cash and goods. The precise functions of historic barns are often difficult to determine. Similar structures on two separate farmsteads may have been used for different purposes, while barns with multiple cribs or rooms sheltered a variety of functions, ranging from stabling to storing feed and equipment. Literature on barns, therefore, commonly categorizes the structures by form or shape, instead of by use. Those built in Arkansas, such as single-crib, double-crib, and transverse-crib barns, are generally like those found throughout the American South.[9]

CATEGORIES OF ARCHITECTURE

Folklorists commonly divide architecture into three nonexclusive categories: elite, popular, and folk.[10] While few buildings are so simple as to be placed into a single category, using categories helps students and scholars understand their subject matter. The goal, however, is not simply to place buildings within categories, but to understand the relationship or flow between categories. For example, in the 1840s, architects Alexander Jackson Davis and Andrew Jackson Downing advocated, through pattern books, the use of board-and-batten siding, particularly for Gothic Revival structures. Since board-and-batten siding was then an old form, the efforts may be viewed as attempts to make popular a folk or traditional construction technique thought appropriate to high-style aesthetics.

Elite

Elite buildings are progressive and "high style." Most often, they are one-of-a-kind structures designed by academically trained architects. An example of an elite building is the Old State House in Little Rock (figure 7). Designed by architect Gideon Shryock and constructed between 1833 and 1836, the Greek Revival capitol is "one of the most individual and original creations of its type."[11] Few houses in the state have fallen into this high-style category. One example, however, is the Matthews house in North Little Rock (figures 8 and 9). Built in 1928, it was designed by architect Frank M. Carmean as a "show house" for the exclusive Park Hill subdivision developed by the Justin Matthews Company.[12] The building's plan, form, and decorative features represent an early demonstration of Art Deco and International styles. In Arkansas, as throughout the nation, elite architecture represents the smallest category of buildings in the cultural landscape.

Popular

Popular architecture is "mainstream" and is associated with the development of mass culture, technology, industry, and modern communications that began in the early nineteenth century. Often originating from the drawing boards of architectural firms, many popular building ideas are distributed to the public through pattern books and magazines. While some popular buildings are built by architects, more are constructed by individuals calling themselves builders and contractors. The architectural firm of Charles L. Thompson was the state's most prominent architectural firm during the late nineteenth and early twentieth centuries. While the firm built many large and stylish buildings, its greatest profit was made from the prolific construction of comfortable, moderately priced houses designed to fit the popular tastes of Arkansans. Using a few basic designs, many of these cottages varied only slightly in scale, ornamentation, and construction materials (figures 10 and 11).[13]

Folk

Folk or traditional buildings are constructed by the members of the society that uses them. They are designed with knowledge passed down from one person to the next. This design knowledge does not necessarily require the use of written plans or drawings. Over time, a few basic designs are found to suit the living requirements of a particular society. These basic designs may be classified into types, including the central-hall house (figure 3). The John Wesley Shaver house, built in Evening Shade in 1854, is an example of a central-hall house. The house is a one-story brick structure covered by a gable roof. The original plan consists of two rooms divided by a central hall. Two decades after Shaver built his house, his son, Charles W. Shaver, built an almost identical house in the same town. (figure 12).[14] While both Shavers may have supervised the construction of their homes, the builders needed no drawings as this type of house had been commonly built in America since the mid eighteenth century. The central-hall house suited the needs not only of two generations of Shavers, but those of families in every region of the state from earliest British-American settlement until well into the twentieth century.

Discerning Folk Architecture

The identification and study of folk architecture is not a simple process. Two examples will illustrate the complexity of the field. Near Blevins in Hempstead County is a house built in 1939 for Dr. Grandison Royston (figure 13). Designed by a St. Louis architect named Gumbrill, the house, in form, is much like a large foursquare. The foursquare house was a "popular" type built throughout the United States in the late nineteenth and early twentieth centuries. To build the Royston house, it took a crew of fifteen, using over two thousand V-notched pine logs. The contractor called the Royston house the largest log house in the United States.[15] The second example, built about 1850 for planter Joel Johnson, must have been one of the grandest houses in the Arkansas Lowlands (figure 14). This Chicot County house, called Lakeport Plantation, is two stories tall and has four large rooms with a central hall on each floor (figure 4). Its front facade is ornamented with an impressive Greek Revival portico rising the full two stories.[16] Which, if either, dwelling may be called a folk or traditional house?

To answer the question, form, construction, and style must be assessed separately. (See discussion below.) Form, or plan and overall shape, is the most significant component in identifying a folk building, but style and construction method may also have traditional aspects.

The initial question should not be, "is this a folk building?" but rather, "what aspects of this building are traditional?" If the structure's form is traditional, then it may be termed folk.

The architect-designed Royston house was built by local craftsman using a construction method derived from traditional building technology. The form of the house has already been identified as foursquare. The foursquare house, which could be purchased from mail-order companies such as Sears and Roebuck, was created by architects seeking an alternative to complex Victorian styles (figure 15).[17] Although built of logs, the Royston house is classified as popular. Lakeport Plantation boasts a very fashionable high-style feature with its Greek Revival portico. The plan and form of the house, however, were a century old when the house was built in the 1850s and were no longer in step with high fashion. True Greek Revival houses were being built in the form of a temple with gable end to the front. The Hanks house in Little Rock is a good example of a temple-form house (figure 16). Lakeport Plantation, despite its pretentiousness, is a traditional house.

Style

Style represents a particular set of features reflecting high aesthetic values. These values are usually associated with a code of standards—political, social, or religious—and are determined by a few individuals having the authority or approval of the power structure. For example, during the Federal period, Thomas Jefferson designed buildings using the principles of Classical architecture to reflect the republican ideology of the new nation. As ideologies and values change, so do architectural styles. Studies of high styles are commonly arranged chronologically, charting the ebb and flow of successive sets of aesthetic features. The various styles constitute periods or eras, and in nineteenth-century America these periods are labeled Federal, Greek Revival, Gothic Revival, Italianate, Queen Anne, etc.[18]

Style as reflected in most folk buildings is usually relegated to ornamentation around doorways, windows, and fireplaces, and to attenuated features, such as porches. However, if ornamentation reflects values basic to a local society's culture and is used generation after generation, not without some change, but with minimal influence from national or international "high" styles, the style may be considered folk. Elements of Arkansas folk architectural style have yet to be identified.

The various high styles in American architecture generally include not only ornament but plan or form as well. Georgian-style architecture, fashionable from about 1725 to 1800, included a set of decorative features, such as triangular and segmental pediments over windows and doors, Palladian windows, and quoins, and a plan that emphasized symmetry and balance (figure 17). When the aspects of style become fully incorporated into the building repertoire of a society and are used after that particular style is fashionable, they may be considered traditional. So, even though decorative features and plans may originate in high fashion, they can "fall" to the category of folk. Such is the case with the many Georgian-plan buildings, like Lakeport Plantation (figure 14), built in Arkansas during the nineteenth and early twentieth centuries.

Also, a building with a traditional or folk plan derived from one high style may have decorative features from another. Most of the pre–Civil War houses, churches, and public buildings in Washington, Hempstead County, exhibit influence from the then-current Greek Revival style. Most of the houses, however, have Georgian or Georgian-derived plans. The buildings in Washington may be thought of as having traditional plans and high-style influenced decorative features.

Construction

Folk building construction reflects technology transmitted from one builder to another. Generally lacking a knowledge of the physics of materials and structural systems, the builder acquired knowledge from his own and his predecessors' experience.[19] Folk construction technology in Arkansas largely reflects European-American forms developed in the multiethnic Mid-Atlantic region, the British-American South, and French Louisiana. In Arkansas, as throughout America, most structures are built of wood. Braced-frame buildings such as the Case-Maxfield house of Batesville (figure 18) exist from the 1840s, while the Wolf house in Baxter County (figure 19), built of logs about 1828, is one of the state's oldest existing structures.

Wood construction may be divided into log construction and frame construction. In the United States, construction with logs is characterized by the use of hewn or unhewn timbers laid horizontally and locked together with notches at the corners of the building (figure 20). Log construction technology is not unique to America, but is rooted in Old World traditions. Debates have long raged over which Old World group is responsible for bringing log construction, as it exists in the south-eastern United States, to the New World.[20] As the technology was common throughout northern and eastern Europe, southeastern log construction is best thought of as a New World hybrid with multiple ethnic origins.[21] Within the United States, there is no doubt that the major source area for log construction technology is the cultural hearth of the Mid-Atlantic region. Beginning in the eighteenth century, the technology was carried south and west by the Scotch-Irish, primarily.[22] Eventually, log construction would be practiced in an area covering the lower Midwest, part of the Mid-Atlantic, and all but the coastal fringes of the South (figure 21). Arkansas exists entirely within this area.

Framing systems may be divided into those of British-American heritage—braced, balloon, and box—and those of French-Colonial heritage—*poteaux sur solle* and *poteaux en terre*. In Arkansas, French-Colonial construction technology is the rarest. Commonly used prior to the American purchase of Louisiana, *poteaux en terre* (frames of upright posts anchored in the ground) and *poteaux sur solle* (frames of upright posts resting on a wooden sill and a masonry foundation, figure 22) are found today in areas where permanent French settlements were maintained after British-American immigration. Such areas include New Orleans, Louisiana, Ste. Genevieve, Missouri, and Mobile, Alabama. No permanent French settlements existed in Arkansas, and as a result no true French-Colonial structures may be found today. After 1803, however, immigrants from Louisiana brought the French-Colonial heritage both in construction technology and in building form.

The Rufus Stone house in Independence County appears to be much like any dwelling of a middle-class British-American family of the 1850s (figure 23). It is a central-hall house with decorative features of Greek Revival influence. Thought to have been built by African-American slaves from Louisiana, it is, however, of *poteaux-en-terre* construction (figure 24). The Stone house is a unique synthesis of building ideas, reminding us that our culture has multiple ethnic origins.[23]

Frame buildings constructed by early British-American settlers were of braced-frame construction (figure 25). This technology employs heavy, hand-hewn upright posts, measuring 4" wide by up to 10" thick, at the corners and intermediate spaces to support window and door openings. Smaller uprights, called studs, usually measuring 2" x 4", give support between the posts. The posts and studs are tied together with horizontal members called sills, at the bottom, and plates, at the top.

The corner posts are given added stability by down-braces, which are diagonal braces running from the posts down to the sills.

Framing members are joined by either mortise and tenon joints or nails. The interior is sealed with vertical boards or lath and plaster, while the exterior is covered usually with horizontal weatherboards. This structural system grew out of a medieval European building technology using even heavier timbers and more complex joinery. It was developed, as used in Arkansas, by the early eighteenth century in the Chesapeake region.[24] Braced-frame construction may be found throughout the state in houses, barns, churches, and other structures built before the Civil War.

Although some braced-frame structures, particularly barns, were built after the Civil War, the technology was generally supplanted in the late nineteenth century by a quicker and lighter framing method. This newer method, called balloon-framing, was made possible by American industrialism, but actually represents only a streamlining of the older technology. Thought to have been first employed in the Chicago area in the 1830s, this construction method spread throughout the country and was popularized by carpentry manuals. The method took advantage of easy access to standardized lumber and cheap mass-produced wire nails. Walls consisted entirely of lightweight two-by-four-inch studs joined to sills and plates with nails and stabilized by interior and exterior sheathing.[25] Most houses built in Arkansas in the late nineteenth century and throughout the twentieth century used this framing method.

Another framing system, called box framing, was used throughout late nineteenth- and early twentieth-century Arkansas (figure 26). Box-framing consists of vertical boards, six to twelve inches wide and usually no more than one inch thick, nailed to sills and plates. Serving as major structural support, the vertical boards also constitute the entire wall, interior and exterior. Window and door casings project into the rooms of the structure. Often, two-by-four-inch studs flank windows and doors to give strength to these openings. The interstices or cracks between the vertical boards are covered by wood strips creating board-and-batten siding. In more substantial or later-improved examples, horizontal weatherboards are added to the exterior, making such houses appear indistinguishable from braced or balloon-frame houses. Box construction is similar to plank construction of medieval England and of seventeenth- and eighteenth-century New England where heavier boards, up to three inches thick, were covered with lath and plaster on the interior and horizontal boards on the exterior. In Arkansas, box construction was considered an economical alternative to other framing methods, and it generally supplanted sturdier but socially inferior log construction.[26]

The state's earliest British-American settlers built not only of wood but also of masonry. Brick buildings constructed in Arkansas prior to the Civil War and stone buildings constructed before the twentieth century were usually load bearing. That is, the masonry walls served as major structural support for the whole building. Stones could be shaped by the stonemason or left unshaped and could be laid to create coursed or uncoursed walls. Brick load-bearing walls consisted of bricks laid in an interlocking pattern of stretchers (bricks turned lengthwise) and headers (bricks turned with the short end facing out). The alternate use of stretchers and headers creates decorative rhythms, making load-bearing brick walls easy to identify (figure 27).[27] The Ringgold-Noland house in Batesville is an early example of a house built of load-bearing brick walls (figure 28). More recent masonry walls consist of only a veneer of stone or brick covering a wood or steel-frame structure. Brick was an important building material for houses, as was stone for commercial buildings. Brick and stone, however, were most commonly used for outbuildings, such as wells and springhouses, and for the foundations and chimneys of wood-frame and log houses.

Brick chimneys may be found throughout the state, while chimneys of stone, mortared and unmortared, are found primarily in the mountainous areas of the north and west. Some chimneys are built of both materials, stone on lower portions, brick on upper portions. In the Gulf Coastal Plain of southern Arkansas, where building stone was not readily available, many chimneys were constructed of wooden frames. These chimneys, built throughout the Lowland South, are similar to the wattle-and-daub chimneys of Europe. Lath or twigs were interwoven between wooden framing members and then covered with plaster. In America they are called mud-cat chimneys (figure 29).[28] Easily damaged by weather and fire, most mud-cat chimneys have been replaced by brick chimneys.

In the history of building technology, roof construction developed independently of wall construction.[29] As a result, roofs on brick, log, or frame buildings in Arkansas are generally constructed in the same manner. As is common throughout the eastern United States, Arkansas roofs are framed with rafters raised in pairs, which are pegged or nailed together at the top, and are unsupported by a ridgepole. Collar beams give added support to rafter pairs and form the horizontal bar in what is generally called the A-frame roof. After the rafters are raised, lath is laid over them horizontally. Wood or metal, in shingles, planks, or sheets, is then nailed to the lath. Gable ends are framed with vertical studs and covered with either horizontal or vertical boards.

Form

Form is a combination of plan, height, and, to a lesser degree, the presence and arrangement of features such as chimneys, windows, and doors. Form constitutes the collective arrangement of spaces that order everyday existence. Considered closer to the basic values of most individuals and groups, form is more enduring than style (decorative ornament), and it tends to be defined geographically, as opposed to temporally, that is, in terms of region as opposed to historical period.

Most of Arkansas's traditional buildings represent, in form, British-American culture of the seventeenth and eighteenth centuries. Seventeenth-century colonists in British North America constructed dwellings based primarily upon late medieval prototypes found in the mother country. In the American South of 1700, most houses contained plans of only one (figure 30) or two rooms, because many domestic functions had been pushed out into an ensemble of ancillary structures. In two-room dwellings, the largest room was called the hall. Derived from the great hall of English medieval houses, this room served as a communal space where household members (family and servants) socialized, worked, and ate together. The smaller room, called the parlor, was a private space used by the family for retiring and sleeping. This dwelling of two unequal-sized rooms is called the hall-and-parlor house (figure 31).[30]

Beginning in the early eighteenth century, major social and economic changes swept through the American colonies. As the culture and its living requirements changed, so did the architecture. Again drawing largely upon English examples, Americans built according to a new set of aesthetics, commonly termed Georgian. The prototypical Georgian house emphasized exterior and interior symmetry and balance. It was a two-story, double-pile (two-room deep) structure featuring a central passage or hallway (or newly defined "hall," for short, figures 4 and 14). Generally, the full-blown Georgian house was too large and too symmetrically rigid for the average Southern planter. So, a set of smaller houses was built. Most commonly, these smaller houses represent geometric subunits of the full Georgian house, including single-story Georgian-plan houses, I houses, and central-hall houses.[31]

Although new types of houses were constructed in eighteenth-century America, earlier post-medieval types were not eliminated from the building repertoire. One-room and hall-and-parlor houses continued to be built. Georgian aesthetics, however, required that these houses appear more balanced, particularly in the arrangement of windows and doors. The facades of smaller houses now had either a window and a door symmetrically placed or a central door flanked by a window on each side. Viewed from the exterior, many hall-and-parlor houses became more or less indistinguishable from central-hall houses (figures 32 and 33).

Georgian aesthetics also influenced the development of two other smaller house types. One is called the double-pen house (figure 34). The two rooms or pens are of equal size and have symmetrical or mirrored fenestrations. Usually, an exterior-end chimney stands at each gable. A variant double-pen form is the saddlebag house (figure 35). Two pens flank a large central chimney having a firebox or hearth for each room. Also drawing upon the Georgian idea of the central hallway is the dogtrot house (figure 36). It consists of two rooms or pens flanking an open passage.

In Arkansas, the one-room or single-pen house was probably the most prominent house form (figure 37). Dimensions of single-pen dwellings range from sixteen to eighteen feet square to larger rectangular dwellings typically measuring sixteen-by-twenty feet and eighteen-by-twenty-four feet. Many single-pen houses, particularly pioneer-phase log dwellings, were considered temporary structures. Even those not thought of as temporary have long since been replaced with newer, bigger dwellings. Some were incorporated into larger structures, but proportionally few single-pen dwellings remain.

Often, as a family's needs for more space grew, rooms were added to single-pen dwellings. Shed-roofed and ell-shaped additions were made to the rear. Others additions, sometimes anticipated, were made to gable ends, creating versions of double-pen houses (figure 38). Two-phase double-pen dwellings may exhibit two construction technologies. As a rule, the pens of an original double-pen house tend to be squarer than those of a two-phase double-pen house. One of the most common folk house forms, the double-pen house is found throughout the state, particularly in rural areas.

A saddlebag house may be constructed complete or it may be the result of adding a new pen to the chimney side of a single-pen dwelling (figure 39). The massive central chimney usually separates the two pens by two to three feet, allowing for closet or storage space on either side. There are few saddlebag houses in Lowland Arkansas. Although the type is more common in Upland Arkansas, even there it is not a dominant type.

Dogtrot houses contain two pens separated by an open passage. The pens are accessible by doors centered in the walls facing the open passage. Usually, both pens were used for domestic space. A contract for the building of a dogtrot made near Washington, Hempstead County, reveals how a dogtrot could serve two functions. On April 24, 1820, two men, Irons and Harris, agreed to build a log dogtrot for two other men, Price and Fisher. One pen was to serve as a dwelling space, the other as a store. The contract also reveals how open areas, porches and passages, were viewed not as negative spaces, but as part of a complete entity.

> Sd Building to be 48 feet long and 34 feet broad, to be well raised from the ground. . . . To consist of a boddy eighteen feet wide with a Gallery on each side the whole length and eight feet broad and divided into three apartments that is one room to be twenty feet long the other eighteen and the space between them ten feet. The boddy of sd building to be of sound Oak logs handsomely dressed six inches thick. . . .[32]

Of the four Georgian house types built in Arkansas, two are generally associated with Lowland areas while two others were constructed throughout the state. The full Georgian house is rare in Arkansas (figure 14). As stated earlier, most were built in Lowland areas before the Civil War, and, because of their association with large-scale plantations, full Georgian houses are usually found in rural settings. More common is the one-story Georgian-plan house, which, like the full Georgian house, is associated with Lowland Arkansas (figure 5). Constructed with increasingly less frequency into the twentieth century, the one-story Georgian-plan house may be found in both rural and urban settings. Throughout the state, the central-hall house (figure 12) and its two-story version, the I house (figure 3), were built in rural and urban settings well into the twentieth century. Room dimensions followed British-American norms; main rooms generally measured sixteen feet by sixteen feet, sixteen feet by eighteen feet, and eighteen feet by eighteen feet, and hallways were ten to twelve feet wide. Most were of frame construction. Brick and stone examples, however, of the central-hall house are known to exist, and there are rare log examples, even of the full Georgian house.

Regardless of the construction technology and the region, Georgian house types tend to be associated with greater socioeconomic aspirations. Of particular note is an association between the dogtrot and central-hall houses. Both forms consist of two rooms divided by a passageway. The dogtrot house, often of less-fashionable log construction, was largely a rural form. The central-hall house, in rural areas, represented agrarian prosperity. When a farmer wished to display economic success, he enclosed the passageway of his dogtrot house and covered the entire structure with weatherboards, turning it into a central-hall house.[33] Georgian house types also tend to reflect, on the part of their owners, greater aesthetic and stylistic awareness. For example, I houses, built throughout the nineteenth century, display decorative features influenced by all of the contemporary Victorian architectural fashions.[34]

As stated earlier, settlers of Arkansas came not only from the British-American east, but also from French Louisiana. These latter post–Louisiana-Purchase settlers, black and white, brought two distinct building traditions. One constituted a complex set of forms reflecting the French-Creole heritage of the eighteenth and early nineteenth centuries. In the early eighteenth century, Creoles from the French Antilles (Caribbean islands under French-Colonial rule) introduced to Louisiana a house form that, modified, would become standard in the Mississippi River valley. One room deep and two to four rooms wide, the house was raised, surrounded by an open gallery, and covered by a roof with two pitches.[35] By the middle of the eighteenth century, Neoclassicism made its impact upon French architecture in the New World. Unlike American Georgian houses, Creole houses, however, lacked central hallways, but did have rooms of equal size with balanced and symmetrical fenestrations. One Creole house, built in Chicot County during the early nineteenth century, featured four rooms with a window-door-window arrangement in each, and two internal chimneys (figure 40). By the early nineteenth century, after a wave of American immigration to Louisiana, American Georgian and Federal aesthetics had a profound impact upon the region's building traditions. Creole houses came to feature central hallways and Federal-style decorative elements,[36] much like Estevan Hall built near Helena in the late 1820s (figure 41).

French-Canadian settlers, who began to arrive in Louisiana in the late 1760s following their ousting from Nova Scotia by the British, adopted and modified a house form that became distinctively Acadian. The Acadian house featured a four-room plan, but unlike the Creole house is double-pile or two rooms deep. The front two rooms are larger than the rear rooms and have symmetrical fenestrations with an entrance to each room. A gable roof with one pitch covers the rooms and a front "built-in" porch (figure 42).[37] In the late nineteenth and early twentieth centuries, the Acadian house was used in Arkansas as housing for farm laborers and tenants (figure 43).

One other dwelling form brought to Arkansas via Louisiana is the shotgun house (figure 44). Generally, this house form has a plan one room wide and two or more rooms deep. A roof, with gable facing the front, often covers a porch. The form is thought to have originated in the French colony of Saint-Domingue and to reflect West African and native-American heritage. Following the revolution that established independent Haiti in 1804, internal strife caused many mulatto Haitians to emigrate to Louisiana. Once introduced to Louisiana, the shotgun house spread with amazing quickness throughout the southeastern United States.[38] Built of frame and sometimes of brick, a few exhibit high-style influence (figure 45). Although the form was adopted by white Americans, it is usually associated with black residents, and shotgun houses were often built as rental property in rows.

It is good to remember that Arkansas is the inheritor of more than one architectural tradition and that one structure may reflect two or more of these traditions. A structure can have the form of one heritage and the construction technology of another. This is the case with the Stone house of Independence County. Its form is British-American, but its construction technology, carried by African Americans, is French-Colonial (figures 23 and 24). Also, a structure can reflect more than one tradition in a combination of forms. The Mundy Friar house of Hempstead County was a log double-pen structure, a construction technology and plan common throughout the British-American South (figure 46). Its roof, however, is of French-American influence. Most roofs on Arkansas houses and outbuildings are generally consistent with British-American traditions. They are either hipped or gable with gable ends to the sides that cover only the main rooms of the house. On the Friar house, cantilevered logs extending six feet over the front and rear facades supported a common house and porch roof. This roof with unbroken pitch is similar to the "umbrella" roofs developed in mid eighteenth-century Louisiana and to the roofs of Acadian houses.[39] Oral traditions has it that the builder of the Columbus-vicinity house, Mundy Friar, was a black man who immigrated from Louisiana just after the Civil War.

SOME GENERALITIES

Folk architecture is often defined in contrast to popular and elite architecture, that is, in terms of what it is not. The three categories do not represent discrete spheres, but rather points on a continuum of influence and interpretation. To understand folk buildings, or any category of architecture, one must understand the wider context of the built environment. And the built environment is important, ultimately, for what it may reveal about culture, about human interaction and human responses to the natural and, for many, the spirit world.

Folklore is not simply the study of traditional customs and artifacts, of how things stay the same; it is also the study of how things change and how people deal with change. It is the study of values and of the decisions people make based upon those values. Change is inevitable in any complex or modern culture, but not all people embrace change as quickly as others. People make decisions daily about what in their lives is to be changed and what, for the time being, is to remain the same. Most buildings in Arkansas are folk buildings. Some reflect the traditions of French-Colonial and African-Caribbean America. Most, however, reflect British-American traditions. What then might Arkansas buildings tell us about Arkansas and its people?

The state's architectural traditions are generally consistent with those of the greater South. Seen in national terms, this architecture must be considered conservative, as it reflects few of the middle-class domestic innovations that spread across the rapidly industrializing free North of the nineteenth century. Many of the antebellum houses surviving in the southern part of the state were built by middle- to upper-class families. These houses, however, may be likened to old candy in new wrappers.

In the early decades of the American Republic, men such as Thomas Jefferson, William Thornton, and Benjamin Latrobe idealized the democracies and architecture of the Classical world. Federal-period architecture reflected a new refining of Classicism and was followed by Greek Revival. In the North, Greek Revival architecture, in ornament and form, took full flower. In the South, where John C. Calhoun idealized not the democracy of the ancient Greeks but the inequality upon which it was based, Greek Revival *ornament* had no rival. Architectural *form*, however, did not change.

Georgian architecture had been ideally suited to the social and economic stratifications of the slave-owning plantation South. Throughout the eighteenth and first half of the nineteenth centuries, Southern institutions became increasingly defined and entrenched. Staple crops changed from tobacco and rice to cotton, but the basic socioeconomic structure remained the same, as did basic architectural form. Greek Revival ornament hung on Georgian houses.[40] Viewed within a regional context, the antebellum architecture of Lowland Arkansas reflected an identification with the plantation South.

In the antebellum Ozarks, there was an obvious lack of one- and two-story Georgian-plan houses. The large house of the Ozarks was the I house. This is consistent with the traditions of the Upland South. The I house is, however, a Georgian subtype found commonly also in Lowland Arkansas. There was also a general commonality in the two areas among smaller houses. Both areas had central-hall houses, double-pen houses, and dogtrots, to the general exclusion of other house forms. Although there may have been some difference in values, Upland Arkansas was tied to the commercial markets and political arenas dominated by Lowland Arkansas. Upland Arkansas is, as most historians and geographers have termed it, a subregion connected to the greater cotton South.

After the Civil War, Arkansans continued to build traditional forms. Houses outside major urban centers such as Little Rock exhibited little influence from the successive Victorian styles. Queen Anne style appears to have had the most influence in rural areas, but it is relegated primarily to porches on central-hall and I houses. One house in Clarendon seems an ideal metaphor for the period. The Renneker house, built in the early twentieth century, is a Georgian-plan house with decorative features influenced by the then nationally popular Neoclassical style (figure 47). It is as though rural Arkansas derived little influence from the entire Victorian era. There are, of course, some houses in urban centers that reflect the Second Empire, Queen Anne, and Eastlake styles in both ornament and form. The Colburn-Baker house in North Little Rock is one example (figure 48). Many examples were built by Northerners who settled in the state after the Civil War.

In the 1880s and 1890s, individuals in rural Arkansas began incorporating some ideas derived from the popular pattern books of mid century (figure 49). These pattern books, aiming to appeal to the middle-class, incorporated new aesthetic and domestic ideals. Romantic America threw off the old architectural ideas of balance based upon symmetry and adopted new ideas of balance based upon an organic asymmtery. This new asymmetry aided the incorporation of new work spaces within the domestic sphere of the home. Stylistically these ideas were associated with Gothic Revival and Italianate. Few of the decorative features advocated in the pattern books were used on common houses. The pattern books did, however, suggest new ways to incorporate spaces that had been previously enclosed in rear shed and ell additions in new, somewhat more fashionable, ways.[41] Among these new forms found in Arkansas were houses with cross wings along one side (figure 50) and those with gabled projections centered on the front facade (figure 51). Collectively termed "bent" houses, the latter form is common enough in the Ozarks to warrant its local name of "prow" house, so-called because the central projection has been likened to the prow of a ship.

The rise of these bent houses on the Springfield Plateau, a fertile area within the Ozark Mountains, has been associated with a shift from subsistence and general farming, which entailed the growing of some wheat and cotton for cash, to the specialized farming of fruit such as apples, strawberries, and grapes. Even for the more well-to-do of these farmers, the bent house reflected a minimum of change of traditional forms. Prow houses are, in fact, double-pen houses with front extensions. The two-story prow house fills the same socioeconomic slot as the I house and somewhat replaces it in the landscape.[42]

In the early twentieth century, smaller cottages of Classical, and later, Craftsman influence, were built in urban areas. It would not be until just prior to World War II that a major change was evidenced in rural Arkansas. The bungalow, in its most basic form, became the predominant house form. By that time, Arkansas had become the only state in the Union to have declared bankruptcy three times. This dubious distinction reflects, at a state level, the general economic plight felt by individuals, particularly in rural areas, of nineteenth- and early twentieth-century Arkansas. These conditions suggest that architectural innovation is tied to the general economy. But, as in the case of the farmers of northwest Arkansas, even in times of economic success Arkansans seem to have preferred old forms to new forms, tradition to innovation.

The above statements are the most general of generalities. Significant conclusions may be drawn only from particulars and from insightful studies of specific issues. Again, the goal of studying folk architecture is to understand what people think of the world around them and how they modify, use, and adapt that world. Elements of the cultural landscape are perceptions as much as realities. We must seek to understand what the built environment means to those who build and use it, and to understand the cultural processes that reflect change in that environment. It is hoped that forthcoming studies on Arkansas architecture will contribute to our understanding of not only Arkansas and its people, but also of culture in general.

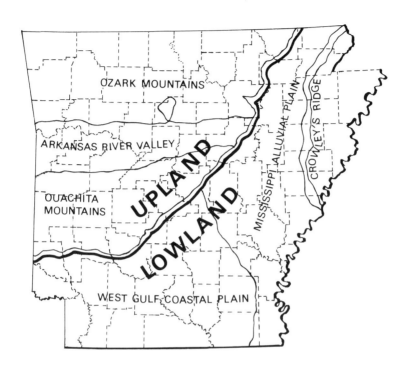

FIGURE 1. *Physiographic and cultural regions of Arkansas. Drawing by Gail Brannen.*

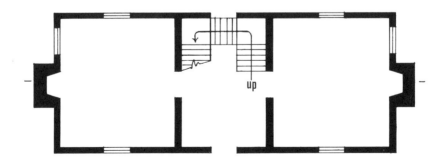

FIGURE 2. *Floor plan for typical central-hall and I houses, consisting of two rooms flanking a central hall. For all plans, — indicates line of roof ridge. Drawing by Gail Brannen.*

Figure 3. *Thomas E. Hess house of Marcella, Stone County. Built in 1900, it is a central-hall I house of frame construction. Photo courtesy of the Arkansas Historic Preservation Program (AHPP).*

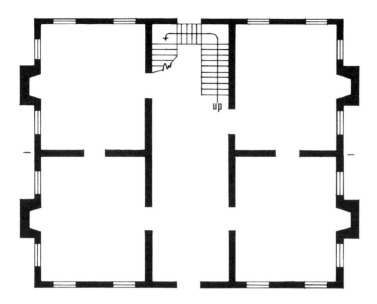

FIGURE 4. *Floor plan for a generic American Georgian house.
Symmetrical balance is the key to this plan with central hallway
and four flanking rooms. Drawing by Gail Brannen.*

FIGURE 5. *Grandison Royston house of Washington, Hempstead County.
Built in the 1840s, it is a Georgian-plan house of braced-frame construction
and Greek Revival ornamental features. Photo by author.*

Figure 6. *Cultural regions and patterns of migration in the eastern United States. Drawing by Gail Brannen.*

FIGURE 7. *Old State House of Little Rock, Pulaski County. Designed by Gideon Shryock and constructed from 1833 to 1836, it is a fine example of Greek Revival architecture in the United States. Photo by Paul E. Pyle, Jr.*

FIGURE 8. *Justin Matthews house of North Little Rock, Pulaski County. Designed by Frank Carmean in 1928, it is believed to be one of the nation's earliest examples of International-style architecture. Photo courtesy of the AHPP.*

FIGURE 9. *Art Deco interior of the Matthews house of North Little Rock, Pulaski County. Photo courtesy of the AHPP.*

FIGURE 10. *One of several classic cottages designed by the Charles Thompson firm. The house, built in 1905, is located in Little Rock. Photo courtesy of the AHPP.*

FIGURE 11. *Another classic cottage, also located in Little Rock, designed by the Charles Thompson firm in 1919. Photo courtesy of the AHPP.*

FIGURE 12. Charles W. Shaver house of Evening Shade, Sharp County, built in 1854. Of load-bearing brick construction, it is a central-hall house with a rear ell. Photo courtesy of the AHPP.

FIGURE 13. Royston house of the Blevins vicinity, Hempstead County, as it appeared in the year it was built, 1939. Designed by the St. Louis architect Gumbrill, it is a large foursquare house of log construction. Photo courtesy of G. D. Royston, Jr.

FIGURE 14. *Lakeport Plantation, located near Lake Village in Chicot County. It is a Greek Revival influenced Georgian-form house, built about 1850. Photo courtesy of the AHPP.*

FIGURE 15. *Illustration of the Chelsea, a foursquare house, as it appeared in the Sears and Roebuck mail-order catalog. Courtesy of The Preservation Press.*

FIGURE 16. *Hanks house of Little Rock. A good example of a Greek Revival temple-form house. Photo by Paul E. Pyle, Jr.*

FIGURE 17. *Westover of James City County, Virginia. Originally built about 1728 by William Byrd, it is an outstanding example of a high American Georgian house. Courtesy of the Library of Congress.*

FIGURE 18. Case-Maxfield (commonly called Garrott) house of Batesville, Independence County. Built in 1842, it is a Georgian-plan house of braced-frame construction. Its original Greek Revival stylistic features were enhanced with Gothic Revival bargeboards in the 1870s. Photo by Diane Tebbetts.

FIGURE 19. Jacob Wolf house of Baxter County. Built of logs about 1830, it is one of the oldest existing structures in Arkansas. Photo courtesy of the AHPP.

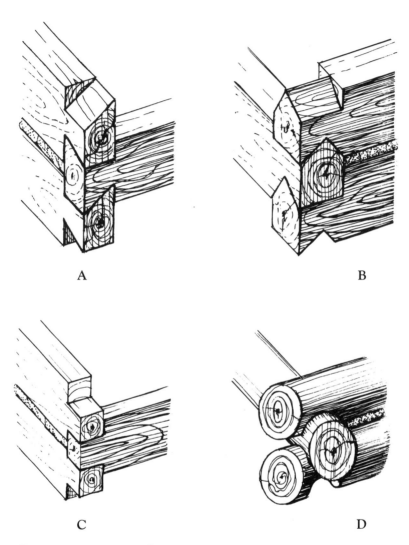

FIGURE 20. *Corner notches commonly found on Arkansas log buildings:*
A) *half-dovetail,* B) V, C) *square,* D) *saddle. Drawing by Gail Brannen.*

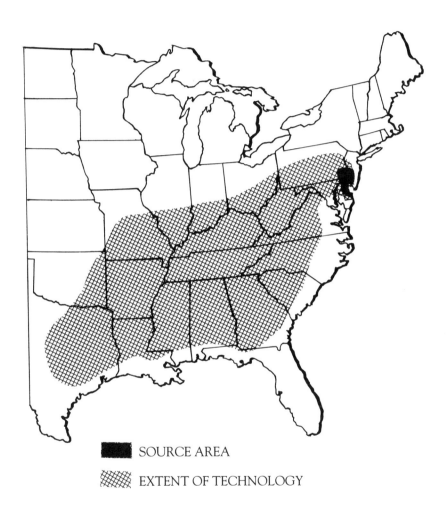

SOURCE AREA

EXTENT OF TECHNOLOGY

FIGURE 21. *Log construction area of the southeastern United States. The technology is thought to have originated in the Mid-Atlantic region during the eighteenth century. From there, it was carried south and west during the late eighteenth to the mid nineteenth century. Arkansas exists wholly within the shaded area. It may be assumed that log buildings were erected over the entire state. Drawing by Gail Brannen.*

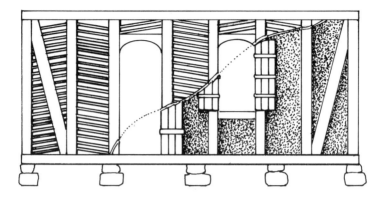

FIGURE 22. Poteaux-sur-solle *(posts on a sill)* construction, featuring large posts and down braces running from plate to sill, and an infill of lath and a clay and straw mixture called bousillage. Drawing by Gail Brannen.

FIGURE 23. *Rufus Stone house near Batesville, Independence County. Built in 1859, it is a central-hall house with Greek Revival stylistic features. Photo by author.*

FIGURE 24. *Corner of the Stone house, showing the cypress earthfast posts used to frame the house. Note that there is no sill and that the posts of the front (on the right) wall have notches for holding the floor joists. This variation of poteaux-en-terre (posts in the ground) construction technology is believed to evidence the knowledge of black slaves whose immediate place of origin was Louisiana. Photo by author.*

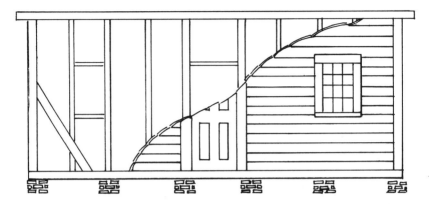

FIGURE 25. Braced-frame construction, featuring large posts with intermediate studs, and down braces. The framing is usually covered on the outside with horizontal weatherboards and on the inside with lath and plaster or with flush boards. It is rare to find historic infill of any material between the interior and exterior coverings. Drawing by Gail Brannen.

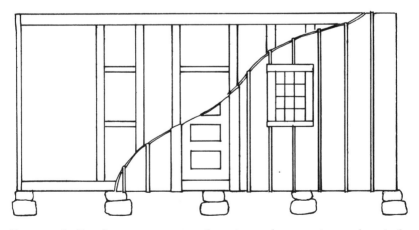

FIGURE 26. Box-frame construction, featuring studs at openings and vertical boards nailed to the plate and sill, serving as both structural support and as exterior and interior siding. The spaces between the vertical boards are often covered with wooden strips or battens, creating board-and-batten siding. Drawing by Gail Brannen.

FIGURE 27. *Portion of a load-bearing brick wall. The bricks with long sides facing out are called stretchers, those with short ends, headers. Varying patterns, or bonds, are made by alternating headers and stretchers. This bond of one header row for every five rows of stretchers is called Common. Drawing by Gail Brannen.*

FIGURE 28. *Ringgold-Noland house of Batesville, Independence County. Built about 1827 by Colonel John Ringgold, it was the principal home of his Southwest Humorist son-in-law, Charles Fenton Mercer Noland. It was a central-hall house with two flanking rooms in Georgian tripartite order. Note that this load-bearing house is of unusual Flemish bond, alternating headers and stretchers in every row. Note too, in this historic photograph, the temporary roof, evidence of the thirty-year effort of three ladies of the Batesville Glass Club to preserve the house prior to its demolition in the 1960s. Photo courtesy of Roberta D. Brown.*

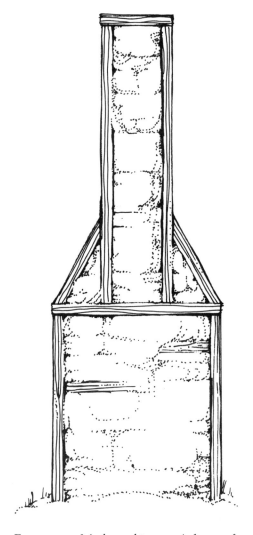

Figure 29. Mud-cat chimney. A frame of
wood is covered with lath, that is then covered
with a clay and straw mixture worked in units
called cats. Historically found in the lowland
part of the state, few exist today. Drawing by
Gail Brannen.

FIGURE 30. *Floor plan of a single-pen or hall house. The hall house could be one, one-and-one-half, or even two stories tall. In Arkansas many surviving examples have boxed-in staircases in a corner. Drawing by Gail Brannen.*

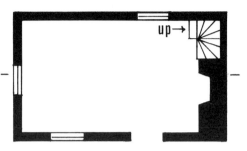

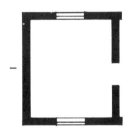 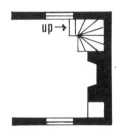

FIGURE 31. *Floor plan of a hall-and-parlor house. The larger room containing the fireplace is called the hall, after the medieval great hall. Drawing by Gail Brannen.*

FIGURE 32. *George Peck house moved to Washington, Hampstead County. The hall-and-parlor arrangement of this house, built about 1840, is reflected in the fenestration of the front facade. Photo by author.*

FIGURE 33. *Monroe house of Washington, Hempstead County. This house, built about 1854, has a hall-and-parlor plan. The parlor is proportionally larger then that of the Peck house (figure 32), making its two rooms almost equal in size. Its fenestration is deceptively balanced, giving the impression of a central-hall arrangement. Photo by author.*

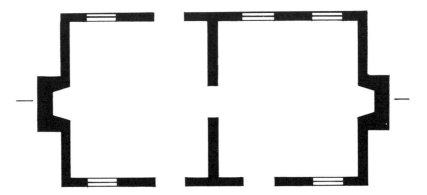

FIGURE 34. *Floor plan of a two-room or double-pen house. The two rooms are of equal size and each room has a doorway to the exterior on the front facade. The arrangement of windows and doors from one room to the other reflects a mirror image. Drawing by Gail Brannen.*

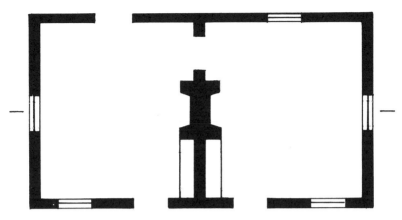

FIGURE 35. *Floor plan of a saddlebag house. The plan, which has a central chimney stack, is a variation of the double-pen plan. Drawing by Gail Brannen.*

FIGURE 36. *Grigsby house, moved to the campus of Arkansas College in Batesville, Independence County. It is a dog-trot or open-passage house of log construction. The logs are hewn on all four sides and square notched at the corners. Photo by Diane Tebbetts.*

FIGURE 37. *Clark-King house, Stone County. Built in 1885, it is a log single-pen dwelling. Photo by Jean Sizemore.*

FIGURE 38. *Albert Blair house, Stone County. This double-pen dwelling was built about 1926. Note that each pen has the same arrangement of window and door openings. Photo by Jean Sizemore.*

FIGURE 39. *Royston log house, built in 1839, moved to Washington in Hempstead County. This saddlebag house contains two rooms, each having an exterior door. The large central chimney has a fireplace for each of the two rooms. Photo by author.*

FIGURE 40. *Historic view of the McDermott house of Dermot, Chicot County. It was a French-Colonial house, containing four large rooms with an exterior entry for each and two interior chimneys which probably had back-to-back hearths. Photo courtesy of the AHPP.*

FIGURE 41. *Estevan Hall near Helena, Phillips County. Built in 1827, this Creole house exhibits Federal-style ornamental features. Photo courtesy of the AHPP.*

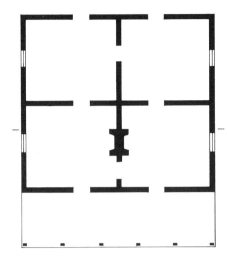

FIGURE 42. *Floor plan for a typical Acadian house, featuring four rooms, a central chimney, two front doors, and a porch under the main roof. Drawing by Gail Brannen.*

FIGURE 43. *Historic view of an Acadian house in Pulaski County. Taken in 1936, the photograph is simply labeled, "a sharecropper's house." Photo courtesy of the Library of Congress.*

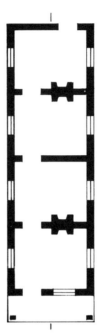

FIGURE 44. Floor plan of
a typical shotgun house,
featuring two or more
rooms arranged in a
linear pattern, running
front to back. Drawing
by Gail Brannen.

FIGURE 45. Shotgun house, Little Rock, Pulaski County. This house with
Colonial Revival stylistic features was built in the early twentieth century and
demolished about 1989. Photo by author.

FIGURE 46. *Mundy Friar house, located near Columbus in Hempstead County. Most recently used as a hay barn, this unique double-pen log house was built by a black immigrant from Louisiana just after the Civil War. Demolished in 1991, it had a Louisiana cantilevered roof. Photo by author.*

FIGURE 47. *Renneker house of Clarendon, Monroe County. Built in the early twentieth century, it is a Georgian-plan house with Colonial Revival stylistic features. Demolished about 1986. Photo courtesy of the AHPP.*

FIGURE 48. *Colburn-Baker house of North Little Rock, Pulaski County. Built in 1898–99, this Queen Anne-style house was constructed for A. E. Colburn, a black jockey. Photo by Paul E. Pyle, Jr.*

FIGURE 49. *Downing's Cottage for a Country Clergyman, elevation and floor plan. Without its decorative ornament, the Cottage looks much like the bent houses built throughout Arkansas in the late nineteenth and early twentieth centuries. Courtesy of Dover Publications.*

FIGURE 50. H. W. Lower house located near Fayetteville, Washington County. Built in 1917, it is a good example of a bent house. Photo by Jean Sizemore.

FIGURE 51. Charlie Williams house located near Elkins, Washington County. Built in 1912, this bent house is an example of what local people call a prow house. Photo by Jean Sizemore.

Customs and Beliefs

Byrd Gibbens

Early Arkansas was quintessential frontier.[1] To live there was to live on what was that narrowly defined line of tension between the known and the unknown. The geography offered a refuge that was both nurturing and challenging. The hills were beautiful, but resistant to the plow. The Delta lowlands were fertile, but prone to flood and disease. The craggy, dense thickets of all areas offered shelter indiscriminately to animals and humans, settlers and outlaws.

Distant from the support services of both Eastern and Southern metropolises, Arkansas pioneers had to be hardy, inventive, self-sufficient people. Their beliefs and customs reveal their strategies for maintaining dignity and independence—with a balance of power and humor.

This chapter on customs and beliefs in Arkansas will not chortle at the so-called magic or superstitions of the hill and Delta families. It will, instead, consider the notion that belief systems and customs are ritual scaffoldings for addressing and living productively in the context of cosmic mystery—perhaps *the* enduring challenge for all human beings. Real folk beliefs and customs of the native Arkansan spring from an independent, resilient people and signify a world view rich in the understanding of the human condition.

Basic to any belief system is a primal impulse to order, to articulate a symbol system that harmonizes and gives meaning to every aspect of a world. Often what we label beliefs are actually customs. They are behaviors continued not for mere pragmatic reasons but because they enable control of the present by creating bonds with a strengthening past or by creating buffers against a threatening future.[2] If we plunge beneath the surface of any so-called folk system, we recognize in its deep structure the same human struggles we experience today and the same kinds of human responses. In reality we are all part of a continuum, a seamless human fabric whose different behaviors are merely variations on age-old ways of struggling with age-old problems.

The customs and beliefs of a group condense community ideals and reveal the values and social mechanisms through which community is maintained.[3] Folklore is a body of material connected by invisible threads through time and space. It can reveal the relatively unconscious motivational forces inside individuals and groups. By listening to contemporary meanings of a custom or belief we tap into "conversations" with the past that are initiations of dialogue with the future.

Arkansans of both the hills and the deltas came from agrarian cultures. The Scotch-Irish connected directly to the religious systems of the Celts and of the early Druids, both of which involved a familiarity with nature magic. The early African, Indian, and French populations still felt the pull of a mythico-religious attitude to external reality, the interrelation of control between mind and matter. "Whoever has brought any part of a whole into his power has thereby acquired power, in the magical sense, over the whole itself."[4] Practically all the charms known in Arkansas had been believed and practiced in the British Isles or in France or Africa for hundreds of years. Attitudes that dealt with the earth as a living spirit were simply replants of the pasts of Europe and Africa onto the soil of the United States.

A recent study on Arkansas Delta families is titled *Hogs in the Bottom*.[5] A family with hogs in the bottom acreage has the proverbial horn of plenty. The identification with the hog is no aberration for an Anglo-Saxon culture. The wild boar was magic and was sacred to the early Norse and to the Celts: it was an animal of fierce power. Boars' heads adorned Viking helmet crests as protective symbols. Often in Welsh stories boars were magicians, shapeshifters, gods, or goddesses in disguise, able both to wreak destruction and to bestow blessing. The other-world feast of the *sidh* (Celtic gods) is alleged to be sustained by magical boars, which, no matter how often they are cooked and eaten, are whole and alive again on the next day, ready to be slaughtered fresh for the next feast. One golden boar of the gods could outrun the fleetest horse, and a boar was ever and in every place a symbol of fertility.

Arkansas tall tales about razorbacks echo the Celtic legends: ferocity (they can lick a pack of wolves), speed (they can outrun the wind and at times fly), shapeshifting (they are gigantic, causing the earth to quake; they are razor thin, slipping through a tiny mountain crack).[6] More than mere tales, though, the razorback stories signify the type of magic, power-presence to earth and life that characterizes the Welsh disposition in their national story cycle, the *Mabinogi*. In one of these tales, "Culhwch and Olwen," an enchanted hog for fourteen days outruns the pursuing King Arthur, who finally sends against the "razorback" an army of mounted horsemen and all the hounds of the land—all of whom fail to kill the triumphant hog.[7] What was transplanted to the Arkansas hills and Deltas was not just a story from the old country, but an archetypal symbol of power, a metaphor for survival. The razorback externalized the early Arkansan sense of self, a link with a transcendent power source originating far from the Arkansas earth. What we see rather collectively in the Arkansan relation to nature are qualities characteristic of the Indian groups that predated the European/African settlers by many centuries: a sense of nature as coextensive with the human body. Both nature and the human body sustain while they are sustained. In Arkansas there is a tangible impulse to be in a synchronic relation with nature, to strike a balance. Nature is not manipulated or controlled; rather, its needs are attended to. In turn, it nurtures and sustains.

A central Arkansas farmer of African descent, a landholder of some thousand acres inherited from his mother, gazed with reverence over his rich soil. I commented on the dramatic difference between his dark, moist earth and the dull, dry dirt of his neighbor's fields. He nodded. His mother had preached to him that a well-prepared soil is three-fourths of a good harvest. This wealthy man did not really *own* his land; he was its partner, its appreciative caretaker.

There are farmers in Sweet Home and Grapevine who continue to use hand plows, though they can afford tractors; the physical contact with the earth is essential to the ritual of planting and harvesting.[8]

The concept of caring for the earth translates into preserving that which nurtures and destroying that which harms. In southeast Arkansas, I watched (heart pounding and palms wet) as three women (in their sixties and seventies) bent with sticks over two long, writhing snakes. The women were deftly prying open the mouth of the one they suspected of being poisonous. When it struck out at them, they simply arched easefully and, as in the rhythm of a dance, repositioned themselves around the snake, their sticks inserted again with precision behind the head and in the mouth. The verdict came: it was poisonous; hence, it must be killed. A single swift knife stroke and the head was severed. One of the women then lifted the still-writhing body on a stick to carry it to a ravine; the other two women continued talking as if this (to me traumatic) interruption had been merely a comma in their conversation. I was shaken and trembling. They were like living, breathing parts of that earth, like human antibodies that with instinctive grace destroyed what was harmful to the whole. These women trace descent directly back to the Quapaw Indians who, when expelled by Andrew Jackson in 1838, hid for a time in northern Louisiana and returned to their Arkansas farmlands when the federal government was not looking.

Hunting rituals/customs illustrate similar modes of being present to nature. It seems characteristic of Arkansas woodsmen *and* women that they hunt their prey in the manner of animals, almost becoming part of the rhythm of that which they hunt. In southeastern Arkansas I was given a turkey beard. The long, coarse-haired goatee seemed a dubious gift to me until I realized it was akin to deer antlers—and a tribute to both the hunter and the hunted.

To match wits with a wild turkey is a feat of intuition, endurance, and marksmanship.[9] Turkeys are often lured with a turkey caller (homemade or bought): a two- or three-inch piece of slate angled against the knee and subtly scraped across with a debarked stick of white oak stuck into a hollowed corncob that serves as handle. The sound produced by a skillful hand is almost identical to the cluck or gobble of a turkey. The turkey will respond to this sound and come to find its source. Sensitive to the slightest breath of alien movement or sound, the wild turkey will stay within shooting range only if the hunter remains "invisible." Such invisibility may entail an entire day of cramped, hidden, statue-like stillness. The hunter who finally kills a wild turkey has, in a sense, honored the prowess of the prey; the turkey beard, then, is a monument to the excellence of the bird, a tribute to a power in nature.

In many parts of Arkansas, women as well as men hunt deer, turkeys, and other wild game. These animals are hunted for food, not merely for sport. Arkansans' hunts are communal affairs marked by ritual: blinds and lookouts are built or repaired seasonally. The first day of the hunting time is marked by celebrations. (In parts of Desha County, there is a special "Ladies Day" feast put on by the women as beginning of fall hunting.)[10]

In times past, Children often learned the properties of roots, barks, flowers, and weeds. Their "scientific discoveries" were often an integral part of their "play." The forest areas in the Delta were filled with delicious seasonal treats to assuage the appetites of energetic young people. There were "sparkleberries," tiny black berries, and also "red-alls" and "black-alls" (sometimes called red or black hawks), tiny date-like fruits with large seeds. There was also the nut-like bull nettle that grew in sandy pastures and would, the children knew, sting *"real bad."* It had a white blossom in the summer and looked like a very small kiwi fruit. It had inner compartments with seeds. Harvesting it was complicated. "You had to take a stick with forked end and lift the bull nettle off the bush, gingerly remove the stinging part. Inside you'd find a kernel with a white head which you had to pull off and then you ate the inside. It was delicious."[11]

Girls *and* boys fixed edible necklaces of "chinkepins" (chinquapins). "They were nuts with stickers outside, like very small lemons. You boiled the nut meat inside and strung the nuts on a thread to make a necklace. You wore this around your neck and ate the nuts whenever you wanted food."

And all the children remembered there was "rattan," a long, slender "wicker-type" vine that runs along the ground or the side of houses and trees. It could be braided, and mothers "lots of times" used it for switches.

All kinds of berries grew in the fields: huckleberries, wild blackberries, dewberries. The berries made wonderful cobblers. "All you needed for a meal was a fish you'd caught in the nearby stream, a blackberry cobbler, and a small salad."

People never threw anything away. They even made good jelly from the hulls of purple peas, boiling down the hulls, mashing them, and then adding sugar and seasoning. To many Arkansans one of the best meals was one of poke sallet. "You got a mess of poke sallet and some lambs quarter (a slick plant with silvery leaves) and some pepper grass which was hot and kind of almond shaped and some wild onions. You would parboil these, drain off the first water which would have the poisons, then put the greens into a big black skillet and cook them. For a really good meal you'd add some eggs to the greens and scramble them into a kind of omelette."[12]

Dried fruits and plants were used to freshen linen closets: the mock oranges, "tiny yellow things the size of a small lemon that grew on a thorny bush," also "calakansas," which was a dark wine magenta color, almost brown, and very fragrant.

Arkansans knew secrets about everything. There were catawka trees that had great big white blooms, "looked like it snowed on the tree." Worms liked to eat the tree leaves, and the trees would become covered with worms, not a disaster to versatile Arkansans who then flocked to the trees to get the worms to fish with.[13]

Buffeted by both gulf and arctic currents, Arkansas weather defies prediction. Even with the meteorological advances of the 1980s, last week's heavy rain forecast was dead wrong: the week was all sunshine; and this week's sun forecast was mocked by thunderstorms. But the media forecasters are "foreigners." Native Arkansans know what their weather will do. They are reticent, though, to push their intuitive knowing, almost as if the state's weather were a cranky relative, capable of wreaking personal havoc if its true inner disposition is exposed to outsiders.

Sensitive to nature as to persons, the Arkansan, even today, knows that when horses in the back quarter or chickens in the yard band together, rain is in the air. A person with a keen eye can discern if the split seed of a persimmon resembles a fork or a spoon. Forks indicate a mild winter; spoons, a harsh one. Since survival in the early days depended on a productive earth, farmers had to hone their reading of nature's weather signals: the cicada sound, the thickness of corn husks, a ring around the moon.

Arkansas teems with weather lore. Some lore seems more of an imprecation of the eccentric climate than a reflection of actual beliefs about the weather. Early Arkansans, like ancient astronomers, attributed the sultry heat of July and August to the influence of the Dog Star, Sirius, of the constellation Canis Major, hence the name "dog days." During this time, according to Arkansas lore, snakes went blind, dogs were more susceptible to rabies, and stagnant water in ponds and creeks became poisonous. Perhaps the underlying, prudent caution here was to be wary of snakes, dogs, and stagnant water in the heat of the Arkansas summer.

There are many early weather control stories that echo early English and even Greek folk beliefs. In Nevada County, for example, early settlers built great fires to break a drought. In rural Britain, similarly, bonfires were built to honor or to placate nature deities. Celtic druids performed a ceremony in which smoke was released to form rain-giving clouds. Another Arkansas rainmaking ritual involved hanging a dead snake, belly up, on a fence. An early English belief held that the serpent was sacred to celestial water gods; by killing a serpent one sacrificed it to the sky deity who should, in turn, bless the earth with rain. (A University of Arkansas at Little Rock student of the 1980s told me, "An overturned snake brings rain. I don't know where I heard this. But I was always careful not to do it."[14]

Stories of treasure buried in the Arkansas earth abound. Whether fact or fiction, their significance lies in their metaphoric value: these stories underscore the rich value Arkansans ascribe to their land. A typical story comes from a woman who lived almost all of her ninety-nine years in Mayfield, Arkansas, some fifteen miles east of Fayetteville. Her great-grandfather moved into the Ozarks in the 1850s bringing with him "quite a lot of gold," which he decided for some reason it would be prudent to hide. He is supposed to have put his money, all gold coins the size of silver dimes, into a dishpan and buried it somewhere on his farm. (A local woman witnessed the action.) This tale was told over and over, not only to the immediate family, but to area residents. For some one hundred years, treasure seekers have dug, searching for that dishpan of gold. As recently as the 1950s family relatives from California traveled to the Ozarks to hunt for the family treasure.[15]

Land is similarly given prominence by association with ghost stories. "A phantasm known as 'Nora' supposedly slain in the 1920s, is said to haunt Fourche Bottoms near Mabelvale Pike." Another spirit frequents Lorance Creek bottoms near the Saline County line: a lovely apparition, dressed in a diaphonous gown, which is said to appear on the anniversary of the girl's burial in December 1863.[16]

On Faulkner Lake, off Interstate-440, a belief circulates that seems clearly a variant of the Hispanic legend of La Llorona, the woman who weeps in New Mexican and Mexican waters for her lost child. A similar legend is found among the Osage and Cherokee Indians. According to the current Arkansas legend, years ago a wreck occurred: a woman and her baby crashed off the lake bridge and were drowned. The belief continues that if someone today stands on the bank of the lake and shouts three times, "Mama Lou, come and get me!" at the third cry, Mama Lou, will, indeed, rise from the water and pull the hapless caller into the waters of Lake.[17] Like the Hispanic La Llorona, the spirit thinks the caller is her lost child.

Other aspects of the relations of Arkansans with nature are interesting (to paraphrase William Wilson's insightful article "Folklore and the Humanities") not just because they reveal what it means to be an Arkansan but because they also reveal what it means to be human.[18] Much of Arkansas "folk" belief and custom involves heightened intuition or instinct. Practices that may seem to the uninitiated to border on magic are but shrewd use of keen awareness.

The widespread practice of water witching (locating underground water sources by means of a forked branch of a tree or bush used as a divining rod) partakes of this human sense of partnership with the earth. Taking one prong of the fork lightly in each hand (palms up) and holding the single end of the stick parallel to the ground, the witcher walks across the land until the stick pulls downward, indicating a subterranean water source. Though definitely not merely an Arkansas phenomenon, water witching seems well known in all parts of the state.[19] Several of my university students (even serious science majors) testify to having witnessed successful practitioners find underground water supplies where none had been identified before. The water witchers do not signify a belief in archaic magic; they signify a more sensitive stance to the properties of the earth. Water witchers are not "creating" water, but responding to its presence much as the women responded to the movements of the snake and the landowner to the nature of the earth. The very term here "witcher" probably came initially *not* from an association with magic and witches, but from the witch hazel branch used for divining.[20]

Folklore in all its guises empowers, provides strategies for negotiating between past and future, reinforces personal identity, and provides buffers against undifferentiated fear. Folk exaggeration can defeat fear by "changing the awesome into a comic monster."[21]

Dangerous bears, wildcats, and poisonous snakes thrive in Arkansas mountains and deltas. A folk impulse adds to the indigenous animals and reptiles fictive ones that serve as cautionary *and* comic devices. Early Arkansans circulated claims about curious indigenous species. In the hills there thrives a remarkable animal, the cattewhampus, that can survive only on the mountainside. This animal, described at times as being covered with shaggy, rough fur, gallops on its four thin legs around and around the steep slopes. Since its legs are of unequal length it cannot survive on level ground. The two legs on one side are very short, while the two on the opposite side are quite long, a natural blessing which enables it to retain balance on the hillsides.[22]

The woods across Arkansas harbor rare species of snakes; for example, glass snakes, joint snakes, coach whip snakes, and hoop snakes. Glass and joint snakes will rejoin parts when chopped or struck with a heavy object. When annoyed, both will inject a virulent poison into anything nearby. (They are easily annoyed.)

The venomous hoop, or coach whip, snake coils under bushes or in tall grass. When prey nears, it slithers out, sets its fangs in its victim and whips it to death with its tail. If the victim tries to flee, the snake grabs its tail in its mouth, forming a hoop, and rolls with lightning speed after its victim.

Such idiosyncratic tales characterize folk landscapes. Knowledge of the stories separates insiders from outsiders and gives the "folk" (in this case Arkansans) a unique bond with their earth.

The mysterious power of the moon that controls tides and influences women's menses presses into human consciousness. Many Arkansans evidence sensitivity to the stages of the moon. Since the 1800s, farmers have planted according to the waxing and waning of the moon.

> Sow peas and beans in the wane of the moon,
> Who soweth them sooner he doweth too soon.[23]

Many people believe that the full moon inserts itself almost as a physical presence into their individual lives. The mid twentieth-century diary of a sharply alert ninety-year-old woman in Hope, Arkansas, marked the "FULL MOON" as a sign of God's beneficence in her life and through the moon she felt a prescience of her own coming death.[24] Vance Randolph noted Ozark wariness of the moon's power. Misfortune surely comes to a baby born in a bed on which the moonlight falls. An adult who sleeps often in the light of the moon will go crazy.[25] A late twentieth-century native of the Ozarks, a high-tech expert, confesses that he never sleeps at all the night of a full moon. "The moon slips into my room and covers and consumes everything." The moon's mysterious influence hints at other mysteries. Pausing over such signification of mystery, of riddle, is an age-old characteristic of human behavior.

The moon as a personified presence seems part of a world view that allows for psychic phenomena. Many Arkansas families treasure several stories of prescient power residing in one member of the family. A wealthy landowner in Sweet Home, Arkansas, recalled his mother's prediction of the death of one of his brothers. One evening at supper the mother (who at that time single-handedly owned and managed an 1,800-acre farm, a cotton gin, and a community store) cautioned her sons: "Be very careful these next few weeks." The sons casually answered, "Sure." Within a few minutes, the mother, with worried countenance, reiterated: "Be very careful in the next few weeks." One of the boys dropped his banter and asked, "Why are you telling us this? Do you know something?" She responded, "One of you is going to die." Within two weeks, the youngest son had a fatal accident.[26]

Faith and psychic power are hallmarks of the folk stance to life. An interesting phenomenon of folk healing here in Arkansas and in other parts of the United States, as well as in other parts of the world, is the bloodstopper.[27] The bloodstopper is precisely that: a person embued with the power to clot blood to prevent hemorrhage. A classic example of folk mystique, the bloodstopper always stands at the most recent point of a long line of such healers. The power is passed down through an unbroken chain of succession. The laws of transmission carry an onus of taboos and vary within narrow boundaries: power is passed directly; the recipient must be of the same sex *or* of the opposite sex; the recipient is often the seventh child of a seventh child; strict secrecy surrounds the words of transmission and also the words of healing.

Bloodstopping is associated with a benevolent power of God. In the United States the words of healing are often phrases from the Bible, most frequently Ezekiel. In Arab countries the phrases come from the Koran. One of my students who researched her own grandmother as a community bloodstopper reflected: "I don't believe any of the people I talked to view the power as a form of witchcraft, yet they feel a power greater than themselves controls it. A quiet reverence and respect seem to go along with the power."[28]

The power can be lost. "My Granny, who practiced the power for over sixty years in Yell County, Arkansas, would not tell me how it works. . . . Though she has not practiced 'blood stoppin' in about twelve years, yet she's afraid if she tells me, then others will lose their power along with her. Granny said she has only told the power to one person. He asked her for the power before he left for the Korean War as a medic. She told him because she was sure he would need it in the war."[29]

Another university student in Little Rock revealed that her mother was a bloodstopper. In the line of succession, the student's sister was the appropriate one next to receive the power. "But all she's interested in is loud music and money, so I'm going to see if there's any way I can become the one to get my mother's power."[30]

The practice existed in the nineteenth-century Ozarks. An instance is cited by Otto Rayburn:

> A person's nose had been bleeding all day; everything had failed to check the flow of blood. As a last resort two young men were sent on horseback to the home of the bloodstopper ten miles away. When he heard their request, the bloodstopper said simply that they should return to their relative, that his hemorrhaging had stopped. Angry at such a simple response after their difficult journey, the young men returned home disgruntled. However, they were met by family members, excited by the fact that the bleeding had stopped. It had stopped, it turned out, at exactly the time the bloodstopper had been telling the young men to return home.[31]

Much energy is put into the preserving of life, into healing. So-called "folk" remedies abound. Almost all the remedies that I have discovered are treatments that science today would support as actually helpful. The keen intuitions that brought rural people to identify the complex cause and effect involved in things like herbal remedies is still a mystery. Operative here is the same knowing evidenced in basic foodstuffs of indigenous peoples all over the world. Remarkably, the basic diet of so-called primitive groups is nutritionally balanced.

Early on, metropolitan areas looked askance at rural healing traditions. As far back as 1840 the "hospital" in Little Rock strictly forbad any practice of herbal or faith healing. But, although the rural "yarb" (herb) and power doctors caused consternation among the urban doctors who held "certificates," the herbal practitioners were usually not quacks, and their remedies often made sound scientific sense. Their healing power likely resulted from a combination of loving concern, confidence, and applied medicine. And while there were *official* doctors and healers, virtually every mother became a compendium of herbal knowledge.

More than the "yarb," power, or urban doctor, it was, in truth, the mother in the home who was responsible for the health of her family. "Skillet bark tea," for example, was used by mothers as a tonic for blue babies and for sluggish adults. Mothers would scrape the bottom of an iron skillet and boil the contents in a rag. What resulted was a healthy iron supplement. Parsley was used as a diuretic; spearmint and horsemint were given as aids to digestion; strong cider vinegar or lemon, honey, and whiskey were prescribed for a sore throat.

Even weeds were used medicinally. "'The jump-on' weed was large and smooth. You beat it flat to make a poultice to put on injuries to pull out poison."[32] For bed-wetting children, mothers made a tea of a sour berry that grows on the roadside. For colds there was pine-top mullein tea made by steeping pine tops with mullein, to which brew some people added whiskey or lemon.[33]

Contrary to popular opinion, there seems to have been very minimal reliance on bizarre, or "magic," home remedies. At times there were questionable concoctions, such as "bessie bug" blood, which was used on a cotton boll to relieve an earache. A resident of central Arkansas recalled: "For years my father lamented that he could not find bessie bugs to use for my brother's earaches. Mother just laughed at him and said he was being silly. She would then put warm coal oil on a cotton ball and cram *that* down in Danny's ears."[34] Near the Texas border people used warm goose droppings on cotton to stuff into aching ears. Similarly questionable might be things worn or carried in pockets as preventives: asafetida ("asfeddity") worn in a bag around the neck to ward off diseases; a buckeye or a potato carried in the pocket to alleviate rheumatism.

Herbal and home remedies did, and do, carry what New Orleanians term "Lagniappe," that bonus or something extra. The "extra" in the earth remedy lies in the tie to a caring tradition. Just as a quilt stitched by a loving grandmother provides not just physical but emotional warmth, so a traditional or earth remedy carries emotional as well as physical healing.

Illness was psychosomatic for rural Arkansans. Bodies and emotions functioned as one. Often physical remedies were accompanied by strictures or practices designed to solace the spirit, to center contradictory, warring emotions. Modern psychology emphasizes positive thinking; biofeedback purports to prove that the mind can control automatic body functions. If nothing else, charms, amulets, and rituals focus concentration on pragmatic results. The midwife who placed a knife, sharp scissors, or even an ax under the pillow of a woman in labor to cut the pains of childbirth did essentially what the acclaimed Lamaze birth method prescribes: they helped the woman in labor concentrate on a physical object to help her relax. The practice has ancient roots: the Greek goddess of childbirth, Ilithyia, placed a sharp object beneath the bed of the woman she assisted with childbirth.

A central ingredient of folk healing was the common admonition: "You've got to believe in it or it won't work."

Numerous taboos shaped housekeeping. There were directives for warding off danger and insuring good. Pillow cases were placed with the openings hung off the side of the bed so that any bad spirits that might cause nightmares would spill out. Only good dreams would come to whoever slept on the pillow. Something silver placed under a pillow also countered nightmares as did a sprig of rosemary. Young women were cautioned to destroy the hair left from combs and brushes because if a bird made a nest of the hair, the owner would suffer terrible headaches. (Such a caution would also facilitate keeping tidy dresser tops for already busy mothers.)

The most pressing, though, of human mysteries is death. That intersection of the known and the unknown confronts all humans with a fearful rupture in continuity. Thus, surrounding death, communities build rituals that echo and reinforce their belief systems. Death rituals address both the here and the hereafter. Aiding family and community to process grief, such rituals provide structures for addressing ultimate mystery. Death rituals both reveal and conceal; they confront the beyond and they buffer the living from its pressing ambiguity.

In many Arkansas Delta areas, as in most rural parts of the United States, death was a family and community ritual. Since death was an expected part of life, it was also well planned for. People bought the clothes they wished to be buried in. The family crafted the coffin: males made the coffin itself and females patterned the lining. A family member prepared the body for burial. In the early days, "you tied the mouth shut."[35] In parts of Arkansas when an infant or young person died, a family member preserved in a small container the "crown of feathers": the child's pillow was carefully opened, and the closely woven feathers from the center, directly below where the small head would have rested, were removed. "The feathers were saved by family or friends to insure the deceased's safe journey to heaven."[36] This gentle practice probably echoes one of the basic principles in mythic thinking, the principle that any *part* of the whole contains the whole—even something casually connected with the whole, like a pillow. Early Greeks, for example, smoothed the bed soon after arising so that no one could use the imprint of the body left on the mattress to bring harm to the body.[37] The preservation of the crown of feathers echoes this sense of identification.

As late as the early twentieth century in Desha County, the dead body was laid out in the person's own home, washed and dressed carefully by family members, and laid out on an ironing board for a night and day of "viewing" while the family and community paid their respects before the funeral.[38]

Graveside rituals allowed for tender family involvement. In both black and white communities, family members, not impersonal cemetery workers, filled the grave with soil.[39] A contemporary resident of Benton, Arkansas, recalls:

> Recently at my great grandmother's funeral a few of us felt as though we were leaving something unfinished and so we stayed a while at the grave. Perhaps we felt vestiges of the old traditions pulling at us, the sense of remorse as if we were leaving our loved one with strangers. But we were forced to yield to new traditions and had to leave so the hired gravediggers, not we family members, could begin filling the grave.[40]

After a death, the older family members went into mourning for at least one year, wearing traditional black mourning clothes. One person remembers having to coerce a very depressed grandmother out of the mourning garb after the year had passed by scheming to wear out all the grandmother's mourning clothes by scrubbing holes in them on the scrub board.[41]

After a death, the family and community often pondered events prior to the death, attempting to discern the signs that presaged the death. People expect that the death was foreshadowed, and that had they but read the signs, they could have anticipated and either staved it off or at least have been more attentive to the deceased. Signs include dreams, irregular behavior on the part of the deceased (coming home to visit a month before the designated time), "feelings" or forebodings of danger on the part of family members, unusual behavior of family pets or farm animals. There is also a general sense that the spirit of the deceased communicates with loved ones for a time, consoling and reassuring them that all is well in the passage to the otherworld. A woman in Marianna felt comfort when, a few days after her sister's death, she saw a strange, beautiful white cat sitting on the windowsill of her living room. The lingering spirit presence does not seem at all ominous; to the contrary, it seems a link of love with the beyond.[42]

Belief in a beneficent power beyond that sustains and assists humans underpins much of the Arkansas way of life. "Little miracles" happen.

> My grandmother was out of chicken feed. There just wasn't any and there wasn't any money to get any. Merlie stood at the kitchen sink pondering this as she washed the breakfast dishes. Without feed the chickens would surely die. Without chickens there would be no chicken to eat and no eggs. Without eggs she couldn't sell or barter. There had to be chicken feed . . . that's all there was to it. So Merlie turned it over and asked the Lord to please provide. Right after that she heard the sound of a truck moving south on Highway 225, which she could see from her kitchen window. It happened to be a feed truck. It hit a large pothole in the road which dislodged one fifty pound sack of chicken feed. It burst open spilling feed across the road. Merlie said, "Thank you, Lord," got her wheelbarrow, and shoveled up her feed."[43]

An eighty-five-year-old resident of Marianna, Arkansas, told me of a time when a neighbor came to her door asking for a cup of cornmeal. Having only a cup herself, which was to have been her children's skimpy supper, she took pause; but reflecting that the Lord would provide, she gave the neighbor her last cup of meal. That evening the miserly woman for whom she worked uncharacteristically invited her to go to the pantry and help herself to a few days' supplies.[44]

Such intervention was expected.

The essence of the folk impulse is the sustaining, enabling presence of the past place or time. The unconscious selects elements of the past to negotiate the future so that no age is ever sprung rootless and wombless ex nihilo. Each age evolves from what came before, trailing with it, as it were, gill slits and tail bones. "A dialogical tension is set up between two idealized extremes: the fondly remembered 'mother culture' and the new culture of new age."[45] The ongoing folk process sustains metaphors of the past place and time, drawing them into the present to enable the shaping of the future. Normative behavior within a group is an accommodating composite of old and new. The folk impulse is not static, but an ongoing dialogue between past and present.

Within any family story or saying lies such negotiation between the old and the new. In folk custom and belief, we can observe individuals and groups coping with change, with movement. We see such dialogue clearly illustrated in stories and sayings that imbibe traditional values. Since people cannot be ready-made, fully experienced citizens of a new age of place, they draw sayings, legends, larger-than-life progenitors, from the past to construct paradigms or blueprints for the present. It is significant precisely which persons, stories, and sayings a family or community invests with legendary stature. These choices, perhaps more than anything else, reveal the essential values of the group.

Increasing numbers of blacks in Arkansas (and other parts of the United States) are aligning their Christmas celebrations with an African celebration of life, *Kwanzaa*. Before the festive meal at her large family gatherings on Thanksgiving, Christmas, and Easter, one Little Rock black university professor reads early Nubian prayers and parables from the *Husia*. She reminds her children and grandchildren of their roots in the ancient culture of kings and calls their attention to the emphasis Nubian (Egyptian) culture put on brotherhood and sharing. It is a proud and socially concerned African-American culture she strives to create through ties to a strong, significant past. One of her granddaughters is named Nia, or Purpose, one of the seven principles of *Kwanzaa*. Arkansans of African descent, in increasing numbers, are giving their children names from African languages.[46]

Sweet Home, Arkansas, in the early nineteenth century was a region in which thousands of acres of fertile farmland were owned and cultivated largely by black landholders. Many of these were blacks who had fled slavery in neighboring states. Ironically, it was after the Civil War that whites began pushing into the area and, through both legal and illegal methods, coercing blacks to sell out. As pressure mounted, only the most shrewd and forceful blacks held out in the manipulated contests.

Those who successfully resisted became legendary figures. Vignettes about them condense strongly held community and family values. One landholder today recounts a story often told of his mother who, widowed in her early thirties, inherited the title and the onus of one of the largest farms in the area. Constant tension existed between her and a neighboring white farmer who was determined to buy out whom he saw as an uppity black woman. But he had met his match. Not only did she refuse to sell, but she defied his authority in other matters. One evening, so the story goes, two eleven-year-old black boys, back from rabbit hunting, traipsed across the outer field of the white farmer, who loosed his two German shepherds on them. Terrified, the young boys shot at the dogs and severely injured them. The following day the landowner brought in the sheriff to arrest the boys and take them to the penitentiary. But the young black widow marched to the landowner's house, accused the sheriff of breaking the law concerning juveniles, and swore that the boys would be taken only over her dead body. The sheriff left, and the boys returned to their own homes. The image of this dauntless black matriarch defeating white opposition continues as a touchstone for the family identify four generations later.[47]

Another elderly black resident of Sweet Home, a man of dignity and low income, recalls a saying of his grandmother that has remained a guideline, enabling him to retain self-respect in a racist society.

> "Feed 'em with a long-handled spoon." That's what my grandmother used to say all the time. And I don't know why but I keep remembering that and I tell it to all my children. I sure didn't know what she meant back then. When I was just a little fellow, we'd be playing in the yard—, my grandmother be setting in her rocking chair on the front porch. And sometimes white children come by and maybe pick a fight or grab our toys. I'd come crying on the porch and want to fight or just go inside. She put her arm round me an' pat my head an' say, "Feed 'em with a long-handled spoon." I couldn't understand that then. I kept seeing a spoon with a long, long handle and me trying to feed someone with it. That was funny to me. But she meant keep your distance with white folks. You may have to associate with them but you don't have to get too close. You don't fight; you don't run away. You just "feed 'em with a long-handled spoon."[48]

The Sweet Home resident did not realize that this proverb traces back to early England, where it was used as a warning to keep distance from the devil.

A sixty-five-year-old retired school teacher in Little Rock told two oft-repeated stories about her father who had died some ten years earlier at the age of one-hundred-and-five. For over twenty years he had daily walked almost fifteen miles to work rather than submit to the humiliation of riding a segregated bus on which he would have been forced to sit in the back section designated "For Colored." In his spare time this same man taught himself to read Greek so that he could read the Bible in that language, which he considered closer to the original Aramaic. He would sit on the front porch for hours, his daughter recalls, deciphering the ancient texts.[49]

This image of the patriarchal figure etched itself into the family memory as an image of values it must sustain. Today the family boasts three lawyers and a NASA space trainee, graduates of Yale, Georgetown, the University of Washington, and Massachusetts Institute of Technology.

A dynamic young black paralegal with East Arkansas Legal Services who divides her sixty-hour work week between clients in Marianna and Helena, sees herself as continuing the tradition of her grandmother and her father. No needy person ever left her grandmother's door without food and clothing. Her father, deceased now for many years, had been manager of the cotton cooperative. An elderly citizen of Lee County recalls that no financially straitened black was ever refused a loan by the manager of the co-op. And there is no record of a loan not being repaid. Such stories acquire the force of tradition and represent communally sanctioned behavior.[50]

Just as architecture has inherent meaning and a place-making function, so customs and beliefs have a deeper significance and a centering function. Not ends in themselves, they reaffirm and perpetuate values through which community is maintained and a group's essential values are expressed.

Modern-day natives of Arkansas publicly dissociate themselves from so-called superstition, lest they be perceived by outsiders as hillbillies or backwoodsy. But, in private, many admit to affection for traditional beliefs and customs. Contemporary Arkansans may, for example, instill a sense of awe and reverence in their children at Christmas, reminding them that at midnight farm animals can speak and herds of deer kneel down. A university professor, and a native Arkansan, confesses to making certain her family's Christmas tree is taken down and out of the house by New Year's Eve just because "that's the way it has to be done. Doesn't everybody do that? To leave the tree up into the New Year would just invite bad luck, wouldn't it!" She also admits to packing fresh Arkansas vegetables to take with her when she travels out of state. "I don't really need them. But they remind me of who I am."

Customs and beliefs are part of a world view, "an encompassing symbolic system in which to locate events and oneself."[51] It is the flavors, the value systems, of the older beliefs and customs that are retained and treasured. In Arkansas such beliefs and customs emphasize the image of a self-sufficient, resilient people, family and nature oriented.

Sorghum Mill. Illustration by Ralph Lawson, used by special permission of The Ozarks Mountaineer *magazine, Branson, Mo.*

Traditional Arkansas Foodways

Earl F. Schrock, Jr.

Varieties of foods, the methods used to prepare them, and the meals at which they are served make a significant contribution to a group's cultural identity. In examining the traditional foodways of a state, in this case Arkansas, several problems emerge. First, the state is not made up of a homogeneous land mass with similar topography, soil types, and water supplies; second, the state was not settled by a single ethnic group with a well-defined cultural cuisine; and, third, the state's settlement over a number of years brought the technological improvements known and practiced by the succeeding groups of settlers.

This chapter, therefore, will include an attempt to point out as many commonalities as possible in the foodways of the entire state: staples in the diet selected from the food supply available or from the foods, both plant and animal, that could be successfully grown in the area; the methods of preparation and preservation of these foods; the use of foods for special occasions and holidays; superstitions associated with certain foods; and the social significance of food.

STAPLES IN THE DIET

Two early accounts—one from a white man's and one from a black man's perspective—dramatize the scarcity of food and the lack of variety of foods in Arkansas. The first is from the song "The Arkansas Traveler":

> My name is Bill Stafford, I come from Buffalo Town;
> I've travelled this wide world over, I've travelled this wide world round;
> I've had my ups and downs in life, but better days I've saw;
> I never knew what misery was till I came to Arkansaw.
>
> It was in eighteen hundred and two, in the early month of June;
> I landed in Hot Springs one sultry afternoon;
> Up steps a walking skeleton and hands to me his paw,
> Inviting me to his hotel, the best in Arkansaw.
>
> I followed my conductor into his dwelling place,
> And poverty was pictured in his melancholy face;
> His bread it was corn-dodger, and his meat I could not chaw;
> And that's the kind of hash I got in the state of Arkansaw.

> He fed me on corn-dodgers as hard as any rock;
> My teeth became all loosened, and my knees began to knock;
> I got so lean on sage and sassafras tea that I could hide behind a straw;
> Indeed I was a different man when I left Arkansaw.[1]

The second account is an anecdote told by an Alabama slave, Henry Green, who relocated in Barton, Arkansas.

> Yes, sir Boss Man, the niggers is easy fooled. They always is been that way, and we was fooled away from Alabama to Arkansas by them two Yankee mens, Mr. Van Fleet and Mr. Bill Bowman, what I told you about, that brung that hundred head of folks the time us come. They told us that in Arkansas the hogs just laying around already baked with the knives and the forks sticking in them ready for to be et, and that there was fritter ponds everywhere with the fritters a-frying in them ponds of grease, and that there was money trees where all you had to do was to pick the money offen 'em like picking cotton offen the stalk, and us was sure put out when us git here and find that the onliest meat to be had was that what was in the store, and them fritters had to be fried in the pans, and that there wa'n't no money trees a-tall.[2]

The true picture of Arkansas foodways in the mid nineteenth century surely lies somewhere between the misery described in "The Arkansas Traveler" and the pipe dream of Henry Green. In 1860 Sir Henry Stanley was invited by a Major Ingham to accompany him from New Orleans by steamer to his home in Saline County, Arkansas. Stanley had the following to say about his reception at the Ingham plantation:

> My welcome from Mrs. Ingham left nothing to be desired. The slaves of the house thronged in her train, and curtsied and bobbed, with every token of genuine gladness, to the 'Massa,' as they called him, and then were good enough to include me in their bountiful joy. The supper which had been got ready was something of a banquet, for it was to celebrate the return of the planter, and was calculated to prove to him, though New Orleans hotels might furnish more variety, home, after all, had its attractions in pure, clean, well-cooked viands. When the hearthlogs began to crackle, and the fire-light danced joyfully on the family circle, I began to feel the influence of the charm, and was ready to view my stay in the western woods with interest and content.

> The next day the diet was not so sumptuous. The breakfast at seven, the dinner at noon, and the supper at six consisted of pretty much the same kind of dishes, except that there was good coffee at the first meal, and plenty of good milk for the last. The rest mainly consisted of boiled, or fried, pork and beans, and corn scones. The pork had an excess of fat over the lean, and was followed by a plate full of mush and molasses. I was never very particular as to my diet, but as day after day followed, the want of variety caused it to pall on the palate.[3]

Stanley's description of food on this southern Arkansas plantation in Warren, Arkansas, does not conform to the stereotypic notion of the lifestyle of the Old South. One has to take into account, however, that Ingham had established his plantation only a few years earlier after having moved to Arkansas from South Carolina; that the visit was made in either October or November (the time of the year when fresh produce was not available); and that the account of the visit was actually written some thirty-five years later, after Stanley had traveled throughout the world.

The most thoroughly documented account of early foods in Arkansas is the description of foods eaten by slaves in Orville W. Taylor's *Negro Slavery in Arkansas*, in which he states that the food eaten by the slaves differed little from that eaten by their masters. The year-round staples, for black and white alike, were meat, corn, molasses, sweet potatoes, beans, peas, and turnips.[4] Meat was synonymous with pork. Beef was eaten occasionally but could not be preserved and kept as pork could be. And, of course, wild game was an important part of the diet of all Arkansans, black and white.[5] Other vegetables and fruits were eaten only when they were in season, with the exceptions of those which could be dried for use during the winter months.

Meat

Pork was the staple domesticated meat in the diet of early settlers in Arkansas, primarily because it could be preserved for use throughout the year. Census records show that hogs far outnumbered any other domestic stock in Arkansas; however, a farmer's reckoning of the number of hogs that he owned would have been at best a rough approximation since, in the early settlement days, hogs were allowed to run loose on open range.[6] A farmer would kill hogs whenever they were needed, never certain whether they were his or his neighbor's. In reference to the open range around Banks and Warren, Ivan Johnson, a black sawmiller and farmer, said, "If [anybody] had a hog in the bottom, he always DID have a hog in there. This year he kill ever' one he had; next year he have a claim in the bottom, he go back there and kill him some MORE hogs."[7] In January 1853, John Brown (plantation owner, lawyer, and businessman) of Princeton, Arkansas, wrote in his diary, "William and myself are hunting wild hogs in the bottom. I have a good deal of pork running wild but it is difficult to get, but the price of green pork . . . makes us industrious. We occasionally get a hog."[8] Warren Farmer Wilhite explained the "hog claim" practiced in Montgomery County in the Ouachita Mountains shortly after 1900:

> The stock all run outside—there was no stock law a-tall. And each settlement had what they called "hog claims." The hogs run wild and eat acorns and roots and bugs and stuff. For two dollars you could buy into this hog claim bunch there, and that gave you the right to the meat whenever they had a hog killing.
> You see, the hogs run loose in the woods. When it got winter and bad weather and the hogs couldn't get as much food as they needed, a fellow on a mule would take some corn over to the spring and strew it around. He'd go every day, usually early of a morning; and that'd get the hogs baited and used to coming up to that place. The people'd choose a place

close by a branch where they could get plenty of water to scald and dress out the hogs. They'd haul up some wood and scalding barrels over there ahead of time to get the hogs used to the wood. Then, come a cold spell, a hog hunt would be organized. They'd get over there—the fellers with the Winchesters—they'd get in there and surround this place and when the hogs came in there to get the corn, then the shootin'd start. And they'd shoot down as many hogs as they thought they could tend to. The hunters would run in with the "sticking" knives and bleed the kill. Then they'd have the scalding barrel and the pots to heat the water in and they'd dress 'em out—out there—and then they'd divide up the meat.[9]

These wild hogs, which were generally black with dirty white spots, were called "hazel splitters."[10] Since many of them were born in the wild and had experienced little contact with humans, they were hunted like other wild animals.

Hogs running wild in the bottoms or through the woods in the mountainous region of the state required no care. They were tough animals and could take an incredible amount of punishment, as exemplified in the following tall tale:

A farmer was clearing new ground—grubbing up the stumps laboriously, by hand. A county demonstration agent came by and showed him how easily and cheaply the stumps could be removed by the use of dynamite. The farmer was delighted. He went to the store, bought dynamite, fuse, and caps. Coming home, he dug a hole by a big white oak stump, set a charge of dynamite under it, lighted the fuse, and went to his house for supper. The fuse went out, but by that time the farmer was clear of the new ground; so he decided to wait until the next morning before lighting it again.

The next morning, early, the farmer's big razorback hog got up and went foraging. He found that stick of dynamite and ate it. Then he saw the farmer about the barn lot and hustled up to see if he could steal a little corn from the mule's breakfast. He broke into the mule's stall, and made for the feed trough. The mule, naturally, kicked at him, and, for the first and last time in his life, connected. The dynamite, at last, went off.

A neighbor heard the explosion and hurried over. He found the owner leaning over the fence of his barn lot, viewing the ruins.

The neighbor heaved a sympathetic sigh. "It looks pretty bad, friend," he said, "pretty bad."

"Yes," said the victim, "it is bad. Killed my mule, wrecked my barn, broke every window out of one side of my house, and, brother, I've got an awful sick hog."[11]

FIGURE 1. *John A. Schrock cares for the hogs that will provide the year's supply of meat for his family (Johnson County, 1940s).*

Later, hogs were marked with different cuts in the ears so that they could be identified by their owners. Sometimes they were brought to the fattening pens by a process called "tolling."[12] Kernels of corn were dropped in a trail from the location of the hogs. Once one of the hogs found the corn and began following the trail, many of the others would follow it home and into the barn lot, where they were "fattened out" on corn before being slaughtered when cold weather arrived.

Following is a description of a typical hog-killing day in the Ozark Mountains in the early years of the twentieth century:

> Killing and butchering hogs was a big job in the old days, when the average family killed as many as twelve or fifteen porkers for their Winter's meat. The neighbors all gathered on the appointed day, and unless there was a very large spring nearby they repaired to the nearest creek and built a great fire of logs, in which a number of large stones were heated. Having no vessels big enough to scald hogs in, they diverted the stream into a suitable hollow or pit among the rocks, and heated the water thus impounded by throwing the hot stones into it. When the hogs were scalded everybody helped to scrape and gut the animals, which were

then cut up by the most proficient butchers in the party. At noon the women provided a big dinner, with fresh pork of all kinds, and the host set out a jug or two of corn whiskey. In the evening there was another big feed, followed by a dance or a play-party. A certain creek-bottom near Eureka Springs, Arkansas, is still known as "Hawg Scald", because it was a favorite place for these hog-killing festivals.[13]

About hog killing, Margaret Bolsterli, who grew up on a Desha County cotton farm in the Arkansas Delta country in the 1930s, wrote: "Hog-killing caused more commotion than anything else around the farm because there was a rush to get it done and cure the meat before the weather changed. Cold snaps in the delta cannot be depended on to hold for more than a day or two and a year's supply of meat was at stake."[14] Because "a year's supply of meat was at stake," hog killing was almost a ritual in the Delta and the mountains alike. It was traditionally done right after the weather turned cold in the late fall or early winter, usually late November or early December. Hog killing was communal work, not the work of a single laborer. It was the work of families or a farmer and his neighbors. In the Delta, white farmers often hired blacks in the community to assist in butchering the hogs.[15] In many parts of the state, however, and certainly in the Ozarks, family and friends would gather to help. They would be rewarded by generous pieces of fresh pork to carry home with them.[16]

At daylight, or before, wash pots were filled with water, and fires were lit under them. When the water reached a boil, the hogs were lured as close as possible with corn and were shot at close range in the head. The shot was to be between the eyes and a little above. If the hog squealed, it wasn't a "proper kill."[17] Then the hog was to be "stuck" with a long, sharp blade at the base of the throat, angling the blade backwards toward the heart. When the animal was "bled," it was dragged to the scalding barrel, which was tilted at an angle, and perhaps partially buried in the ground. While this process was being completed, someone else dipped the boiling water from the pots and poured it into the barrel. The hog was lifted and shoved into the barrel head first and turned over in two or three minutes. If the hair "slipped" when it was pulled, the hog was pulled from the barrel, turned around, and shoved into the barrel again, butt first. More boiling water was added to the barrel. Then the hog was pulled from the steaming barrel and scraped to remove all of the hair.

To suspend the hog, a man exposed the tendons in the rear of the hind legs just above the foot with a sharp knife to allow something to be inserted, either the beveled end of a gamboling stick or the hooks of a double-tree. Then the hog was hoisted into the air. A sharp knife was inserted at the base of the belly between the back legs and carefully pulled down to the throat where the first cut had been made. This cut was a delicate one, for the person wielding the knife had to exercise extreme care to avoid cutting through one of the intestines.

A wash tub was placed under the carcass to catch the intestines as they were removed. At this point, the carcass was washed thoroughly and removed to a flat place, a rock or a bench, to be cut into pieces. Generally, by then, another hog had been killed and was being dragged to the barrel for scalding.

Usually the process described above was exclusively the work of men. It was carefully synchronized work; bodies had to move harmoniously together to minimize the back-breaking labor. Certain tasks in the process had to be carried out quickly; there was no time for loitering or letting one's mind wander. A year's supply of meat was at stake. Young boys were at the scene intently observing the process, helping where they could, fetching and carrying for the men, and learning to carry on the tradition.

After the hog was "gutted," the women joined the work. The liver and lights (lungs) were removed from the other entrails and placed in another container. The small intestines were cut into sections, turned inside out, and cleaned, to be used later as "casings" in which to stuff freshly ground sausage. Chitterlings, or "chitlins," were often made from the small intestines.

The head was split open lengthwise with an ax, and the brains were removed to be scrambled with eggs for the next day's breakfast.[18] The head and feet were then placed into a large kettle to be boiled for souse-meat or head cheese.

All of the fat scraps were collected in a large pot and rendered down for lard. The pieces of lean meat and skin that floated to the top in this process were skimmed off; these cracklings were added to corn meal batter to make crackling cornbread.

The men took the hams, shoulders, and sidemeat to the smokehouse, where it was "salted down" and later smoked. The backbone, tenderloin or pork chops, ribs, liver, and lights were generally divided out among those who had come to help, to be eaten as fresh pork.

The lean scraps were collected, run through the sausage mill, and salted and spiced with red and black pepper and sage to suit the family's taste. While one person was seasoning the ground meat, another was

FIGURE 2A. *John A. and Earl F. Schrock, Sr., with freshly killed hog (Johnson County, around 1950).* B. *One day's kill (Johnson County 1940s).* C. *Cad A. Patterson butchers hogs just outside the smokehouse (Holly Springs, Dallas County, 1943).*   A

B

C

frying samples to determine whether the seasoning was just right. The sausage was stuffed into the cleaned intestines or into white cloth bags. These were then hung with the other meat in the smokehouse to be smoked. Some people fried the sausage, packed it in layers in a stone jar, and poured grease over it; this method of preserving the sausage was referred to as "lardin' it down."[19]

This traditional hog-killing method changed little over the years. Friedrich Gerstäcker, a German from Bremen who traveled extensively throughout Arkansas in the late 1830s, described scalding pigs "Arkansas fashion."

> The weather set in very cold, and we resolved to kill and salt the pigs we had bought, weighing about 200 pounds each. . . . The neighbors were called in to help, the pigs driven into the enclosure, shot, stuck, scalded, cleaned, and carried into the house. Not having any large caldron to scald them, it was done Arkansas fashion. A cask with the head out was half sunk in the earth, and filled with cold water, and a large fire made close by and covered with stones. When these were hot enough, they were thrown into the water, and the cask covered with a blanket. The water was soon hot enough for our purpose: the pig was dipped once or twice in the water, and five or six pairs of hands soon removed all the bristles. By evening all was finished and part of the fat laid aside, out of reach of the dogs for making soap. . . . Next day the pigs were cut up, salted, and suspended in the smoking house.[20]

There is little mention of beef among the writings of the early settlers. Although cattle were kept on the farm, beef simply did not have the important place in early Arkansas foodways that pork had. When a calf was slaughtered, the meat had to be used immediately since there was no method of preservation except drying. Newman Sugg, from Chickalah Mountain in Yell County, said: "Most of the time when they'd kill a beef in the summertime, why they'd just dress it and they'd cut off what they wanted and they'd start peddling it out among the neighbors, you know. And maybe a week or two from then some other guy would kill one. By doing that in the community—somebody killing one ever week or ten days—they'd have fresh meat all summer."[21]

On August 4, 1890, Nannie Stillwell Jackson of Watson (Desha County) wrote the following entry in her diary: "Clear & warm, Mr. Jackson killed whiteface my tiny cows yearling & sold it for beef, he got the money for most of it, sent his ma a piece gave Mr. Morgan 15 lbs & sent Aunt Lucinda Black a piece, Lizzie Sue & I cleaned the tripe & feet, we did not get to eat breakfast until after six oclock & Mr. Jackson did not get all the beef sold until most sundown. . . ."[22]

Hog killing was a winter time activity. The accounts of the butchering of cattle by both Sugg and Jackson refer to its being done in the summer time. Probably more cattle were slaughtered in the late summer because supplies of cured pork had been exhausted and cattle had fattened from grazing on summer vegetation. The practice of cooperative slaughtering provided the only method by which people could have beef on the table throughout the year.

Small flocks of chickens were kept by most farmers to provide eggs and meat. Chicken provided an occasional change from a steady diet of pork. And eggs could be sold to bring in a little additional income. Although nowadays people think of chicken only as a part of a noontime or evening meal, it was often served in earlier times for breakfast: "Thursday June 26, 1890 . . . Lizzie caught & killed & picked the little duck leged rooster for to cook for Mr. Jacksons breakfast in the morning it is one of the little chickens that I kept all through the overflow there are 3 left now, one rooster & 2 pullets."[23]

Early settlers in Arkansas found an abundance of game both in the Delta and in the mountainous regions. Wild animals and fish supplemented the supplies that the settlers brought with them and remained an important part of their diet even after self-sufficient farms were established. Allsopp writes:

> Arkansas has been, and is yet, a hunter's paradise. When Presley Huckaboy moved to Green County, in 1867, all the people depended upon their gun for a living, to a great extent. Game was plentiful everywhere. When Huckaboy wanted fresh meat, he sent his children to a thicket about 300 yards from the house and shot a good deer from the drove they started up. His method for trapping turkeys was unique. Building a square pen of logs near where he fed his stock, he covered it with poles, and dug a slanting passageway under the logs. He scattered corn along the passageway. The turkeys had to stoop a little to get under the pen, but as soon as they were inside they flew up to the level ground, and, instead of looking down to get out, would always look up. He said he often caught as many as eight or ten at a time in this manner.
>
> Coons and squirrels were so thick that a man could take a rifle and kill fifteen or twenty a day. Bears were so plentiful that their meat was used instead of bacon, and was cured for the season in much the same way as pork.[24]

FIGURE 3. *Jack Bonner (Baxter County) with wild turkey. By permission of Mary Ann Messick.*

Ducks, geese, quail, turkeys, squirrels, rabbits, raccoons, possums, deer, and bear provided food for the table and sport for the hunter. Possums were hunted by many only for their hides, but others prized the flavor of this particular animal if it was cooked in the proper way. Tom Patrick of Madison County said, "We put it in the pot and biled it; and then put it on and baked it."[25] From the Slave Narratives comes this entry: "Possums! I should say so. Dey cotch plenty of 'em and after dey was kilt Ma would scald 'em and rub 'em in hot ashes and dat clean't 'em just as pretty and white. OO-oo-oo but dey was good. Lord Yessum."[26]

Game was so abundant in the 1850s that a plantation owner in eastern Arkansas hired a white employee whose only duty was to hunt wild game to be used in feeding the slaves. "Slade['s] . . . duty . . . was to hunt all night. He slept in the day time. He could not bring in all the game he would kill, hence the hands on our place would divide themselves into squads and take time about hunting with Slade at night until he had killed a load of coons, and they would then carry them home and go to sleep, leaving Slade to make the rest of the night alone. . . . Such was the abundance of wild life in those days that whole families could subsist on game if they desired."[27]

Corn

The main food crop for the early settlers in Arkansas was corn.[28] It grew well throughout the state, it was less trouble than wheat or other grains, and it was nutritious. Because of its versatility, corn was the favorite crop. Besides the many foods that corn provided, it could be fed to the stock, sold, or made into whiskey in a still; the shucks could be used for chair bottoms, horse collars, mats, brooms, or mattress stuffing; and the cobs were used for fuel, pipes, or dolls for the little girls in the family.[29]

The earliest settlers had to exercise their ingenuity because of the lack of grist mills. Following is a description of a makeshift contraption devised for the grinding of grain:

> A tree was felled, so as to leave a large stump with a level surface. Then a fire was started and kept burning on the top of the stump, until a large bowl was formed, the outer rim of the stump being kept from burning by constant wetting. The hole was cleaned out and scraped, and then a pole with one end hinged to a forked post was set near the hollow stump and extended horizontally over it. A maul or rock fastened to the pole hung over the stump completed the pioneer grist-mill. The corn was placed in the hollow opening, and was ground by moving the loose end of the pole up and down.[30]

FIGURE 4. John A.
Schrock with grand-
children Patricia and
Earl Schrock, Jr., in
cornfield (Johnson
County, late 1940s).

Schoolcraft encountered this primitive method of grinding corn in Arkansas in 1818.[31] Where a water source was available, people used a pounding mill, called a "Lazy Tom," to beat their corn by water power:

> The mill was made by getting a large log of timber about fifteen feet long, making a trough at the butt end, three feet long, to hold as much water as possible, leaving the balance of the log some four inches square, hanging it on a pivot near the trough. They fixed a pestle at the other end and then a mortar to hold the grain. The trough was about four feet above the ground. The spout carried water from the spring into it and when the trough was full it sunk down, raising the pestle some ten feet high. When the water poured out, the pestle fell with a vim on the grain in the mortar. They were slow but sure, running day and night, and were called "Lazy Tom's," and were enclosed with palings to keep out fowls and wild animals.[32]

In 1860, more than 17,000,000 bushels of corn were produced in the state in amounts ranging from 88,295 to 663,540 bushels per county.

Corn grew well in all areas of the state: the four leading corn-producing counties were Washington, Independence, Phillips, and Hempstead, located in the northwest, northeast, southeast, and southwest quadrants of the state respectively. Large planters produced meal for their own use in their own water- or animal-powered grist mills and, at times, ground corn "on shares" for small farmers in the vicinity. The 1860 census shows that 254 men in Arkansas reported their occupation as miller.[33] It is apparent, therefore, that grist mills by this date were no longer in short supply.

As testimony to the phenomenal success of growing corn in Arkansas, Friedrich Gerstäcker was told by a farmer in the first half of the nineteenth century that "he had but a small tract of land, but it was the best and most fertile in the whole world; that he could grow everything on it except common garden beans, because the corn grows so fast that it drags the beans out of the earth."[34]

And Vance Randolph relates the following "windy" about how well corn grows in Arkansas:

> . . . the boy climbed up the stalk in dry weather, but was unable to return because a sudden shower made the corn grow faster than he could descend. The boy's father tried to fell the stalk with an axe, but the damned thing was growin' so fast that he couldn't hit it twice in the same place. Two men came running with a cross-cut saw, but they only pulled it once through the rind when the saw was wrenched from their hands and disappeared into the darkness overhead. When I heard this story in Russellville, Arkansas, in August, 1934, the boy was still aloft. He was living on green corn without salt, and had thrown down more than four bushels of cobs already. "If Tommy can just hold out till frost," a neighbor told me, "the damn thing is bound to stop growin', an' we'll surely be able to git him down somehow."[35]

Corn was harvested by hand, loaded on wagons with sideboards, and transported to the corncrib, generally a small structure made of logs with a cedar-shake roof. In Arkansas corn was stored "in the shuck," with the shucks being removed as the corn was used. Occasionally families had corn huskings to which neighbors and friends would be invited to share the work of shucking the corn. If a boy found a red ear of corn, instead of the usual yellow or white, he won the privilege of kissing the girl of his choice.[36]

As wheat became more abundant and less expensive, people began to eat less corn everywhere except in the South. Bolsterli argues that the continued use of corn meal as a staple in the South is the key to under-standing the effect of African influence on Southern eating habits. Since blacks were the only immigrants who came to this continent with an already-established tradition of eating maize, she contends that the con-tinued popularity of corn meal as a staple in the South is linked to the region's partial African heritage.[37] For whatever reason, corn has played a very important role in the traditional foodways of Arkansans, and today corn-on-the-cob, fried vegetables and meats rolled in corn-meal batters and coatings, and cornbread are regularly served on Arkansas tables.

Molasses

Sugar was a scarce and expensive commodity for the settlers in Arkansas. Before the introduction of sorghum grain, they relied heavily on wild honey as their primary "sweetening." By 1860, however, Arkansas pro-duced 115,604 gallons of sorghum molasses, more than any other state of the lower South.[38] Poured over cornbread or biscuits, it provided a nutri-tious dessert, rich in calcium and iron, for any meal.

Sorghum making was another of fall's chores to be added to corn gathering, cotton picking, and hog killing, but, according to Warren Farmer Wilhite, it "was usually a joyful time of the year with the folks. We always looked forward to sorghum-making because usually you had done run out of sorghum by this time and you was glad to have some new syrup."[39] Like hog killing, sorghum making was a communal activity that required as many hands and strong backs as were available.

Early fall, generally September, is sorghum-making time in Arkansas. The rich, reddish-gold syrup made from sorghum cane (not sugar cane) was referred to as sorghum, molasses, sorghum molasses, or "long sweet-enin'"; the latter term was used to distinguish sorghum from honey, which was called "short sweetenin.'"[40] To ensure the best quality syrup, the farmer had to cut the cane at the proper stage of ripeness before frost. The outer leaves of the stalks were stripped with wooden paddles, designed for this purpose. All members of the family old enough to work in the field were recruited for this time-consuming job. The task was not a pleasant one: the work was hard, September days in Arkansas are gen-erally hot and muggy, and the cane plant cut fingers and arms and irri-tated the skin. The cane was stacked, loaded on wagons, and carried to the mill, where it was fed, a few stalks at a time, into the cane press The juice extracted from the cane as it was crushed in the press ran into a barrel. The press was operated by a long pole, or "sweep," attached

Figure 5. *Clifford Sides of Dardanelle (Yell County) feeds the press which extracts the juice from the cane. Photo by Louella Norris for the* Courier-Democrat.

Figure 6. *Courtney Campbell of Dardanelle oversees the cooking of the syrup in the copper pan. Photo by Louella Norris for the* Courier-Democrat.

to mules, which would walk for hours on end around and around the press.

At least three people were needed in making the sorghum: one to feed the cane through the rollers of the press and two to watch the cooking pan and tend the fire. Whenever the landscape allowed, the pole and press were set up on a knoll so that the juice could run downhill through a hose or a pipe to the cooking pan.[41] A wood-burning furnace built of bricks or stones was topped by a long, flat copper cooking pan that was built with a maze of baffles through which the syrup must pass in the cooking process. To obtain just the right color, taste, and consistency, the sorghum maker had to carefully regulate the hickory fire under the pan. Too much heat would scorch the molasses, and too little would make it strong and dark.[42] As the juice came out of the press into the barrel, it was strained, generally through a piece of burlap, and the remaining impurities were skimmed from the surface of the liquid during the cooking process with a device called a strainer. As the cane juice moved through the baffles, its color changed from a pale green to a deep green and gradually to a golden brown, and it thickened as the water cooked out of it. When the syrup reached the right color and consistency, recognized only by the expert sorghum makers, the stopper was pulled from the spout on the end of the pan, and the syrup was forced out into cans, jars, or barrels. At the same time, the next section of juice was being released into the "cooking off" area.

Sorghum millers took a toll of the finished product, usually one-third or one-fourth. A farmer tried to raise enough sorghum cane to supply his family, pay the toll, and have enough left over to provide a little cash.

After the sorghum was made, families would often gather for a candy pulling. Lourinda Hoggard of Faulkner County recalled, "Lots of young folks would get together and they'd make sorghum molasses candy. They'd boil the syrup down and before it got quite done they'd put a little soda in it and that'd make it foam up, you know, and get brittle. And then they'd take and pull that until it'd get just as white and bright."[43] The anticipation of the social activity to follow doubtless helped people to get through the very difficult work required in supplying their households with food.

Sorghum is still made here and there throughout the state. The horse or mule is often replaced nowadays with a motor of some kind or a tractor, but the rest is all hand work and is done in the same way it has been done for generations. The demand for the tasty syrup is still great enough

FIGURE 7. *Molasses making in Baxter County. By permission of Mary Ann Messick.*

that the few people who continue to make it usually have it all sold before a single gallon is produced.

The early settlers who made Arkansas their home brought with them a taste for pork, corn, and molasses—the basic food staples—and the state provided an environment in which these staples could be produced in great abundance. There was plenty of mast everywhere to provide forage for the hogs; therefore, the production of large supplies of meat was neither expensive nor time consuming. The first farmers were faced with the clearing of land before it could be plowed and sown, and clearing was a slow process. The choice of which crops to plant probably depended upon two things—the foods which, through tradition, settlers had grown in the past and those which would produce the highest yields from the land available to them. Corn and, later, sorghum cane fit the bill, and they had the added advantage of serving as food for men and beasts alike. There was no waste in these two crops; everything could be used.

Other year-round staples that are frequently mentioned in the early diaries and journals were peas, beans, potatoes (both Irish potatoes and sweet potatoes), and turnips. These are high-yielding, hardy garden crops that store well. In the early 1830s, Gerstäcker observed in the Ozark Mountains in Johnson County:

> . . . a turnip field, about sixty paces square, from one corner of which I saw smoke rising. As there was no trace of a building or of a human being to be seen, I was anxious to discover where the smoke came from, and on reaching the corner of the field, I found myself looking straight down a chimney. The house was built in a little hollow in the rock, probably to avoid encroaching on any part of the useful ground. But what could induce people to settle in such a hole, when so much good land was to be had in Arkansas, was more than I could divine.[44]

Figure 8. *John A. and Savelle Schrock (Johnson County, 1940s) with a morning's picking of blackberries—over fourteen gallons.*

What caught Gerstäcker's attention apparently was the smoke rising from the corner of the turnip field, but, in relating this incident, he gives us a little piece of evidence about the farmer's livelihood. If a man's pace is three feet, sixty paces square would be roughly three-quarters of an acre, a good-sized turnip patch! Turnips, like grain sorghum and corn, provided food for both people and livestock.

In addition to these vegetables and others which could be grown and eaten in season, a wide variety of wild fruits and nuts could be found, then as now, throughout the state. Most Arkansans, at least those living in rural areas, are familiar with hickory nuts, black walnuts, chinquapins (the American chestnut), native pecans, plums, cherries, persimmons, possum-grapes, muscadines, dewberries, blackberries, and wild strawberries.

Preparation and Preservation of Foods

The first farmers in Arkansas probably longed for spring and summer in a way not known to us today. The spring vegetation brought a welcome change to their unvarying winter diet made up only of those foods that they could preserve by salting, pickling, drying, or burying in the ground. Spring meant that greens could be added to a meal of meat, dried peas or beans, boiled turnips, and cornbread. Both wild greens and cultivated ones added variety to the winter menus.

Two types of greens—one wild and one domesticated—are worthy of mention, poke sallet and leaf lettuce. Many wild greens (wild lettuce, lamb's quarter, sheep sorrel, and dandelion) were sought out and used by early settlers, but none of these had the widespread popularity of poke sallet. The tender shoots of this plant push through the ground in March and April and can be found in great plenty in old fence rows, beside stumps, and in areas from which brush has been cleared. This plant was considered by many old-timers as a necessary spring tonic for the whole family.[45] The greens are parboiled, drained, and placed in a skillet of hot pork grease; to this mixture, three or four eggs are added. This dish, served with pinto beans and cornbread, is a favorite of many Arkansans today. Salads as we know them were not a part of the diet of our ances-tors. Fresh vegetables were not mixed together; instead, they were sliced and served separately on the table. "Garden sass," some people called it—tomatoes, cucumbers, and green onions that were washed, cut up, and put on a plate with no dressing of any kind.[46] "Sallet" meant either poke sallet or wilted lettuce, a tasty dish made by pouring sizzling hot bacon grease and a little vinegar over chopped lettuce leaves and green onions.

Boiling and frying were the two methods of cooking most common in the settlement period of the state. Meat was sometimes roasted over an open fire, but baking was difficult to accomplish in an open fireplace. Baking was made possible by the use of the Dutch oven, a heavy-lidded iron pot that could be placed in the fireplace and covered with coals.

Sweet potatoes were generally baked or roasted in ashes. This popular vegetable was carried by workers to the field, by men who went on all-day hunting trips, and by children to school to provide a snack or, in some cases, a full meal. Most other vegetables were either boiled or fried.

Boiled vegetables were cooked for long periods of time. Beans, peas, cabbage, and all greens (turnip greens, collards, etc.) were invariably cooked with a piece of fat pork for seasoning. "Pot-likker," often mentioned in the early writings, was the broth containing the juices of the meats and vegetables that had been boiled together. Often cornbread was crumbled into a dish and the pot-likker was poured over it.

Other vegetables were fried. Irish potatoes, okra, eggplant, and squash could be boiled alone or added to stews, but they were most often fried, after being sliced and rolled in corn meal, in sizzling hot fat.

Corn was eaten in a variety of ways and appeared in some form at every meal. It was picked just at the right time and boiled on the cob as "roasting ears," it was cut off the cob and boiled or fried, often with butter or cream added, it was used to make hominy and grits, and it was ground for corn meal. The ground corn meal, either white or yellow, was used for mush, cornbread, fritters, and as a coating in which to roll fish, squash, okra, and green tomatoes before frying them.

Ruby Forbus of Ozark provided the following description of the preparation of hominy:

> The way I made hominy was with lye. Eagle Eye, was that the name of it? I like white corn; I never did make any out of yellow corn. But of course you can buy white and yellow hominy both. Now I don't remember the proportions or anything. Guess it was all guess work. It was made outside in a kettle. We filled the kettle about half full of water and put the lye in there, which I said was just guess work, and then you put your corn in, and you cook it long enough for the lye to make the husks come off. Then when it was cooked long enough for the husks to be removed easily, why you took it out of that hot lye and water and washed it and washed it and washed it and, with your hands, you got all the husks off. Then you put it back in the kettle in clear water and cooked it till it was done. In the wintertime, why you could keep it several days without canning it.[47]

Hominy was often dried and ground into a coarse meal to become grits. Grits were boiled into a thick porridge and often served along with meat and eggs for breakfast. Upon cooling, this porridge congeals and can be sliced and fried in hot grease. Garlic, butter, cream, and a little cheese can be added to form a mouth-watering main dish referred to as "garlic grits."

The daily bread for the earliest settlers was cornbread. Wheat was not grown extensively in the state, and flour is always mentioned among the staples that had to be bought. In 1819, Thomas Nuttall noted: ". . . there is not, however, yet a grist mill on the Arkansa, and flour commonly sells above the Post, at 12 dollars per barrel. For the preparation of maize, a wooden mortar, or different kinds of hand or horse-mills are sufficient. Sugar and coffee are also high priced articles, more particularly this year."[48] Although it is difficult to know how twelve dollars a barrel compares with today's cost of flour, it is apparent that Nuttall considered it a very high price. About the availability of flour in the period of the late 1830s and early 1840s in Sevier County, Nancy Cooper Holoman Guinn wrote, "Wheat flour was a luxury we did not often enjoy, for we had to send to Washington [Hempstead County] for it, paying $20.00 a barrel for it."[49] As a consequence of the scarcity of wheat flour, its use among the less affluent was probably sporadic at best, perhaps on Sundays or two or three times a week.[50] It was more often used for pie crusts, cakes, and pancakes rather than for the preparation of everyday bread.[51]

The most common wheat bread in the traditional diet of most Arkansans was biscuits, a quick bread using baking powder or soda as the leavening agent depending upon whether the bread dough is made with sweetmilk or buttermilk. As wheat became more available and more affordable, biscuits became a regular variation from the routine baked or fried cornbread.

Although not so common as biscuits, yeast breads—both loaves and rolls—were prepared by many nineteenth-century housewives. Yeast could be bought, but it was generally prepared at home. The flowers from hops and potatoes were mixed together to provide a homemade yeast. A mixture of flour, potato water, hot water, salt, and sugar left uncovered for several hours to ferment provided another type of rising agent.[52] Still others kept a supply of "everlasting," a liquid starter made by adding sugar and water to a piece of the dough saved from the previous baking.[53]

Before the days of refrigeration, short-term preservation of foods that had to be kept chilled was accomplished by submersing them in cold well water. Milk, butter, and fresh meat were placed in a container, generally a lard bucket with a tight-fitting lid, and lowered into the well or placed in the spring that served as the family's water supply.

FIGURE 9. *Laura Carroll (Pope County, 1930s) brings the cow home at milking time.*

Root vegetables were most often preserved by storing them in earthen mounds. The farmer would dig a pit, line it with a thick layer of straw or hay, and put in the vegetables. The vegetables would then be covered with something solid—a board or a tarp—another layer of hay, and finally the dirt that had been removed to form the pit. Vegetables would usually keep all winter stored in this manner.

Other foods were preserved by drying, fermenting, smoking, and salt curing. Drying was the most common method of preservation for many fruits and vegetables. Beans were sometimes strung on a thread and dried to make what most people called shuck beans or "leather breeches."[54] Fruits, particularly peaches and apples, were sliced, seeded, and placed out of doors to dry. Generally, they were spread out on a sheet, often on the top of one of the outbuildings, so that they could be brought in at night. After the drying process was completed, they were put in cloth bags and hung in the attic. To keep bugs out of them, some people would put chinaberry twigs and leaves into the bags with the dried fruit.[55] Pumpkins were often dried in the house rather than outside:

Nearly everybody raised pumpkins—by the wagonloads. Because they was all used up one way or another. To dry them you cut them crossways there, in rings. Hanging right next to the fireplace there was a framework hanging down—like the quilting frames used to hang down from the ceiling.

You'd cut these pumpkins in these rings, oh, about three quarters or an inch thick; then of course you'd peel off the outside hull part; and then you'd have sticks that you'd put these [pumpkin circles] on and set 'em up on this frame there—kinda like drying tobacco in the tobacco barns. And you'd put 'em up there and every day or two you'd turn 'em so it all dried uniformly all around. You utilized the heat from the fireplace. And that, now, is delicious when it's cooked.[56]

Through the fermentation process, men made wines from practically any kind of fruit, and they made persimmon beer, and, of course, moonshine whiskey. Cabbage was preserved by fermenting or souring, the end product being sauerkraut. Pauline Harvey of Clarksville described the traditional method of preparing kraut taught to her by her mother:

She used a five gallon or ten gallon stone jar, whatever amount she wanted to make. She would bring her cabbage in and trim 'em nicely and shred it on this cabbage shredder. Then she would put it down in a stone jar, add so much salt mixture, and continue this shredded cabbage and salt on the cabbage until it was filled.

Then she would pack it down real good until it would make its own brine, and then when she filled her jar, she would put a weight on it, a heavy weight. I think maybe she used a nice clean rock that she had washed real good. And then she would put a cloth over it and set it aside for a period of time until it would ferment. Then she would check it every few days. When it had been in this churn the desired length of time, why she would can it. She would put the kraut in a dishpan on the stove and bring it to a boiling point, and then put it in her glass jars and seal it.[57]

At apple-canning or drying time, the peelings and cores of the apples were kept and boiled down, and part of the juice was used to make vinegar:

To make vinegar Mama sweetened the apple juice with sorghum molasses, sometimes adding a bit of honey, if we happened to have any at the time. To the best of my recollection, Mama didn't actually measure either the juice or the sweetening. After pouring in some thick, golden sorghum, she would taste the mixture to determine whether or not to add a little more sweetening.

Upon finding the taste satisfactory, she would securely tie a clean white cloth, usually a thick flour sack, around the top of the jar to keep out any dust or insects, particularly the "sour gnats" that would hover around the jar when fermentation of its contents began to take place.

During the process by which the fermented juice and molasses became vinegar, a gelatinous scum, called "mother," would appear. It would take the vinegar several weeks "to make" and to reach the proper stage of acidity for use.[58]

The importance of vinegar was that it was the primary ingredient in the pickling of fruits, vegetables, and meats.

Salt curing, sugar curing, and smoking or a combination of these were used as methods of preserving pork. The hams, shoulders, and side meat were the cuts that could be successfully preserved. The meat was thoroughly rubbed with salt or a salt mixture (some people added other ingredients to the salt such as molasses, black pepper, and red pepper) and placed on waist-high shelves in the smokehouse or in curing boxes or barrels. The length of time that the meat was left in the salt coating

FIGURE 10. *Gladys Richardson (Yell County) canning apples.*

varied greatly from one individual to another. People checked the meat daily and moved forward in the process when the meat "looked right" or "felt right." If the meat were left in the curing mixture for too short a time, it would spoil; if it were left too long, it would be hard. Some preferred to hang the hams and shoulders with the hocks down to preserve the juices.

Fires were built in the smokehouse with hickory and oak or corncobs. If the smokehouse had a dirt floor, the fire could be built right on the floor; if it had some other kind of floor, the fire was generally made in an iron wash pot. A slow fire was kept constantly burning until the meat was thoroughly smoked.

When the family needed meat, someone would cut off the amount that was needed, wash the salt off, soak it overnight, and then cook it.

Canning was practiced in the United States from early in the nineteenth century, but no evidence of its use in Arkansas was found until much later.[59] After it became known in the state, it became one of the most important methods of food preservation. Vegetables, fruits, and even meat and fish were preserved by canning. The amount that any family "put up" was limited only by the number of jars that they owned.

Maya Angelou's description of her childhood experiences with food preservation in Stamps, Arkansas, is indicative of rural life throughout the whole state in the 1930s:

> In Stamps the custom was to can everything that could possibly be preserved. During the killing season, after the first frost, all neighbors helped each other to slaughter hogs and even the quiet, big-eyed cows if they had stopped giving milk.
>
> The missionary ladies of the Christian Methodist Episcopal Church helped Momma prepare the pork for sausage. They squeezed their fat arms elbow deep in the ground meat, mixed it with gray nose-opening sage, pepper and salt, and made tasty little samples for all obedient children who brought wood for the slick black stove. The men chopped off the larger pieces of meat and laid them in the smoke house to begin the curing process. They opened the knuckle of the hams with their deadly-looking knives, took out a certain round harmless bone ("it could make the meat go bad") and rubbed salt, coarse brown salt that looked like fine gravel, into the flesh, and the blood popped to the surface.
>
> Throughout the year, until the next frost, we took our meals from the smoke house, the little garden that lay cousin-close to the store and from the shelves of canned foods. There were choices on the shelves that could set a hungry child's mouth to watering. Green beans, snapped

always the right length, collards, cabbage, juicy red tomato preserves that came into their own on steaming buttered biscuits, and sausage, beets, berries and every fruit grown in Arkansas.[60]

FOODS FOR SPECIAL OCCASIONS AND HOLIDAYS

When people gather together to work or to have a good time, some type of food is almost always served. People seem to be much more relaxed and at ease when conversation is accompanied by food, possibly from association with family meals, where most of the communication within families takes place. The hospitality of a host is often measured by the amount and quality of food that is provided for guests. To show the gratitude to neighbors who had volunteered to help raise a barn, clear a field, or kill hogs for a year's supply of meat, the recipients almost always provided food for the entire group, putting out the very best they had. Allsopp says about an Arkansas quilting party:

> The news would spread from house to house that Mary Jane Smith's "Spread Eagle" quilt was finished and was to be quilted the next night. Invitations were scattered broadcast, not alone to the mothers and daughters, who were expected to ply their busy needles. The children also were bidden to come and "play" and "eat at the table." Often more eating than quilting was done at these parties, especially after the men arrived for supper. The dinner was hard to describe—such piles and heaps of sausage, spare ribs, turnover pies and transparent custards, sliced ham, chicken pie, all the vegetables of the season, pig's feet, jelly, syllabub, and pound cake. No one went away hungry from the quilting party![61]

Many quilting groups exist to this day; many are associated with churches, and almost all have regular "quilting days" when the members gather, sew the quilts, share gossip, and eat a potluck dinner (noon meal).

The box supper and the pie supper were purely social events for the purpose of raising money for some cause that the community considered worthy. One man recalled that: "The teacher would announce the time and place and every woman and girl would fix a box supper for two people. These were auctioned off by the teacher. Usually each man bought his favorite girl's box. Sometimes they would bring as high as twenty-five dollars, and this was the talk of the country."[62]

Another man reminisced about an experience at a box supper that didn't turn out as he had planned it:

One time I went to the box supper at the school. And see, the highest bidder would get this box. Well, there was a girl there named Beulah Kane. She put one up on a shelf, and I just knew it was hers. So I started biddin' on it. I bid the last dollar I had, ten dollars I believe it was. I bid the last dollar I had—if it'd been a nickel more I couldn't a got it. Well, to cap it all—it was a married woman's with an old man there and seven kids. And I had to sit down and eat supper with them![63]

Because pies are such a popular Southern dessert, pie suppers were, and still are, well attended in rural communities throughout the state. Held at schools, churches, or community buildings, they feature homemakers' best creations—fruit pies, nut pies, cream pies topped with mounds of meringue, mincemeat pies, and the more old-fashioned chess pies, buttermilk pies, and vinegar pies. Ruby Forbus of Ozark commented:

Well, all pie suppers I'm thinkin' was planned and put on for a good cause. To help the needy or to help some organization or something. And it was customary for the girls to bake the pie and the boys to bid on 'em, and the girls dressed up a box and made it fancy thinkin' that it'd bring more. But usually the pie that brought the most would be the girl's who had a sweetheart that wanted it very badly and the boys ran it up on him and, if he wanted it and had enough money, he just kept bidding. And it was customary for the pie to be cut and the girl and the boy to eat what they wanted and if it wasn't all eaten and passed out, then she took the rest of it home with her.[64]

A pounding is another traditional gathering where people bring gifts of food to a new family that has recently moved into the community. The gifts were generally staples, either store-bought or homemade. The following is a description of a pounding in the little community of Alpena:

We have the pounding each time a new preacher arrives to preach at our church. We might even have the pounding for each new year he stays.

We have our monthly fellowship supper second Monday of each month at which time the preacher and his family also attend. When he starts his year of preaching we set the date of the pounding first supper after that. The congregation brings anything they wish in foodstuffs— garden produce, fresh fruit, eggs, staple goods such as coffee, sugar, meal or frozen meats and canned goods. We gather this in one lot in boxes and bags. We delegate someone to make a short speech of presentation, generally a man, after we have our supper. In turn, the preacher and his wife express their thanks. We then visit, sing hymns, or have short meetings or commissions.[65]

The time-honored custom of providing food for a family on the day of a funeral is still very common throughout the state. If a woman were asked why she was carrying food to a funeral dinner, she would probably answer, "Because the family won't feel like cooking." But the real reason is surely that she is providing an outward symbol of the grief that she shares with the family. The food is sometimes carried to the home and simply left for the immediate family and those family members who have come from other places. At other times, the food is taken to the church, especially to churches that have their own cemeteries, and the family is joined at the meal by everyone in attendance at the funeral. Even though the occasion for the gathering is a sad one, people begin to eat and converse and soon are reminiscing about the old days, telling old hunting stories, or recalling happier occasions that they had shared in the past. Often the noise level rises to a crescendo and peals of laughter can be heard. The simple "breaking of bread together" can have a telling effect upon us, elevating us from deep sadness to levity, at least for a while.

Feasts were often a part of a wedding celebration. In the German community of Augsburg, in western Pope County, the weddings were held after the church service. After the wedding, the bride and groom, their families, and the invited guests went to the bride's home for the wedding dinner and celebration. The meal began as near midday as possible and continued as long as it took to get everybody filled up. The *Hochzeitsbitte*, a close friend or relative of the bride who had been in charge of inviting guests and who served as an honorary master of the festivities, passed out homemade beer to all of the guests. There was no stinting on food or drink. They ate and drank and danced sometimes all night long. Describing her sister's wedding on March 17, 1917, Lucy Dietrich said, "I know my mother baked bread for a whole week when my sister got married, and I don't know how many hams she had. She cooked the hams in the huge washpots in the yard."[66]

Decorations and homecomings are traditional in the small communities throughout the state. In the spring the weekly newspapers are filled with reports of family community homecomings. This is the time of the year when people travel great distances to visit friends and relatives. Homecomings are often held simultaneously with decoration at a church cemetery or small community cemetery. Families make this annual pilgrimage to clean up the cemetery, to repair any damage that grave markers have sustained, and to put fresh or artificial flowers on the graves of their loved ones. The slate of activities varies, but there is generally singing, and there is always a meal, which is eaten in the church, under a pavilion, or spread on the ground.

Outdoor activities are very popular in Arkansas. Weekends find the many parks scattered throughout the state completely filled with campers and picnickers. Churches, civic organizations, and often towns sponsor special picnics on the Fourth of July. Gerstäcker described an Arkansas Fourth of July picnic that he attended in the late 1830s:

> Meantime a long table was laid out before the house and surrounded with chairs, benches, &c.: but as it was impossible for all to find seats at once, the ladies were accommodated first, and waited upon by the gentlemen. The dinner consisted of roast beef, roast pork, potatoes, sweet potatoes, maize bread, cakes, and coffee and milk, and went off very well. Rutkin had brought a case of wine for the ladies, which was soon emptied. After dinner, a speech was made to the assembled public, in honor of the birthday of the United States, and then dancing commenced again. Picturesque groups were formed here and there, occupied in various ways. In one place, a party of strong-built, sunburnt figures lounged at full length on the grass, relating their shooting adventures; further on, two figures, astride a fallen tree, were playing a game of cards; in another place, a party leaping with a heavy stone in each hand, to give them more impetus; and a row of big fellows were taking their siesta under the trees, only moving to avoid the too intrusive rays of the sun, as he declined towards the west.[67]

This account of a picnic, which was held on the Fourche LaFave River, contains an interesting comment about the serving of the food: the men served the women and the women ate first. This practice was indeed unusual; at another place in the description of his travels through Arkansas, Gerstäcker comments on the fact that women ate only after the men had finished their meal:

> These calumnies were put an end to by the announcement, "Supper is ready." Boxes, chairs, and logs were placed around the table for seats. Turkey, venison, pork, opossum, maize, bread, and the favorite beverage of the backwoodsman, coffee, disappeared so rapidly that soon nothing was left but the bones of the animals, the remembrance of the bread, and the grounds of the coffee. One after another rose when he had had

enough, and then the woman-folk, who had wisely kept something for themselves, took their places. This is one of the customs of the West which always displeased me. The hostess seldom sits down to table with the men, except now and then at tea or coffee.[68]

The similarities of the 1830s picnic held by a group of white people on a river bank and a 1930s picnic held by a group of black people in a clearing by a pond are striking:

> The summer picnic fish fry in the clearing by the pond was the biggest out-door event of the year. Everyone was there. All churches were represented, as well as the social groups (Elks, Eastern Star, Masons, Knights of Columbus, Daughters of Pythias), professional people (Negro teachers from Lafayette County) and all the excited children.
>
> Musicians brought cigar-box guitars, harmonicas, juice harps, combs wrapped in tissue paper and even bathtub basses.
>
> The amount and variety of foods would have found approval on the menu of a Roman epicure. Pans of fried chicken, covered with dish-towels, sat under benches next to a mountain of potato salad crammed with hard-boiled eggs. Whole rust-red sticks of bologna were clothed in cheese-cloth. Homemade pickles and chow-chow, and baked country hams, aromatic with cloves and pineapples, vied for prominence. Our steady customers had ordered cold watermelons, so Bailey and I chugged the striped-green fruit into the Coca-Cola box and filled all the tubs with ice as well as the big black wash pot that Momma used to boil her laundry. Now they too lay sweating in the happy afternoon air.
>
> The summer picnic gave ladies a chance to show off their baking hands. On the barbecue pit, chickens and spareribs sputtered in their own fat and a sauce whose recipe was guarded in the family like a scandalous affair.
>
> However, in the ecumenical light of the summer picnic every true baking artist could reveal her prize to the delight and criticism of the town. Orange sponge cakes and dark brown mounds dripping Hershey's chocolate stood layer to layer with ice-white coconuts and light brown caramels. Pound cakes sagged with their buttery weight and small children could no more resist licking the icings than their mothers could avoid slapping the sticky fingers.
>
> Proven fishermen and weekend amateurs sat on the trunks of trees at the pond. They pulled the struggling bass and the silver perch from the swift water. A rotating crew of young girls scaled and cleaned the catch and busy women in starched aprons salted and rolled the fish in corn meal, then dropped them in Dutch ovens trembling with boiling fat.[69]

Figure 11. *Scenes from the annual Mountain Home Picnic (Baxter County). By permission of Mary Ann Messick.*

Three organized picnics or suppers grew rapidly and became favorite stumping places for politicians, especially during election years—the Polk County Possum Club Banquet, the Mt. Nebo Chicken Fry, and the Gillette Coon Supper. For many years the Polk County Possum Club, formed in 1913, held an annual dinner of possum and all the trimmings, which in 1940 attracted 600 guests from as far away as New York.[70] The Mt. Nebo Chicken Fry, a yearly poultry festival in Yell County, is one of the largest annual food festivals in the state. It is an all-day affair attracting scores of local and state politicians who pass out cards, shake hands, and kiss babies throughout the day. In 1936 farmers from the Gillette area (Arkansas County) gathered for a meal of raccoon and chicken pie. Fifty years later, in 1986, the Gillette Farmers' and Businessmen's Club served 2,012 pounds of raccoon, 10 bushels of sweet potatoes, 100 pounds of barbecued rice, 14 large hams, 2,000 rolls and numerous cakes to the 1,200 guests from Arkansas and five other states. Among those present were Governor Bill Clinton and former Governor Orville E. Faubus.[71]

Other holidays, especially Easter, Thanksgiving, and Christmas, are memorable in large part because of the different foods associated with them. Traditions vary from family to family because of their ethnic backgrounds and their religious beliefs.

Finally, the noon meal on New Year's Day is as closely associated in the South with black-eyed peas and hog jowl as Thanksgiving is with roast turkey. No matter how simple or elaborate the meal is, this dish can almost always be found somewhere on the table. It is usually accompanied by cornbread. This meal, which guarantees luck, success, and happiness throughout the rest of the year, makes use of three of the staples of the state's early settlers and perhaps serves as a reminder of the simple foods that were enjoyed, or repetitively endured, by our ancestors.

SUPERSTITIONS ASSOCIATED WITH FOODS

The "thou shalt nots" associated with certain foods are legion. Conventional wisdom had it that, if a person drank sweet milk at a meal of fried fish, he would sicken and die; buttermilk was an acceptable drink, however. Such warnings about cause and effect or condition and result were scrupulously heeded by a great many people, and many others put stock in them because there wasn't any sense in taking chances.

Otto Earnest Rayburn said that, in the Ozarks, "regardless of the coming of automobiles and radios, thunder continues to sour milk."[72] Vance Randolph, in his discussion of household superstitions, listed the following beliefs about foods:

— If you help yourself to something at table, when you already have some of the same stuff on your plate, it means that somebody is coming who is hungry for that particular article of food.

— If you accidentally drop a bit of food on the floor, you will have a visitor who is hungry.

— If coffee grounds cling to the sides of a cup, high up, it is a sign that company is coming with good news.

— If you run completely out of salt, your family will experience a full year's poverty and privation.

— If the salt shaker is full on New Year's Day, prosperity for the coming year is assured.

— It is bad luck to lend salt; lending salt causes some kind of "fraction" - between the lender and the borrower.

— If a woman burns bread until the crust is black, she will fly into a rage before the day is over.

— If a person eats blackened bread, he will have good luck and will never be troubled by intestinal worms.

— If a woman burns pancakes or biscuits, it means that her "old man" is angry.

— It is bad luck to give away yeast.

— It is bad luck to cut cornbread with a knife. It should be broken.

— Cake batter should always be stirred in the same direction. Stirring it first one way and then the other will spoil the cake for sure.

— Two people should not stir the same batter. If two try to divide the labor, they might as well throw the cake away.

— In making vinegar from molasses and rain water, the Ozark housewife hastens fermentation by putting in nine grains of corn, which she "names" for the meanest, sourest persons of her acquaintance.

— Cider or wine should not be made when the moon is waning; it will turn sour every time.

— A menstruating woman can perform all of her ordinary household tasks save one—she can't pickle cucumbers.

— A bad woman can't make good applesauce; it will always be mushy and not sufficiently tart.

— If a woman opens a jar of fruit and some of the juice spatters into her face, she will hear some welcome news very soon.

— Walnut shells should not be burned.

— Lightning often strikes a cookstove, but never one that has a fire in it.[73]

Although hunting is practiced by a large part of the population, both male and female, in the state, many hunters would not think of shooting a dove because of the religious symbolism associated with this fowl.

Social Significance of Food

Food keeps us alive; it helps to keep us healthy if we eat the proper types; and it gives us great pleasure when it looks, smells, and tastes good. Food has a much greater impact upon our lives than simply providing sustenance, however.

In earlier days when a woman spent almost all of her time in the home, the preparation and preservation of food provided an outlet for her to display her artistic abilities to be enjoyed by her family and guests. Compliments she received on a special dessert that she carried to a church social or a Fourth of July picnic gave her a sense of worth outside the home, where she spent most of her time. Often a certain dish won such acclaim that it became her specialty, her unique contribution to communal celebrations. The county fair raised canning almost to an art form with competition among women to produce beautifully arranged fruits and vegetables in pint and quart jars. Patrick Dunahoo writes, "[W]hen the canning was finished, the mistress, dabbing at her moist face with a handkerchief, often would survey the rows of jars as proudly as if they were a picture she had painted, which in a manner they were, for each of the glass jars glowed with a captured bit of the glorious color and natural richness of a Delta summer."[74]

The early settlers of Arkansas sometimes considered sharing food a social duty. Common decency dictated that travelers who knocked at the door be offered lodging for the night and the same food that the family ate. Though the travelers might never see their hosts again, they remembered the hospitality that was extended to them, and they showed the same kindness to other travelers who stopped at their homes.

People in communities served by a resident pastor usually considered it their duty to share food from their fields, gardens, and smokehouses with the minister's family. Following the biblical precept that "The laborer is worthy of his hire," the congregation provided a monetary salary of some sort through their offerings, but they also brought the minister lavish gifts of food. Louise Harms, from the Lutheran community of Augsburg, said: "Let me tell you, they didn't go hungry, they got fed good. We all had hogs, and they'd get ham, they'd get sausage, and potatoes. My dad used to load that hack full of cabbage and everything and bring it to the preacher."[75] Since the community's economy was entirely dependent upon the land, it seemed proper and satisfying for the parishioners to directly offer the fruits of their labor to Christ through His vicar.

A gift of food, more than most other kinds of gifts, conveys affection and concern. The custom of taking food to the homes of people who are ill, who have had a death in the family, or who have suffered a loss of some kind still continues. Never mind that the family may not need food, that they may be better off financially than the giver; food, especially personally prepared food, means nurture, comfort, and friendship.

Before modern times small groups of women who lived within walking distance of one another developed special ties—sharing work, delivering babies, and nursing the sick. Sometimes presents of food exchanged by these women were personal gifts, not to be shared by the family.[76] Entries in Nannie Stillwell Jackson's diary make frequent mention of such personal gifts:

> Fannie ate dinner here she made me a vinegar pie & it was so good, she gave me some fresh butter milk for my dinner. . . .
>
> Fannie came this evening & brought me a bowl of blackberries & oh they were so nice I just ate all I wanted gave the children some. . . .
>
> I made a berry pie for Fannie & sent it up there for dinner. . . .
>
> Mrs. Smithee came & brought me a cup of good pot licker & some greens & a piece of corn bread O but it was so good, & I did enjoy it so much. . . .
>
> Pete Willis sent me some fish & I sent him some milk. I sent 3 of the fish to Fannie after I fried them. Tony sent me a bucket of blackberries & I did enjoy them so much, I sent Fannie a saucer full of them. . . .[77]

Such small tokens of personal affection must have been especially meaningful to women who were often called upon to subordinate their own needs, comfort, and interests to those of the family.

Gifts of food were sometimes extended to large groups of people. John Gould Fletcher remembers how the women of his household provided patriotic support to a group of Arkansas soldiers in 1898, during the Spanish-American War: "The next year, the year of the Spanish-American War, patriotic meetings were in order; and I recall still vividly how our home bustled with vast preparations; hundreds of luncheon boxes were filled with fried chicken, biscuits, delicious jellies, and other good Southern things, all prepared for a company of volunteers going off to Cuba."[78]

Lucy Dietrich, daughter of German immigrants who moved into the Augsburg community in the 1870s, comments that the old ways of providing basic needs are worth remembering. "They knew how to help themselves. Butchering hogs, that was usually a big affair; neighbors would get together. . . . And anybody that needed a house raised, everybody went. The women folks went and cooked; the men, they built the house."[79] Any sort of job that required, or lent itself to, a community effort was an occasion for sharing food as well as labor. Working together and eating together strengthened the bonds between mutually dependent neighbors.

Recalling the foods one ate as a child invites nostalgia and a whole loosely related chain of reminiscences. Familiar smells of the family kitchen, the scent of fresh bread, the steam from a pot of soup on a cold, dark day—these are evocative memories for everyone, everywhere, Southern or Northern, American or not. And when the natives of a region or a state share more or less identical memories of food, the nostalgia translates into a powerful element of regional identity.

Having a common food heritage with someone we meet may not in itself make us like and trust him, but it never does any harm. Jeff Davis, son of a prosperous Pope County attorney and businessman, served as governor of Arkansas from 1901 to 1907. His political success lay in his ability to identify himself with the common man, the farmers in the villages and crossroads stores.[80] The farmers and laborers loved Davis's language and his descriptions of their way of life—particularly their eating customs.

> If some of them high-collared, fly-weight dudes of the East had sense enough to set down to a big dish of turnip greens, poke sallet, and hog jowl, they might sweat enough of that talcum powder off to look a little like a man.

> I have got eight children and nine pointer dogs in Little Rock. If any of you farmers should come to the city, come to my house and make it your home. The fatted calf will be killed, and I will roll down a few big yellow yams, fry some country hams and cook about two dozen eggs and we will eat eggs until we have every old hen in Arkansas cackling. Just come down there and act like you had good sense.

Old Armour and Cudahy never raised a sow and pigs in their life. Yet the prices of meat are so high that I can hardly buy breakfast bacon in Little Rock enough to support my family. I just buy one little slice, hang it up by a long string, and let each one of my kids jump up and grease their mouths and go to bed.

Many a moonlight October night, I have turned my hounds out o'er the hills and valleys of good old Pope county, and the most beautiful music that could come from the keys of an organ, would come from those long, flop-eared hounds of mine. I have picked cotton, possum hunted and raised great big old yaller yam potatoes and pumpkins. Mr. Chairman, isn't your mouth watering?[81]

Indeed, a special meal prepared by a good Arkansas cook will make anyone's mouth water. Fast-food chains such as McDonald's, Pizza Hut, and Kentucky Fried Chicken create the illusion that there is a uniform American cuisine. This illusion can be quickly dispelled by having a "company" meal with an Arkansas family: it might include fried chicken, potatoes and gravy, corn-on-the-cob, a fresh garden salad or "garden sass," homemade pickled beets, and fresh apple pie, or perhaps baked ham, red-eye gravy, rice, baked sweet potatoes, fried okra, steaming hot rolls, and peach cobbler or pecan pie. Everyday fare, of course, is not quite so sumptuous. Although food preferences change when a greater variety of foods becomes available, many Arkansans still enjoy an everyday meal of boiled beans and turnip greens, both heavily seasoned with a chunk of fat pork, and cornbread. The popularity of this meal, called a "poorboy supper" when sponsored by churches and civic clubs as a fund raiser, attests to our continued taste preference for the staples in the diet of our ancestors.

Folk Festivals and Celebrations

Michael Luster and Robert Cochran

Every year thousands of Americans flock to events that their sponsors call "festivals." There are classical music festivals, pop festivals, and an array of what are advertised as "folk festivals."[1] Representatives of this last category usually consist of an outdoor concert featuring several blues, gospel, bluegrass, old-time country, and/or ethnic performers as well as some singer/songwriters and several craft and food offerings. Most of the performers at these events are excellent—the very best in the business—and folklorists are frequently to be found among the festival-goers and can be seen having a fine time, for these can be extraordinary occasions. In fact, with the proliferation of "public sector" folklore jobs,[2] the odds are very good these days that a folklorist may have had a hand in putting the program together.

Yet folklorists, be they promoters or ticket holders, should sense a certain irony in such gatherings. On the one hand, these "folk festivals" offer excellent opportunities to present to the public the "stars" of American traditional music, performers whom most of the festival-goers might not otherwise see. And there can be little doubt that the exposure does a tremendous job of increasing public awareness and appreciation of traditional performers. On the other hand, though, the whole idea of presenting traditional performers to an audience of "the public" contradicts what folklore, folklorists, and specifically folk festivals have historically been about.

For folklorists the key word is "folk." As in all areas of life to which this adjective has been applied, *folk* festivals have been viewed as those celebrations or observations that take place within a folk group—possibly a family, a community, a group of co-workers or co-worshipers, or people of common ethnic identity. Folklorists have thought of them as "insider" events involving participants who were taking part according to a shared sense of proper action. Festivity has been seen to differ from other genres of folklore in that it is occasional, that it is tied to a specific occurrence, and that it provides a setting or frame for many of the other genres such as song, dance, music, storytelling, games, and foodways. As the defining features of folk festivals, folklorists have taken two key concepts: group participation according to rules and linkage to a specific occurrence.[3]

The occasions for folk festivals fall into two broad categories. The first category of festivity consists of those celebrations that French anthropologist Arnold van Gennep called "rites of passage."[4] These are ceremonies that mark the transition from one state of being to another. Birth, adolescence, coming of age, marriage, parenting, and death are a few of the more crucial transitions. Others might include baptism, confirmation, conversion, graduation, promotion, inauguration, installation, and induction or acceptance by the members of a club, lodge, or fraternity. In each of these transitions a person or persons must move from a familiar state into one that is unfamiliar to the mover. For many of these transitions, appropriate festivities have developed to either ease the passage or highlight the passage's importance. The other broad category of folk festivals includes "calendar customs," celebrations that occur temporally—for instance, in association with the regularly recurring periods such as school years or hunting and fishing seasons. Our first in-depth example is of a rite of passage. This particular instance reveals how a folk group will cooperate to create an appropriate festival when one of its members faces an important life transition.

RITE OF PASSAGE: RETIREMENT PARTY

For Al Jamison, a custodial supervisor at the University of Arkansas, Fayetteville, June 30, 1983, was a work day, but a work day with a difference. Tomorrow, and all the succeeding tomorrows, would be off days.

FIGURE 1. *Group Photo. Front, John Abbott. Second row, left to right, Al Jamison, Roy Reed, David Mitchell. Third row, left to right, Tommy Rose, Mick McKinnis, "Jake" Phillips. Back, Sherrall Cheatham. Photo by Mick McKinnis.*

There would be no more work, for Al Jamison, after this penultimate rite of passage. It was his last day on the job; he was retiring.

The University, Mr. Jamison's employer, had no official, campuswide procedure for the commemoration of this event. Instead, an annual Service Awards Banquet, usually held in April or May, focused attention on the length of employee service by presenting pins to those with ten, twenty, and even thirty years on the job.[5] Al Jamison knew about these affairs—he'd picked up his own ten-year service pin at one of them.

What Al didn't know about was a ceremony in his honor arranged not by his employers, technically his superiors, but by his co-workers, technically his subordinates. Seven men, the entire custodial crew for the Communications Center (now renamed Kimpel Hall), had been preparing for several weeks, and they were busy with final arrangements even as Jamison arrived for work. Things had started out simply enough, according to Mick McKinnis, one of the project's two principal organizers: "Well, everybody liked Al, and here he was retiring. I knew a little about the dinners the University gives every year or two, when they give out those little pins, but I wasn't sure if they invited everybody that had retired since the last one. And even if they did, you could wait maybe two years, you know, before you got that, if you live to get it. Anyway, I just went in there one night and asked the boys if they'd thought about getting him something. Everybody said it sounded like it'd be a good idea."[6]

"Something," after some discussion, became a wristwatch, a "gold wristwatch," according to John Abbott, the project's other prime organizer.[7] "I mentioned that Wal-Mart's had a sale on fairly decent watches—wristwatches—and that it wouldn't cost us very much apiece if we got him one of them and had it engraved on the back," said McKinnis. Purchase of the watch was quickly approved, but this was only the beginning. The memories of the participants differ as to details, but the "party"—as the organizers were now beginning to call it—soon involved plans for a cake and a "gag gift." Most participants recalled the cake as the second item agreed upon, and all remembered it as proposed by Abbott, who had experience as a cake decorator and did the lettering for Al Jamison's cake himself. Some, however, remembered the "gag gift," unanimously credited to McKinnis, as preceding the cake.

Whatever the order, it is clear that the party was acquiring both a temporal dimension and a tone in the minds of its planners. The "gag gift" would be a cap—that seems to have been understood from the beginning. "At one time we were gonna get him a hat that said 'Goodbye and good riddance,' " said McKinnis. "Then I decided that the other one would be more appropriate." The "other one" was still a cap, but the insulting valediction had been replaced by the more gnomic capital initials HMFIC with Retired written just below.[8] The party, everyone understood, would begin with the cap. "It just—just popped in my mind we'd get him something small like that, throw it at him first, and then come in with the big one," said McKinnis.

Temporal priority, in this instance, would also serve tonal purposes. They would begin with a joke; the man they would honor they would first mock. This is a standard procedure, after all. One who would be president must first run for president, must kiss babies, press flesh, suffer fools. Rituals of reversal, where the highly placed wash the feet of the lowly—these are familiar to students of culture. Here jocularity would make intimacy possible. The ceremony would open upon its own repudiation. We wanted to get you a nice gift, Jamison's co-workers would say, but all we could afford was this cheap cap with its obscene and contradictory message. There would be a final test: before the "big one" could be bestowed, its givers must bring in their "gag gift" and "throw it at him

FIGURE 2. Cake. Lettering by John Abbott. Photo by Mick McKinnis.

FIGURE 3. Cap with HMFIC lettering. Watch. (Billfold is gift from B.A. crew.) Photo by Mick McKinnis.

first." There would be one moment, then, when Jamison could not be certain, on grounds other than faith in his friends, that this "gag" was not all, that this travesty of ceremony was not the only ceremony that would be his. In his willingness to be the butt of their joke, he would demonstrate again that he was worthy of their honor, of the great pains they had taken to salute him.

The plan was by this time nearly complete. The watch had been purchased and suitably engraved: "It just said 'Good Luck, Al, From the Gang at CC,'" recalled Abbott. "And we put the date on it, too." The cake was also taken care of, as was the HMFIC cap. But then Abbott and McKinnis had another idea; neither gives it to the other or claims it as exclusively his own. They'd get some girls! It wouldn't be hard. After all, they were on a university campus, a place crawling with good-looking women who would be willing to help them out. They'd get two of them (it would be easier for the girls that way) and have them in bathing suits. Bathing beauties! They could carry in the watch, all wrapped in a huge box. Sure, and they could wrap it up "Chinese box" style, boxes inside boxes, so it would take Al forever to open it. Right, and the girls could have bright red lipstick and plant kisses on Al's bald head, and somebody could take pictures, and . . .

It was a great idea. Everybody loved it. The only problem was to find the girls. This portion of the party not only has a prominent place in the event's photographic record, but the fine adventure of arranging it is told with great relish and in considerable detail by the participants. Here is McKinnis's account:

> John said that he thought he knew a girl that would do it. Fine, we said. Go to it. He wasn't able, as it turned out, to get the particular girl, but someplace along the line he got in contact with one of the girls here in the drama department. And she agreed to do it. I'd say this was about two weeks before the party. So everything was set up. We had left messages for her to get in touch with us two or three days ahead of time, so we'd get it set up for sure.
>
> But we never did hear from her, so we thought maybe she might have backed out. And the night of the party—Al was already here and had gone over to B.A. (the adjacent Business Administration building, where Al's other crew worked)—we noticed across the street there was three young ladies over there, fooling around out on the lawn. John said maybe we ought to go talk to them, and I said go ahead, so we did. And he was over there for a little bit. Then I went over, and two of the three girls, when we explained what we were doing—they thought it sounded like a real good idea, and they agreed to go along with it.
>
> So we made arrangements to meet them about a quarter to eight here in the building. At the time they were supposed to be here, they were, and about that time, the other one showed up, the one we hadn't heard from. So here we got three girls. So I told John—I says, "What the hell. The more the merrier!" So that's how we ended up with three girls.

By this time it was nearly eight o'clock. Al was back from B.A., in his office on the first floor, ready for dinner. It was time for the party. "We all got together in the office," recalled Abbott, "and we give him the hat. That was the first he knew, because we didn't all come in at once, you know. We filtered in like one at a time, staggered in, here and there, to throw him off guard so he wouldn't get suspicious. And when all the guys were there, then the hat came out. Then the cake came out. Mick brought the hat out. I brought in the cake."

According to McKinnis's recollection, Al accepted the hat with good grace: "When we gave him the hat, we told him that was all we could afford. 'Well,' he said, 'that's all right.' Then, if I remember right, that's when John came in with the cake, and after we all gave him that, John and I excused ourselves for a minute to go bring in the girls." Thus far, everything had gone according to plan. The "gag gift" had served its multiple purposes well, not only letting Al prove himself a fine fellow once again by taking the joke in good spirit, but also establishing a "light" tone before the serious heart of the party opened with the presentation of the cake with its straightforward compliments, its words and very substance the product of John Abbott's labor. Already, with the "big one" still to come, Al Jamison's retirement party, created and shaped in every detail by his friends, had ranged from the hilarity of the joke with Al as its good-natured butt, to the deep intimacy of shared nourishment, one taking food from another's hand.

But now, with the "bathing beauties" on their way, bearing Al's "big" gift in its comic "Chinese boxes" wrapping, there was an unexpected complication, the arrival of an uninvited guest, not only an outsider but an outsider from above, a boss. His name was Glenn Grippe, and he was, in Abbott's description, "the immediate supervisor over all custodians, custodial supervisors, and everyone else in the custodial department. He's the custodial manager. He was Al's boss." Suddenly, with Grippe's appearance, a new element was introduced—the surprisers were themselves surprised, and the carefully orchestrated order of their party was imperiled. "For a few minutes it caused a lot of excitement," recalled Abbott.

McKinnis's memory centers here upon his own reaction to Grippe's presence: "So when I went back in through the door, there set Glenn. And the first thing I said was, 'Oh shit!' And I just turned around and went back to where the girls was—and John—and I told 'em, I said, 'Glenn's in there.' And John—he said, 'Oh shit!' And then I said, 'Well, we're here. Go for it.' And so we went for it." One of the girls entered the office first and said that she was looking for a Mr. Al Jamison. When Jamison identified himself, she told him there was a present for him and the other girls then entered carrying the large box (a "toilet tissue box," according to McKinnis) with the watch inside. The girls not only presented the gift, along with wishes for Jamison's happy retirement, but also, following specific instructions from Abbott and McKinnis, "lifted up his cap and kissed him on his bald head." The photographs of the party, taken by McKinnis, include one close-up of a lipstick print clearly outlined on Jamison's temple. As it turned out, Glenn Grippe was no problem. While all participants stressed his initial surprise, nearly equal emphasis was given to his positive response. McKinnis's account, in fact, gives most attention to Grippe's general assessment: "He was really surprised. As a matter of fact, I think he was in a state of shock for about ten minutes. But he stayed until about the last dog was bit. . . . About

FIGURE 4. *Left to right, Al Jamison, unidentified bathing beauties, Tommy Rose. Photo by Mick McKinnis.*

FIGURE 5. *A just-kissed Al Jamison, with lipstick print on forehead. Photo by Mick McKinnis.*

the most important thing he said was that out of all the retirements that he had been to, he'd never found one that showed as much initiative and planning as we'd done for this one."

John Abbott's recollections are remarkably similar. "He (Grippe) said it was—a lot of work was put into it, and he also said that, 'Al, this is the way the men show their appreciation to you.' He said he had seen lots of parties—Al said he's been to a lot of retirement parties—but neither one had ever been to one like this. Glenn or Al. He said, 'This topped it all.'"

Glenn Grippe, then, was a happy accident, a real addition to the party's highlights. A potential destroyer, he added the stature of his position to the celebration, and by his words of compliment he commended both its organizers and the man they honored. Grippe was able, by virtue of his position and experience, to introduce a comparative note. This was not his first retirement party. He was familiar with the tradition, knew its understood though unspoken rules. His voice, assuring Abbott, McKinnis, and the others of the excellence of their effort, was the voice from above, the official voice, the voice of authority. Just as he was leaving, Grippe even managed to add his own gift to the occasion. He was leaving, he said, headed for the other side of the campus. He didn't plan to return. The message was clear: Get your work done, and go home early.

With the appearance of the girls, the presentation of the watch, the cutting and eating of the cake, and the congratulatory remarks by Grippe and by Jamison himself, the party came to an end. It ended as it had begun—with its ceremonial core disguised in jocularity, just as the watch, with its explicit message of affection and regard, was hidden beneath layers of packaging and presented in a toilet paper box. As the cake had been preceded by the "gag gift" hat, so the watch was preceded by the girls in bathing suits. The requisite balance, a matter of considerable delicacy, was maintained throughout. It's all a big joke, we say, as we hand you our heart. Just a good laugh, we say, but under the surface, unstated, is a matter of sufficient importance to be worth several weeks of planning and preparation.

At bottom, retirement is a matter of departure, of separation, of loss. The cohesiveness of a group is ruptured; a place at its table is empty, soon to be filled by a stranger. Where Al Jamison was yesterday at home he will tomorrow have no place. His voice, that yesterday gave orders, will tomorrow be still. Whatever its benefits, retirement's costs most obviously include a disruption of routine, that valued illusion, true order's false cousin. So precious are routine's comforts that we are not surprised to learn of released hostages who exhibit great concern for the fate of their captors, of long-time prisoners who find it difficult to leave their cells. Time is a mostly modest power, moving quietly, like termites or undetected cancer. It is only when the obvious day comes, when the house falls down, when our fingers first notice the lump, when the alarm goes off and there's no job to wake up for, that time gets our attention. The retirement party, viewed in this light as a rite of passage, as an edge in experience, is a heavy-laden festival, designed at least in part to ease a difficult time. The group itself, in such moments, is threatened. This, at bottom, is what offended McKinnis and his colleagues in the official recognition policies of the University of Arkansas—they made too little of a man's departure, treated it too casually, and in so doing made light of their association, paid insufficient attention to the bonds they had formed in all those nights at work together in the nearly empty building, sharing their evening meals in the small office together, leaving in the late dark together. In Abbott's passing reference to "the guys," or McKinnis' to "the boys," there is adumbrated an awareness of association, of solidarity. In the creation of their indigenous ceremony, with its complex and delicate balancing of messages, they not only honored their retiring leader, they insisted too upon themselves.

Al Jamison's co-workers, in their recollections of the event, were articulate and explicit with regard to motive. As John Abbott put it, the party was important "to show our appreciation to him. . . . We would have done it for anyone, I'll put it that way, but we wouldn't have went to the extremes that we did. In our book, all of us would say the same thing: he's the greatest." Mick McKinnis's remarks, cited earlier, are quite similar ("Everybody liked Al"), adding primarily the note of dissatisfaction with official University of Arkansas policy. In other remarks, however, McKinnis made clear his understanding of the event's ambivalent nature:

> A man reaches retirement age, supposedly that's what people work for. It's the day that they can say goodbye, you know, I'm done with you, I'm gonna do what I want to do. That would be reason for a party. . . . You're done, you know, you've served your debt to society, more or less.
>
> Then, on the other hand, as the time draws near, and I noticed this with Al, the closer he got to that retirement, the more he was having second thoughts about it. Because he would no longer be the head dude. He'd no longer come to town. He won't see us as much any more. He sees me quite frequently because I live by him and I go by and see him. You know, he's not been down here since he left.

(McKinnis goes on to discuss the possibility that Al will return to work.) He'll want something to do. Winter time's coming, you know, out there on that little old five acres of his, when it gets cold. . . . He's got a wife, (but) she's gone a lot playing bingo. She ain't home very much at night. He'll want something to occupy his time.

Motive and message are thus clear. Al Jamison's co-workers knew why they organized a party for his retirement, and they also knew what they wanted that party to "say" to him. But means are a different matter. Asked why they chose a hat, say, for the "gag gift," or why they selected a watch for its "serious" counterpart, or why the addition of the girls in their bathing suits seemed such a good idea, even Abbott and McKinnis, normally so voluble and articulate, had virtually nothing to say. Asked later if they didn't find a watch a strange gift to give a retiring co-worker ("Why give a man a watch when you could say the whole point of retiring is you don't need to know what time it is anymore?"), man after man simply noted that "everybody" gave watches to people when they retired. Why? Nobody seemed to know.

It was the same with the hat, and its inscription, though McKinnis did stress the importance of the word *Retired:* "Now, we put *Retired* underneath that—he wasn't it no more, you see. He was retired." There was no mention, despite the obvious claims of authority made by the inscription, of the hat as a traditional badge of rank, a symbolic crown. In fact, all attempts to elicit from the organizers any statement concerning the deliberate manipulation of symbolic elements were met with emphatic rejection. "Yeah, I don't know whether it's traditional or not. It just—just popped in my mind," said McKinnis of the basic idea for the "gag gift." Even the interviewer's suggestion that the decision to photograph the party could be seen as an index of its importance, a gesture of respect for Al Jamison, was viewed with vigorous skepticism. "Well, I don't know whether it's a sign of how important it is," said McKinnis. "It's just a way of remembering it."

The impulse to act on their colleague's behalf, to prepare a party in his honor with care and delicacy sufficient to their purposes, this impulse was shared, like the labor and cost of its realization, by John Abbott, Sherrall Cheatham, Mick McKinnis, David Mitchell, "Jake" Phillips, Roy Reed, and Tommy Rose, who also shared a disinclination to analyze the event beyond a consideration of its purpose. The analytic impulse, right, proper, and indeed inevitable to their calling, belonged nonetheless to the interviewers alone. They alone were struck by the conspicuous deployment of power's emblems on the occasion of their surrender; they alone were moved to note the gentleness in the festival designed by Al Jamison's co-workers to mark the transfer of his authority. As folklorists, the researchers were impressed also by the "homemade" character of the event. It was a festival created by the celebrants themselves out of a shared competence in such matters that was no less real for being largely unspoken. It was a true "folk festival" in a world where the term is so often misapplied to chamber of commerce productions, a celebration of the group itself as much as its departing member.

On how many occasions at the end of breaks or of their dinner hour, had Al glanced at his watch and said it was time they were getting back to work? It was one face of his power, one face of power in general, this control over others' time, clocks and hourglasses being to time what keys are to space, so that the traditional giving of a watch to those relinquishing whatever powers they have until that time held is a resonant and empathetic gesture. So too with the hat, with its assertion of authority made explicit by the inscription, and even with the girls. It's David, remember, as an aged king, who is visited by Abishag the Shunamite, a famous beauty. It's a mark of his rank. Not every old man is so lucky.[9]

Such things have little to do with "need," as any reader of *King Lear* will recognize, but everything to do with desire. Al Jamison was no foolish monarch—where Lear throws a tantrum and banishes Kent, Jamison submits in good spirit to the "gag gift" joke at his expense—but he had reached the time to "shake all cares and business" from his age. That's what retirement is. You give up the power and you are freed from the responsibility. Lear's folly, in part, consists in not understanding the deal. Al Jamison was smarter, and he had better luck in his professional "family." Because they liked him, they surrounded his loss of position with all the traditional regalia of that position. He was no longer their boss, but he was HMFIC. He wouldn't be in charge of their time in the future, but he would still hold the clock. He was an old man, but lovely young women would still praise him, plant kisses on his brow, and wish him well. In a stroke of good fortune, the whole occasion was witnessed and praised by an outsider of high station and wide experience, in whose eyes both Al and the group he headed were recognized as excellent. The awkwardness of such open expressions of regard and affection was skillfully managed by the successful imposition and periodic maintenance of a comic surface. Not only, in light of such insights, is Al smarter than Lear, his co-workers are better inheritors than Goneril and Regan, more successful loyalists than Cordelia. Al understood retirement—he was unloading responsibility and relinquishing power. The two went together. He asked for no knights, but his co-workers, who were his friends, designed out of their own sense of appropriate festival and their insistence upon the importance of their shared life a ceremony to ease his departure, to give him as he left "the name and all the additions to a king."[10]

CALENDAR CUSTOM: GOSPEL ANNIVERSARY

Our second case study focuses on a calendar custom, an occasion for festivity that recurs on a regular basis. The Union Memorial Temple sits at the corner of Eleventh and Plum Streets on the Texas side of the city of Texarkana. Despite its rather grand name, the temple is a modest frame structure, a converted house, in a neighborhood of other modest structures, most of them the homes of low- to moderate-income black families. A sign in the corner of the temple's grass-and-mud lot tells the seeker or the passerby that this is the home of the Arkansas and Texas Quartet Union and that this is the site of one annual meeting, twelve monthly gatherings, and an unspecified number of anniversary programs.

Inside the building is another sign, a piece of yellow paper tacked to the far wall of what most observers would take to be a church—with its draped podium and rail and its rows of pews littered with paper fans. But this is not a church. It is a singing center, and the piece of paper at the front lists the names of gospel singing groups affiliated with the union and the dates of their anniversary programs. There are fourteen groups listed—"quartets" by a loose definition—and the dates are all in the form of Sundays in each month: for example, the first Sunday in July or the second Sunday in October. The date listed is understood to include the preceding Friday and Saturday nights. On these occasions, a celebration takes place, a patterned performance in honor of a group which has traveled that tough old road out there another year and kept on keeping on.

The union itself has hung tough some forty years. The oldest members say it began sometime in the late 1930s as a prayer band, a small group of the faithful who gathered for praise and song outside the context of any particular church. The same time period also saw the rise of the popularity of male quartets singing bluesy, expressive "gospel" rather than the stiffly syncopated "jubilees" that had previously comprised the quartet repertoire. So the prayer band became a prayer band with quartets like many others at that time in east Texas and south Arkansas. The prayer band affiliated itself briefly with the Texas Singing Convention, a branch of gospel pioneer Thomas Dorsey's National Singing Convention, but the members soon felt they were being lost in the shuffle. In 1948 they decided to go it alone, forming the Arkansas and Texas Quartet Union, applying for and receiving their tax-exempt status and acquiring and converting their modest structure, the Union Memorial Temple. At the same time, a similar progression was occurring in much of the surrounding area, a fertile crescent of gospel that extended from east Texas through southeast Oklahoma, south Arkansas, and north Louisiana over into northwest Mississippi.

According to the members, the principal reason for needing a union and a temple was jealousy on the part of some of the ministers. The new quartets were flashy, well dressed, and attractive, and it wasn't long before some of the preachers decided they didn't like the competition. Suddenly there was nowhere for the quartets to go, so they made themselves a home and took to the road, going out to sing to other singers at other temples and singing centers as well as singing occasionally at a welcoming church.

It was indeed a tough old road where, as one singer put it, "Some folks come out just to see what you've got on." But there were also friends who knew the cost of gasoline and matching outfits and sympathized with the sheer effort of traveling long miles to sing two songs and sit down. They knew the dedication it took to persevere when jobs or school, spouses or parents, were always asking, "Why bother?" They knew.

From that understanding developed a tradition of paying back the performers one weekend each year by celebrating the singers in song. For three days the groups and soloists you had met out on the road would be invited to come to your home singing center and sing for you and give you a little money in order to tell you, "You are appreciated." These anniversary programs came to follow a particular order, to have their own aesthetic, their own rules of behavior, all of which worked together to honor the particular group, the larger community of singers, and the love of God that unites them.

The celebration begins with the arrival of the participants, stunningly dressed in brightly colored outfits of sateen and sharkskin, the members of a group identifiable by their matching green suits or black feather boas. Then others drift in, greeting old friends, checking others out, picking up programs, selecting their seats. If they are members of a singing group—as most of them are—they stop at the door and pay their "representation" fee and have their group name printed on an index card to be given to the master of ceremonies. An appointed hour is usually printed on the program, but this is a time to begin arriving, not a curtain time, and people will continue to come and go throughout the evening.

When the moment seems right, a person of importance—usually the president of the union—will take to the stage and announce that this is the anniversary program of the Starlights, the Chariettes, or whoever it may be. At this moment the group being celebrated may either be already seated in a place of importance, perhaps with a glittery sign bearing its name on the wall above the members' heads, or the group may come down the center aisle toward the front, singing "We Are Marching to Zion" and using a distinctive step-stop-step-stop march to arrive at their place.

This accomplished, the greeter will then say, "You are now in the hands of the Devotional Committee." The devotional survives from the old prayer meeting and is the deepest, most devout portion of the celebration, in which the oldest traditions are touched and offered up. The assembled celebrants are a diverse group made up of Baptists, Methodists, and representatives of various Pentecostal and Holiness denominations. Consequently, the first thing the Devotional Committee must accomplish is to remind them of their commonality. A song is begun, sung by all assembled as a congregation. The song is deliberately chosen as one everyone will know or can pick up without difficulty—perhaps "Jesus on the Main Line" or "Jesus Is Getting Us Ready for That Great Day" with their simple repetitive texts. This is followed by a reading from the scripture, usually Psalm 23 or 105, well-known and appropriate words that serve to remind those present of the centrality of the Bible.

Next is the "lining hymn," one of the deepest of African-American song traditions, a style of singing that stands as a model of the whole coming together of African style and Christian content. The text is always from the very bedrock of English hymnody, the beloved "Dr. Watts" hymns from the early eighteenth century. In Texarkana they especially love to hear Justenora White sing,

> When I shall read my title clear
>   to a mansion in the sky,
> I'll bid farewell to all my fields
>   And wipe my weeping eye.[11]

But Mrs. White does not sing it alone. She leads the audience in a manner more reminiscent perhaps of Africa than of England. First she sings the first line and then joins the congregation in the response, a very slow, melismatic repetition of that line, each syllable "worried" into five or six. So slow is that response, in fact, that each repeated line becomes a full verse of pure ornament. For the fourth and final line, everyone stands, and as the last syllables trail off, some other member of the Devotional Committee will begin a long prayer, moving from speech toward a song-like chant, building in intensity, eliciting words of response and echoes of affirmation from the others in the room, before closing with a softly spoken, "These things we ask in Jesus' name. Amen." The devotional closes with another congregational hymn.

At this point the members of the devotional committee take their seats, and the greeter announces, "You are now in the hands of the Master of Ceremonies." The emcee takes the stage, index cards in hand, and signals by a humorous remark or a casual acknowledgment of how handsome or lovely the guests of honor look that the time of deep reverence has passed and that the time for fun and celebration of a different sort has arrived. He or she begins by asking for someone from the union to extend a formal welcome. The welcomer, perhaps one of the guests of honor, perhaps someone else, stands and delivers a short speech, which traditionally begins with the observation that "welcome" is a short little word with only seven letters and ends with the triple repetition, "You are welcome, welcome, welcome." The emcee then calls for some visitor to accept the welcome. Someone rises to express his or her gladness at being present and to extend an invitation to visit his or her singing center. The emcee may pause to chide gently the performers to be ready when they are called, to show their respect and appreciation, and not to leave as soon as they've finished their own selections. And then the emcee announces each group from the cards they have filled out with a show-business flourish: "And now, all the way from (wherever), make welcome none other than (whoever) for an A and a B selection."

The first groups called are usually those including children or the elderly, and they'll most likely be followed by local groups. For each the pattern will be basically the same: the introduction, the taking of the stage, the addressing of the guests of honor with some variation of the "keep-on-keeping-on" speech that slides into a short bit of preaching based on the text of the song they are about to sing. The second number or B selection will likewise be preceded by a short bit of preaching, again based on the lyrics of one of the two songs, either the one they've just completed or the one they are going to sing. They may end the B selection by singing all the way back to their seats, and some of the older groups may have begun their A selections back in their pews, singing their way up to the front and ending the same way.

Two types of songs are sung, and frequently the groups will perform one from each category. First are the fast "shout" or "jubilee" numbers. Frequently these have two parts, a more or less standard verse-chorus structure followed by a shouting section—often introduced by an "off" chord—in which the leader "catches fire" and the backup singers launch into a chanting response. Such numbers occasion much handclapping and provide the contexts when people in the room are most likely to "fall out." These songs act out conversion. In a song such as "Over in Zion/I've Got a New Walk" done by Little Rock's Hearts of Joy, the level of intensity becomes particularly intense when the singers chant, "I've got a new walk, got a new walk, got a new walk," as they join hands to form a protective circle around the dancing, weeping, whirling leader. The other principal type of song is slow and bluesy, referred to as a "spiritual" by some singers. However, it should not be confused with the songs of the nineteenth century to which that term is familiarly applied. Instead, these songs are the intensely personal sort that Thomas Dorsey began writing in the 1920s. Examples such as "Stand By Me," "I'm Going Home to Jesus," and "Ain't Gonna Let My Religion Down" may be reminiscent in performance to the outsider of the great soul performances of the sixties. These songs build their intensity in a different way than the shouts. Rather than the accelerated pace, they build on the tension between the groove laid down by the electric guitars, piano, drums, and backup singers and the leader's ability to create an expressive, dramatic vocal that rises above that groove. Often during these numbers the lead vocalist will leave the stage to "get down with the people" and will heighten the drama by roaming the center aisle, waving his arms, and ignoring the constraining microphone. The crowd, in turn, shouts words of encouragement—"That's all right!" or "Tell it, son!"—and wave their hands or fan themselves in response to the heat the singer generates. Both types of song integrate the total event, breaking down barriers between performers and audience, stage and stands, speaking and singing.

About halfway through the program, the emcee will pause and ask for a couple of volunteers to take up an offering. This is a very "up front" collection by most church standards. Instead of passing a plate, the volunteers stand behind a draped table moved to the head of the center aisle and watch as row by row all come forward to lay their money on the table. Once everyone has done so, the volunteers count the money, announce the amount, and declare that it is not enough. Then begins the pressure to "bring it up to a decent amount" or "round it off." "Who'll give another dollar?" they ask. "You know you've got more money than that," they insist. After some fumbling in pockets and purses, people come forward to put down a little more. A second tally is made, and the result, rarely approaching the targeted figure, is again announced, this time perhaps including the representation collected at the door. Finally the whole is ceremoniously or surreptitiously presented to the guests of honor. Quite likely, this is the only money that gospel singing will afford them all year.

The call always follows the offering. The master of ceremonies will ask some minister in the house to officiate. The minister or—if one is not present—the union president will say, "Let it not be said that we gathered together in the Lord's name without giving some lost soul the chance to come to Jesus." This is usually a perfunctory call, a fact emphasized by the one time the researcher witnessed a person actually coming forward. Everyone in the room was astonished by the behavior of this obviously disturbed individual, and the minister exclaimed, "Isn't this something! To accept Jesus at a *singing* program!" On that occasion suitable procedures were carried out, but everyone seemed slightly mystified and was happy to return to the familiar program of singing.

On most occasions after the call has been dutifully offered, the emcee will begin again calling on the groups to come forward for the "A-and-Bs." This second section of singing performances usually consists of the out-of-town and/or more polished performers. For these groups "A-and-B" is interpreted more liberally, and the bands are more likely to stretch out a bit. Often the slickest groups, hot acts, such as the Mighty Sons of Joy from Tyler, Texas, will close the program, bringing the audience to its feet with showy center aisle shouting. Most nights it all makes for a terrific time, and if it is a Friday, there are still more programs to attend before the weekend is over.

By the time the last group has shouted, everyone is starting to look a little tired. Children are falling asleep on the pews, and some of the elderly have already begun to leave. The emcee rises once more to ask if there are any announcements, and many of those that remain will stand and tell about the appearance they are going to make at this or that church or about their own imminent anniversary. Frequently the guests of honor will be asked to offer their own pair of selections before the prayer of benediction.

The cycle is complete. The anniversary has been marked. A year of singing and giving money to others is repaid in a single weekend, and the guests of honor have been encouraged to carry on. The whole celebration has carried a message of integration—from the easy transitions between inside and outside the building to the deliberate coupling of seemingly opposite pairs: prayer meeting and performance, performer and audience, singing and speaking, the stage area at the front and getting down with the people in the center aisle.

The final mission of integration, the feeding of the body as well as the spirit, has been taking place throughout the evening and accounts for much of the flux in the room. In Texarkana, it occurs in the "cafe," a long, table-filled room where a traveling singer can enjoy some catfish or a sandwich at a modest price. After the program, the room becomes the equivalent of the post-game locker room where the musicians, now in their street clothes, can talk of "axes" and "licks" or speak with the female singers over a Shasta or a cup of instant coffee. After all, they may meet again at the next anniversary program.[12]

These two examples—one a rite of passage, the other a recurring calendar custom—represent the kinds of folk festivals and celebrations folklorists study. But what about those "folk festivals" that thousands anticipate every year in Arkansas at Mountain View or Eureka Springs? Is a "folk festival"—so labeled by its boosters—ever a folk festival as the term is understood by folklorists? Perhaps the answer is "sometimes." Such festivals are periodically recurring events. Those in attendance can sometimes develop a sense of community. That sense of community is accompanied by a shared sense of proper celebration: rules for listening, clapping, whooping, when and what requests to scream out—as well as any activities, such as jam sessions, sing-alongs, and parking lot "picking," that suggest that the affair is not just a concert for a passive, non-participating audience.

A Selective Bibliography of Books on Arkansas Folklore

This is a lightly annotated listing of some commonly encountered titles dealing with Arkansas folklore. The brief annotations are designed to give the reader an idea of the contents and are not necessarily evaluative. In addition to these and other books, one frequently finds articles on Arkansas folklore in the journal *Mid-America Folklore*, which is published by the Mid-America Folklore Society. For further information about this journal, contact Editor, *Mid-America Folklore*, Arkansas College, Batesville, Arkansas 72501.

Abrahams, Roger D. *A Singer and Her Songs: Almeda Riddle's Ballad Book.* Baton Rouge, Louisiana: Louisiana State University Press, 1970.
> The biography of Ozark singer Almeda Riddle (1898–1986) that includes words and music of fifty songs with commentary. Although based on a number of taped interviews with Mrs. Riddle, Abrahams fails to tell anything about his editorial practices.

Allsopp, Fred W. *Folklore of Romantic Arkansas.* 2 volumes. New York: Grolier Society, 1931.
> A hodgepodge of newspaper clippings assembled while Allsopp was managing editor of the *Arkansas Gazette.* Contains a variety of genres of folklore including songs, ballads, place-name information, tall tales, stories and anecdotes, and beliefs.

Botkin, Benjamin A. *Lay My Burden Down, a Folk History of Slavery.* Chicago: University of Chicago Press, 1945.
> An edition of interviews with former slaves, collected by WPA workers in the 1930s and selected and edited by Botkin from manuscripts in the Library of Congress. Most of the material was collected in Arkansas and Oklahoma. Many items of folklore are scattered throughout the volume. The book was reprinted in 1968.

_____. *A Treasury of Southern Folklore.* New York: Crown Publishers, 1949.
> A hodgepodge of materials from all parts of the South, taken mainly from printed sources. A number of references to Arkansas tall tales are included.

Deane, Ernie. *Ozarks Country: A Collection of Articles About Folklore, Places, People, Customs, History and Other Ozarks Subjects.* Branson, Missouri: The Ozarks Mountaineer, 1975.
> A collection of essays from Deane's *Ozarks Country* column, which was syndicated and used in various newspapers in Arkansas and Missouri. Several of the articles deal with traditional musicians and craftsmen from Arkansas.

Dorson, Richard M. *Negro Tales from Pine Bluff, Arkansas, and Calvin, Michigan.*
Bloomington, Indiana: Indiana University Press, 1958.
    Approximately the first half of this book deals with the Arkansas mate-
    rial, all of which was gathered in just eight days of collecting. This book
    was later incorporated into a paperback titled, *American Negro Folktales.*
Hogue, Wayman. *Back Yonder, an Ozark Chronicle.* New York: Minton, Balch &
Company, 1932.
    Hogue was from Van Buren County, Arkansas, and this is essentially a
    biography. He includes a great deal of information about folklore includ-
    ing songs, play-party games, beliefs, legends, and various other items.
Jackson, Thomas W. *On a Slow Train Through Arkansaw.* Edited by W. K.
McNeil. Lexington: University Press of Kentucky, 1985.
    Annotated reprint of a 1903 publication that is the best-selling Arkansas
    title ever. Actually, the title notwithstanding, the book has very little to
    do with Arkansas. It is, instead, a collection of folk jokes that were popu-
    lar in 1903; the annotations trace the histories of many of the jokes. The
    introductory comments by McNeil discuss Jackson's methods of collect-
    ing and of testing out his material; sometimes his techniques were quite
    similar to those of today's folklorists.
Masterson, James R. *Tall Tales of Arkansaw.* Boston: Chapman & Grimes, 1943.
    Excellent survey of the entire field of Arkansas humor, much of which
    deals with folklore. A 1974 reprint was given the misleading title
    Arkansas Folklore.
McDonough, Nancy. *Garden Sass: A Catalog of Arkansas Folkways.* New York:
Coward, McCann and Geoghegan, 1975.
    Popularly written book dealing mainly with the Ozarks and the Ouachitas.
    Some good material but the volume gives a misleading impression about
    folklore because it is written from a nostalgic, survivalistic viewpoint.
McNeil, W. K. *The Charm Is Broken: Readings in Arkansas and Missouri Folklore.*
Little Rock: August House, Inc., 1984.
    A collection of essays that is about equally divided between pieces deal-
    ing with Arkansas and those dealing with Missouri. This book is intended
    for use by high school students and for the general public as well. The
    articles range in age from 1892 to the 1980s. An introduction provides a
    general discussion of folklore and how one should go about collecting it.
_____. *Ghost Stories from the American South.* Little Rock: August House, Inc.,
1985.
    A collection of approximately one hundred texts gathered from Southern
    oral tradition. An attempt is made to provide ghost stories that are repre-
    sentative of Southern folk tradition, and they are categorized according
    to what the author discerns are the major themes of Southern ghostlore.

A sizeable percentage of the texts were collected in Arkansas. A trade
edition was issued in 1987.

_____. *Ozark Mountain Humor*. Little Rock: August House, Inc., 1989.
Approximately two hundred jokes collected from Ozark oral tradition.
The individual jokes are arranged in the categories that are most promi-
nent in Ozark folklore. Annotations are provided for each joke.

_____. *Southern Folk Ballads*. 2 volumes. Little Rock: August House, Inc.,
1987–1988.
A collection of ballads taken from Southern folk tradition, most of them
being gathered since 1955. They are arranged in several thematic categories with extensive discussion of the history of each song. Extensive, but
not complete, discographical and bibliographical listings are provided.

Nelson, Joseph. *Backwoods Teacher*. Philadelphia: J. B. Lippincott Company,
1949.
An account of a teacher's life at a rural Arkansas school near the
Missouri border. Much folklore is presented including songs, folk speech,
customs, anecdotes, and beliefs.

Ohrlin, Glenn. *The Hell-Bound Train, a Cowboy Songbook*. Urbana, Illinois:
University of Illinois Press, 1973.
Texts and discussion of one hundred favorite songs of Glenn Ohrlin, a
cowboy singer from Mountain View, Arkansas. Also included is an
extensive bibliodiscography by Harlan Daniel.

Randolph, Vance. *The Devil's Pretty Daughter*. New York: Columbia University
Press, 1955.
A collection of brief tales collected mostly in Missouri and Arkansas.
Comparative notes are included.

_____. *Hot Springs and Hell and other Folk Jests and Anecdotes from the Ozarks*.
Hatboro, Pennsylvania: Folklore Associates, 1965.
A collection of several hundred jokes and anecdotes from Missouri,
Arkansas, and Oklahoma. Extensive annotations are included.

_____. *Ozark Folksongs*. 4 volumes. Columbia: State Historical Society of
Missouri, 1946–1950.
One of the great American folksong collections, this set contains over
sixteen hundred texts and eight hundred tunes. The entire collection,
minus fourteen songs, has been reprinted by the University of Missouri
Press (1980).

_____. *Ozark Superstitions*. New York: Columbia University Press, 1947.
A collection of folk beliefs from Missouri, Arkansas, and Oklahoma. This
book was reprinted under the title *Ozark Magic and Folklore* (1964).

_____. *Pissing in the Snow and Other Ozark Folktales*. Urbana: University of
Illinois Press, 1976.

A collection of one hundred bawdy tales, primarily from Missouri and Arkansas, that were deleted from the original folktale publications by Randolph.

_____. *Sticks in the Knapsack and Other Ozark Folk Tales*. New York: Columbia University Press, 1958.
A collection of ninety-seven tales recorded mostly in Arkansas and Missouri. Annotations and comparative notes are included.

_____. *The Talking Turtle, and Other Ozark Folktales*. New York: Columbia University Press, 1957.
One hundred tales collected mainly in Missouri and Arkansas. Comparative notes are included.

_____. *We Always Lie to Strangers*. New York: Columbia University Press, 1951.
A volume entirely devoted to tall tales found in the Ozark Mountains.

_____. *Who Blowed Up the Church House? and Other Ozark Folk Tales*. New York: Columbia University Press, 1952.
One hundred tales collected in Arkansas and Missouri. Comparative notes are included.

_____, and George P. Wilson. *Down in the Holler: A Gallery of Ozark Folk Speech*. Norman, Oklahoma: University of Oklahoma Press, 1953.
The most extensive study of the subject yet published. This volume was reissued in 1978 by the University of Oklahoma Press.

Rayburn, Otto Ernest. *Ozark Country*. New York; Duell, Sloan and Pearce, 1941.
Part of the American Folkways Series edited by Erskine Caldwell, this volume includes some examples of just about every genre of folklore found in the Arkansas Ozarks. Unfortunately, the material is placed in a fictionalized setting rather than being presented exactly as found in oral tradition.

Wilson, Charles Morrow. *Backwoods America*. Chapel Hill: University of North Carolina Press, 1934.
Dated book about life in the Southern Appalachians and the Ozarks. It includes examples of songs and ballads, games and play-parties, tall tales, stories and anecdotes, beliefs, legends, and fiddle tunes.

_____. *Stars is God's Lanterns: An Offering of Ozark Tellin' Stories*. Norman: University of Oklahoma Press, 1969.
Mostly literary reworkings of traditional legends and narratives.

Wolf, John Quincy. *Life in the Leatherwoods*. Memphis: Memphis State University Press, 1974.
Nostalgic, but absorbing, account of nineteenth-century life in a small section of the Arkansas Ozarks. Wolf (1864–1949) originally wrote this manuscript for a Batesville newspaper, his son edited this edition. Information is included on folk dance, tall tales, stories and anecdotes, and folk speech. A new edition was published in 1988 by August House.

SELECTIVE DISCOGRAPHY OF RECORDINGS OF ARKANSAS FOLKLORE

This is by no means a complete listing of commercially available records dealing with Arkansas folklore. It is, instead, a citing of some commonly encountered titles, most of which are still in print. For more detailed listings see various back issues of *Mid-America Folklore*. Not surprisingly, the same emphases found in publications on Arkansas folklore are also pronounced in recordings of folklore. That is, the Anglo-American traditions of the Ozarks have been greatly emphasized while various other traditions have been virtually ignored.

Arkansas Blues: Keep it to Yourself. Rooster R7605.
> An important survey of various blues performers found in Arkansas in the late 1970s. It was intended to be one of a series of records on Arkansas's blues tradition but, apparently, only this initial album was ever issued.

The Armstrong Twins. *Hillbilly Mandolin.* Old Timey 118.
_____. *Just Country Boys.* Arhoolie 5022.
> Two fine albums featuring one of the better old-timey country duets from Arkansas. *Hillbilly Mandolin* is a reissue of several sides they cut in the late 1940s while *Just Country Boys* contains recent recordings.

Cowden, Noble. *Songs My Family Loves.* Arkansas Traditions 002.
> A selection of some of the favorite songs from the repertoire of Noble Cowden, Cushman, Arkansas, as chosen by her family.

Echoes of the Ozarks. County 518–520.
> Despite the title, these three albums include only Arkansas string bands who made commercial recordings in the 1920s and 1930s. At least, that was the intent of the album's producer, but the attempt was not entirely successful. A number of string bands and performers who were not from the Ozarks or even from Arkansas are included on the set, most of these errors occurring on County 520.

Gilbert, Ollie. *Aunt Ollie Gilbert Sings Old Folksongs to Her Friends.* Rackensack RLP 495.
> Unfortunately, the only recording devoted entirely to Ollie Gilbert (1892–1980), one of the best-known folksingers from the Mountain View area and possessor of a huge repertoire. The album is no longer available.

I'm Old But I'm Awfully Tough: Traditional Music of the Ozark Region. Missouri Friends of the Folk Arts. MFFA 1001.
> Excellent two-record set featuring performers from the Arkansas and Missouri Ozarks, with a slightly greater emphasis given to instrumental music than to vocals. Unfortunately, the album is out of print.

Music from the Ozarks. Folkways 3812.

> Collection of several vocals and instrumentals recorded in Delaney, Arkansas, by two men who happened to be passing through on their way from Fayetteville. For the most part, this is mediocre material, and the album is unimportant except that it does make the point that folk musicians do use electric instruments, a fact that some folk music "authorities" deny.

Music of the Ozarks. National Geographic Society 703.

> Poorly done compilation of material from Stone County, Arkansas. There are a few very traditional performances heard here, but they are mingled in with some bad folk revival presentations with no distinctions made between the two. Now out of print.

Not Far From Here: Traditional Tales and Songs Recorded in the Arkansas Ozarks. Arkansas Traditions 001.

> Two-record set with the first LP being devoted to traditional narratives and the second to traditional songs. This is the only commercially available recording of Arkansas folk narratives.

Ohrlin, Glenn. *Cowboy Songs*. Philo 1017.

_____. *Wild Buckaroo*. Rounder 0158.

> Fine performances by Ohrlin of Mountain View, who is one of America's best-known traditional cowboy singers. The Philo LP is no longer available.

Riddle, Almeda. *Songs and Ballads of the Ozarks*. Vanguard VRS 9158.

_____. *Ballads and Hymns from the Ozarks*. Rounder 0017.

_____. *More Ballads and Hymns from the Ozarks*. Rounder 0083.

_____. *Granny Riddle's Songs and Ballads*. Minstrel JD-203.

_____. *How Firm a Foundation and Other Traditional Hymns*. Arkansas Traditions 003.

> Almeda Riddle (1898–1986) of Greers Ferry, Arkansas, was one of America's best-known folksingers and one of the most frequently recorded. Her large repertoire merited such recording, and there is very little duplication on the five records listed here. The Vanguard album is no longer available, and the Arkansas Traditions LP is Riddle's last, recorded in 1984, two years before her death.

The Williams Family. *All in the Family: The Williams Family of Roland, Arkansas*. Arkansas Traditions 004.

> A small sampling of the traditional repertoire of a central Arkansas family band.

Record Companies

Arhoolie and Old Timey, 10341 San Pablo Avenue, El Cerrito, California, 94530.

Arkansas Traditions, Box 1097, Mountain View, Arkansas, 72560.

County, P.O. Box 191, Floyd, Virginia, 24091.

Folkways, Office of Folklife Programs, Smithsonian Institution, 955 L'Enfant Plaza, Suite 2600, Washington D.C., 20560.

Minstrel, 35–41 72nd Street, Jackson Heights, New York, 11372.

Rooster, contact Flying Fish Records, 1304 West Schubert, Chicago, Illinois, 60614.

Rounder, One Camp Street, Cambridge, Massachusetts, 02140.

Selective Filmography of Arkansas Folklore

This brief listing of films contains only the most commonly encountered titles dealing with Arkansas folklore. Documentation of Arkansas folklore in print and on sound recordings has been far more extensive than in commercially available films, probably because films are generally more expensive to produce.

Bear Dog, Bulldog: Talking Traditions and Singing Blues in Arkansas Schools. Co-Media, Inc. 1984. 30 minutes.
    Filmed in 1982 this videotape shows two traditional narrators at a sixth-grade class at Big Flat, Arkansas, and a blues musician in an eleventh-grade class in DeVall's Bluff, Arkansas.
Folklore Research. University of Iowa. 1954. 28 minutes.
    Film dealing with the ballad collecting of Mary Celestia Parler (1905–1981) who, for more than three decades, was associated with the University of Arkansas. Originally aired on CBS-TV, November 14, 1954, under the title *The Search*, this film is a very romanticized account of folksong research that should not be taken seriously.
I Heard It Through the Grapevine. Talking Traditions. 1984. 22 1/2 minutes.
    Fictionalized account of an elementary classroom in which a young girl dreams of discovering her family's folklore in her parents' house.
Musical Holdouts. Phoenix Films. 1978. 51 minutes.
    Brief look at surviving, acculturated, and revived forms of music from Afro-, Anglo-, and native-American cultures. In one section of the film Glenn Ohrlin of Mountain View, Arkansas, discusses the changing nature of the life of a traditional cowboy.
National Folk Festival, Part 3. National Audiovisual Center. 1950. 10 minutes.
    Survey film showing various performers at the National Folk Festival, one segment shows an Ozark ballad singer.
Now Let's Talk About Singing. Talking Traditions. 1986. 28 minutes.
    Video dealing with the life and career of Almeda Riddle (1898–1986), Arkansas's best–known ballad singer. Riddle is seen performing at a variety of venues around the United States.
They Tell It For the Truth. Pentacle Productions, Inc. 1981. 57 minutes.
    This two-reel film features a number of tall-tale tellers from throughout the Arkansas Ozarks. The featured narrator is Hubert Wilkes (1905–1984) of Cave City.
What All I Could Tell. Talking Traditions. 1984. 17 minutes.
    Video made up of material filmed at a storytelling project held at the Senior Center in Big Flat.

FILM COMPANIES

Co-Media, Inc., and Talking Traditions, 1018 Rock Street, Little Rock,
    Arkansas, 72202
Pentacle Productions, Inc. 1408 West 50th Terrace, Kansas City, Missouri,
    64112
Phoenix Films, 470 Park Avenue South, New York, New York, 10016.
National Audiovisual Center, General Services Administration, Washington,
    D.C., 20409
The University of Iowa, Audiovisual Center Media Library, C-5 East Hall, Iowa
    City, Iowa, 52242

NOTES

Notes to Introduction

1. Francis James Child, *The English and Scottish Popular Ballads*, volume 3 (1888–89; reprinted New York: Dover, 1965), 379–99.

2. The historical background on "The Four Marys" is presented in Child, 382–84, and in Tristram P. Coffin, *The British Traditional Ballad in North America*, rev. ed. (Philadelphia: American Folklore Society, 1963), 115. Almeda Riddle describes how she relearned the ballad, which she had known as a child, from hearing it sung by folksong popularizers in the 1960s in *A Singer and Her Songs, Almeda Riddle's Book of Ballads*, ed. Roger D. Abrahams (Baton Rouge: Louisiana State University Press, 1970), 132–36. She sings a version of "The Four Marys," recorded in 1972, on *Ballads and Hymns from the Ozarks* (Rounder Records 0017).

3. In October 1986, Mann Alberson tried his hand at hewing out a crosstie for the camera. The result is a videotape, *Tiehackers of Cross County, Arkansas* by Paul Summitt, Larry Ball, and William Clements (Department of Radio-TV and Mid-South Center for Oral History, Arkansas State University). See also Larry D. Ball and William M. Clements, "Tiehacking in the Northeast Arkansas Bottomlands," *Southern Folklore* (forthcoming).

4. A thorough lexicon of the distinctive vocabulary of University of Arkansas students is available in Gary N. Underwood, "Razorback Slang," *American Speech* 50 (1975): 50–69.

5. Jan Calhoon collected a text of this legend from Maurice Lewis of Magnolia in 1960. The text appears in W. K. McNeil, ed., *Ghost Stories from the American South* (Little Rock: August House, 1985), 106.

6. These and other traditional remedies collected from black Arkansans from the Delta appear in Donald Morson, Frank Reuter, and Wayne Viitanen, "Negro Folk Remedies Collected in Eudora, Arkansas, 1974–1975," *Mid-South Folklore* 4 (1976): 11–24; and Freddie Vaughn and Frank Reuter, "Negro Folk Remedies Collected in Southeast Arkansas, 1976," *Mid-South Folklore* 4 (1976): 61–74.

7. William J. Thoms, in *Athenaeum* 22 August 1846, 862–63; reprinted in Alan Dundes, ed., *The Study of Folklore* (Englewood Cliffs, N.J.: Prentice-Hall, 1965).

8. Maria Leach and Jerome Fried, eds., *Funk & Wagnalls Standard Dictionary of Folklore, Mythology and Legend*, one-volume ed. (New York: Funk & Wagnalls, 1972), 398–403.

9. These traits are suggested in Jan Harold Brunvand, *The Study of American*

Folklore, An Introduction, 3d ed. (New York: Norton, 1986), 7. Brunvand's volume is one of the standard college-level textbooks in folklore studies.

10. See Tristram P. Coffin, "'Mary Hamilton' and the Anglo-American Ballad as an Art Form," *Journal of American Folklore* 70 (1957): 208–14; reprinted in Jan Harold Brunvand, ed., *Readings in American Folklore* (New York: Norton, 1976).

11. "The Hook" is treated in Jan Harold Brunvand, *The Vanishing Hitchhiker, American Urban Legends and Their Meanings* (New York: Norton, 1981), 48–52.

12. A thorough study of this migratory legend appears in Brunvand, *The Vanishing Hitchhiker,* 24–40. For Arkansas texts, see McNeil, *Ghost Stories from the American South,* 95–98.

13. In *American Balladry from British Broadsides, A Guide for Students and Collectors of Traditional Song* (Philadelphia: American Folklore Society, 1957), 267, G. Malcolm Laws indexes this ballad as P35. He treats its evolution from the broadside source—which he reproduces in its forty-four-stanza entirety—on 104–22.

14. Ballad commonplaces are discussed in Roger D. Abrahams and George Foss, *Anglo-American Folksong Style* (Englewood Cliffs, N.J.: Prentice-Hall, 1972), 32.

15. For a listing of Vance Randolph's folktale publications, see Robert Cochran and Michael Luster, *For Love and for Money, The Writings of Vance Randolph: An Annotated Bibliography,* Arkansas College Folklore Monograph Series No. 2 (1979).

16. A full text of this ballad (without music) appears in Mary Celestia Parler, *An Arkansas Ballet Book* (n.p.: Norwood Editions, 1975), 2–3. In *Native American Balladry, A Descriptive Study and a Bibliographic Syllabus,* rev. ed. (Philadelphia: American Folklore Society, 1964), 266, G. Malcolm Laws indexes this ballad as dE34 under the title "Harrison Town."

17. See the chapter entitled "The Power Doctors" in Vance Randolph, *Ozark Superstitions* (New York: Columbia University Press, 1946), 121–61. This volume was retitled *Ozark Magic and Folklore* when it was reissued by Dover in 1964. For a survey of the pervasiveness of threefold patterning, see Alan Dundes, "The Number Three in American Culture," in *Every Man His Way, Readings in Cultural Anthropology,* ed. Alan Dundes (Englewood Cliffs, N.J.: Prentice-Hall, 1968), 401–24.

18. Threefold repetition and other stylistic and schematic formulas employed in *Märchen* are treated in Axel Olrik, "Epische Gesetze der Volksdichtung," *Zeitschrift fur Deutsches Alterum,* 15 (1909), 1–12; reprinted as "Epic Laws of Folk Narrative" in Dundes, ed., *The Study of Folklore.*

19. Patterns of vocabulary formation among University of Arkansas students are treated in Gary N. Underwood, "Some Characteristics of Slang Used at the University of Arkansas as Fayetteville," *Mid-South Folklore* 4 (1976), 49–54.

20. Laws, *American Balladry from British Broadsides*, 21–22. See also Anne B. Cohen, *Poor Pearl, Poor Girl! The Murdered-Girl Stereotype in Ballad and Newspaper* (Austin: University of Texas Press, 1973).

21. The fundamentals of this pattern are suggested in V. Propp, *Morphology of the Folktale*, trans. Laurence Scott (Bloomington: Indiana University Press, 1968).

22. This is motif F1041.7, "Hair turns gray from terror." See Ernest W. Baughman, *Type and Motif-Index of the Folktales of England and North America*, Indiana University Folklore Series No. 20 (The Hague: Mouton, 1966), 237.

23. W. K. McNeil identifies the composers of "Put My Little Shoes Away" in his notes to *Songs My Family Loves, Favorite Folksongs of the Cowden Family, Cushman, Arkansas* (Arkansas Traditions Recording 002).

24. Phillips Barry introduced the concept of communal re-creation in "Communal Re-creation," *Bulletin of the Folk-Song Society of the Northeast* 5 (1933): 4–6.

25. These categories are based loosely on the scheme proposed by Roger D. Abrahams in "The Complex Relations of Simple Forms," *Genre* 2 (1969): 104–28; reprinted in Dan Ben-Amos, ed., *Folklore Genres* (Austin: University of Texas Press, 1976).

26. For the distinction between these two types of gestures, see Loretta A. Malandro and Larry L. Baker, *Nonverbal Communication* (New York: Random House, 1983), 117–22.

27. For many more examples of Ozark pronunciation, vocabulary, and usage, see Vance Randolph and George P. Wilson, *Down in the Holler, A Gallery of Ozark Folk Speech* (Norman: University of Oklahoma Press, 1953).

28. The most thorough treatment of the ethnic dialect of African Americans is J. L. Dillard, *Black English, Its History and Usage in the United States* (New York: Random House, 1972).

29. These examples come from an unpublished student collection by Edna Shadowens done among high school students in Lake City (Craighead County) and deposited in the Arkansas State University Folklore Archives.

30. The occupational language of pizza parlor employees is the subject of an unpublished collection by Barbara Wess deposited in the Arkansas State University Folklore Archives.

31. The examples come from Randolph and Wilson, *Down in the Holler*, 122–86.

32. These and other instances of folk speech in frontier Arkansas appear in Edward Everett Dale, "The Speech of the Pioneers," *Arkansas Historical Quarterly* 6 (1951), 117–31; reprinted in W. K. McNeil, ed., *The Charm Is Broken, Readings in Arkansas and Missouri Folklore* (Little Rock: August House, 1984).

33. F. P. Wilson relates this widely known proverb to a maxim in the Greek of Erasmus. He reports English usage of it in William Langland's *Piers Plowman* in 1362. See *The Oxford Dictionary of English Proverbs*, 3d ed. (Oxford: Clarendon, 1970), 682.

34. Collected by Willie Treat from Kenneth Pemberton in Big Flat (Baxter County) and annotated by W. K. McNeil in "Folklore from Big Flat, Arkansas, Part I: Rhymes and Riddles," *Mid-America Folklore* 9, no. 1 (Spring 1981): 12.

35. Vance Randolph, *The Devil's Pretty Daughter and Other Ozark Folk Tales* (New York: Columbia University Press, 1955), 105–07.

36. This story is indexed as Type 1535, "The Rich and the Poor Peasant," in Antti Aarne and Stith Thompson, *The Types of the Folktale, A Classification and Bibliography*, 2d revision, FFC No. 184 (Helsinki: Suomalainen Tiedeakatemia, 1964), 440–41, where an overview of its Old World distribution may be found. For North American variants, see Baughman, *Type and Motif-Index of the Folktales of England and North America*, 38.

37. Richard M. Dorson, *American Negro Folktales* (Greenwich, CT: Fawcett, 1967), 109.

38. Elwin L. Goolsby, ed., *The Teeth on the Bradley-Rushing Building and Other Stories, A Collection of Legends, Tall Tales, Exaggerations, and Factual Lore of Grant County, Arkansas* (Sheridan: Grant County Museum, 1978), 59. This is motif X1113, "Shooting off the leader's tail," in Baughman, *Type and Motif-Index of the Folktales of England and North America*, 462.

39. Robert Cochran, "The Interlude of Game: A Study of Washers," *Western Folklore* 38 (1979): 71–82; reprinted in McNeil, ed., *The Charm Is Broken*.

40. The standard works on children's games are William Wells Newell, *Games and Songs of American Children* (1903; reprinted New York: Dover, 1963); and Paul G. Brewster, *American Non-Singing Games* (Norman: University of Oklahoma Press, 1953). "Red Rover" is treated in Mary and Herbert Knapp, *One Potato, Two Potato . . . , The Secret Education of American Children* (New York: Norton, 1976), 49, 54. See also the recent survey by Simon J. Bronner: *American Children's Folklore* (Little Rock: August House, 1988).

41. For the Senior Walk tradition, see Mary Celestia Parler, "Folklore from the Campus," *Arkansas Folklore* 8, no. 1 (February 1958), 4–9; reprinted in McNeil, ed., *The Charm Is Broken*.

42. The widely known practice—in the South, at least—of eating black-eyed peas on New Year's Day is catalogued as items 2827–2831 in Wayland D. Hand, ed., *Popular Beliefs and Superstitions from North Carolina, The Frank C. Brown Collection of North Carolina Folklore*, Vol. 6 (Durham: Duke University Press, 1961), 365–66. Hand's work is the standard index of folk beliefs.

43. Quilting traditions in Arkansas are treated in Joanne Farb, "Piecin' and Quiltin': Two Quilters in Southwest Arkansas," *Southern Folklore Quarterly* 39 (1975): 363–75.

44. Frank Reuter, "John Arnold's Link Chains: A Study in Folk Art," *Mid-South Folklore* 5 (1977): 41–52; reprinted in McNeil, ed., *The Charm Is Broken*.

45. For an account of the basketmaking craft of a native of Pocahontas (Randolph County) who expatriated to Missouri, see Howard Wight Marshall, "Mr. Westfall's Baskets: Traditional Craftsmanship in Northcentral Missouri," *Mid-South Folklore* 2 (1974): 43–60; reprinted in Brunvand, *Readings in American Folklore*.

46. For the folklore of dyads, see Elliott Oring, "Dyadic Traditions," *Journal of Folklore Research* 21 (1984): 19–28; and Regina Bendix, "Marmot, Memet, and Marmoset: Further Research on the Folklore of Dyads," *Western Folklore* 46 (1987): 171–91.

47. For family folklore in Arkansas, see Deirdre LaPin (with Louis Guida and Lois Patillo), *Hogs in the Bottom, Family Folklore in Arkansas* (Little Rock: August House, 1982); George E. Lankford, "Ozark Family Legends," *Mid-America Folklore* 9, no. 3 (Winter 1981): 89–92; and William M. Clements, "Some Functions and Dysfunctions of Family Folklore," *Mid-America Folklore* 14, no. 1 (Spring 1986): 26–35. The examples of family folklore were collected by students Blanche Sanders, Judy Gibson, Katherine Lemay, Mary Susan Chester-Seawell, Karen Watson, and Mary Ann Watson and deposited in the Arkansas State University Folklore Archive.

48. Sources on the Italian presence in Arkansas include Jeffrey Lewellen, "'Sheep Amidst the Wolves': Father Bandini and the Colony at Tontitown, 1898–1917," *Arkansas Historical Quarterly* 45 (1986): 19–40; Diane Tebbets, "Food as an Ethnic Marker," *Pioneer America Society Transactions* 7 (1984): 81–88; and Louis Guida, "The Rocconi-Fratesi Family: Italianata in the Arkansas Delta," in LaPin, Guida, and Patillo, *Hogs in the Bottom*.

49. Useful treatments of folklore fieldwork methodology are Kenneth S. Goldstein, *A Guide for Field Workers in Folklore* (Hatboro, PA.: Folklore Associates, 1964); Edward D. Ives, *The Tape-Recorded Interview, A Manual for Field Workers in Folklore and Oral History* (Knoxville: University of Tennessee Press, 1980); and Bruce Jackson, *Fieldwork* (Urbana: University of Illinois Press, 1987).

50. Evaluations of the work of these two folklorists appear in Cochran and Luster, *For Love and for Money*; Robert Cochran, *Vance Randolph, An Ozark Life* (Urbana: University of Illinois Press, 1985); and George E. Lankford, "John Quincy Wolf, Jr.: An Appreciation," *Mid-America Folklore* 13, no. 1 (Winter–Spring 1985): 3–8.

Notes to Folklore Studies in Arkansas

1. There were travel writers in Arkansas before Nuttall, but none left any extensive comments on folklore and folklife. Typical is Timothy Flint, a

Harvard graduate and Congregationalist from Massachusetts, who spent the years 1816–19 in the vicinity of St. Charles, Missouri, taking time off for several trips into Arkansas. During his three-year stay, Flint conducted church services at Arkansas Post. Several years later, in his book *Recollections of the Last Ten Years* (1826), Flint discussed the natives he encountered on his sojourns into Arkansas. He found them polite and attentive but in the main irreligious savages who "are certainly more rough and untamed than the people of the state of Missouri, or of more Northern and Western regions." (Boston: Cummings, Hilliard & Co., 1826, 269–70) He concluded that his services were not of much utility. Beyond his few negative comments on the nature of the people he encountered and some mention of the mosquitoes and malaria that abounded at Arkansas Post, Flint offered no remarks about Arkansas.

2.   Thomas Nuttall, *A Journal of Travels into the Arkansas Territory During the Year 1819*, Savoie Lottinville, ed. (Norman, OK: University of Oklahoma Press, 1980), 88.

3.   Nuttall. The Quapaw traditions are discussed on 93–99 and the Cherokee traditions on 142–48.

4.   Nuttall, 136.

5.   Ernie Deane, *Arkansas Place Names* (Branson, MO: The Ozarks Mountaineer, 1986), 111.

6.   Henry Rowe Schoolcraft, *Scenes and Adventures in the Semi-Alpine Region of the Ozark Mountains of Missouri and Arkansas* (Philadelphia: Lippincott, Grambo & Co., 1853), 235.

7.   Henry Rowe Schoolcraft, *Journal of a Tour into the Interior of Missouri and Arkansaw . . . Performed in the Years 1818 and 1819*, in *New Voyages and Travels: Consisting of Originals and Translations* (London: Sir Richard Phillips & Co., 1821), IV, 64.

8.   James R. Masterson, *Arkansas Folklore: The Arkansas Traveler, Davey Crockett, and Other Legends* (Little Rock: Rose Publishing Co., Inc., 1974; reprint and retitling of a book originally published in 1942), 306–07.

9.   Friedrich Gerstäcker, "Women in the Backwoods," *Early American Life* 13 no. 6 (December 1982): 16. This article, translated by Ralph Walker, was originally published in a German magazine in the 1840s.

10.   Octave Thanet, "Folklore in Arkansas," *Journal of American Folklore* 5 (April–June, 1892): 121–25. This essay is also reprinted in W. K. McNeil, *The Charm Is Broken: Readings in Arkansas and Missouri Folklore* (Little Rock: August House, Inc., 1984), 30–35.

11.   McNeil, p. 34.

12.   Allsopp's other books, which are of varying degrees of interest to folklorists, include *Little Adventures in Newspaperdom*, *History of the Arkansas Press* (both 1922), *Rimeries* (1926), *Albert Pike, a Biography* (1928), *The Poets and*

Poetry of Arkansas (1933), *Rhymeries* (1934), and *The Romance of Books, with an Arkansas Bibliography* (1936).

13. Fred W. Allsopp, *Folklore of Romantic Arkansas*, 2 vol. (New York: Grolier Society, 1931), I, 65–107.

14. Allsopp, I, 108–200; II, 46–140.

15. Only one chapter, in II, 121–128, is wholly devoted to superstitions, but there is much information on the subject in several chapters scattered throughout both volumes and ostensibly devoted to other topics.

16. This was the title of an article by Wilson that appeared in *Atlantic Monthly* 144 (August 1929): 238–44.

17. Finger's books of interest to folklorists include *Sailor Chanties* and *Cowboy Songs* (1923); *A Book of Strange Murders* (1925), *Ozark Fantasia* and *Frontier Ballads* (both 1927), and *Adventures Under Sapphire Skies* (1931).

18. Vance Randolph, *Ozark Folklore: An Annotated Bibliography*, Vol. I (Columbia: University of Missouri Press, 1987; reprint of a work originally published in 1972), 512.

19. There is some disagreement about Turnbo's dates. Most sources give the year of his birth as 1842, but Desmond Walls Allen, who has edited nine volumes of Turnbo's work, gives 1844.

20. To date the following nine titles based on Turnbo's manuscripts have been published under the general title *Turnbo's Tales of the Ozarks* by Arkansas Research, P.O. Box 303, Conway, Arkansas 72032: *Biographical Stories; War and Guerrilla Stories; Schools, Indians, Hard Times and More Stories; Incidents, Mean Tricks and Fictitious Stories; Bear Stories; Deer Hunting Stories; Wolf Stories; Panther Stories; Snakes, Bird & Insect Stories.* All of these volumes have been edited by historian Desmond Walls Allen, who also edited Turnbo's *History of the Twenty-Seventh Arkansas Confederate Infantry.* Lynn Morrow is currently editing Turnbo's manuscripts housed at the Greene County Public Library, Springfield, Missouri, for publication.

21. Fred High, *It Happened in the Ozarks* (Berryville, AR: Braswell Printing Co., 1954), 20.

22. This revision is by Abrahams and Debora Kodish and will be published by the University of Illinois Press.

23. *Ozark Folksongs and Ballads collected and sung by Max Hunter of Springfield, Missouri.* Folk-Legacy Records, Inc., FSA-11.

24. *Southern Folklore Quarterly* 39 (1975): 363–75.

25. *Mid-South Folklore* 5 (Spring 1971): 3–23.

26. Child gave this song the title "The Gypsy Laddie."

27. The articles are "Some Survivals of British Balladry Among Ozark Folk Songs," (Autumn 1946): 246–62, and "The Native American Influence in Folk Songs of North Arkansas," (Summer 1947): 165–79.

28. The revised version of the thesis is titled "Dreams of the Past: A Collection of Ozark Songs and Tunes" and appears in *Mid-America Folklore* 11 (1983): 1–79.

29. Carr's articles, all published in *Dialect Notes* and all titled "A List of Words from Northwest Arkansas," appeared in the following issues: 2 (1904): 416–22; 3 (1905): 68–103; 3 (1906): 124–65; 3 (1907): 205–38; and 3 (1909): 392–406. The fourth article was co-authored by Rupert Taylor and is more comparative than the other essays. Carr and Taylor compare their Arkansas material with that collected by others from Cape Cod, central Connecticut, southern Illinois, and southeastern Missouri.

30. In addition to his work in folk games Brewster also did some publishing in the area of folk speech, folk narrative, and superstition.

31. Robert Cochran, "The Interlude of Game: A Study of Washers," *Western Folklore* 38 (1979): 71–82. The article is also reprinted in McNeil, 177–86.

32. Frank Reuter, "John Arnold's Link Chains: A Study in Folk Art," *Mid-South Folklore* 5 (Summer 1977): 41–52; Diane Tebbetts, "Earl Ott: Fishing on the Arkansas," *Mid-South Folklore* 5 (Winter 1977): 101–12. Both articles are reprinted in McNeil, Reuter's on 187–201, Tebbetts's on 111–25.

33. William M. Clements, "The Rhetoric of the Radio Profession," *Journal of American Folklore* 87 (October–December 1974): 318–27; _____, "Conversion and Communitas," *Western Folklore* 35 (1976): 35–45.

34. Nevertheless, when Rose Publishing Company reprinted the book in 1974 they gave it the misleading title *Arkansas Folklore*.

35. Masterson, vii.

36. George E. Hastings, "Annie Breen from Old Kaintuck," *Publications of the Texas Folklore Society* 6 (1927): 207–08.

37. The book is Robert Cochran and Michael Luster, *For Love and For Money: The Writings of Vance Randolph* (Batesville: Arkansas College Folklore Archive, 1979).

38. This set was republished with all but fourteen of the songs in the original retained. Those fourteen were deleted because of potential copyright problems.

39. See my Introduction to the 1980 reprint of *Ozark Folksongs* (Columbia: University of Missouri Press), 26, for one instance of unsubtly expressed dissatisfaction.

40. McNeil, Introduction, 28.

41. Janet Lynn Allured, "Families, Food and Folklore: Women's Culture in the Post-Bellum Ozarks," Ph.D. diss., department of history, University of Arkansas, 1988. Abstract, 2.

42. McNeil, 9.

Notes to Singing and Playing Music in Arkansas

1. Collected in 1979 by W. K. McNeil from Bob Blair, Pleasant Grove, Arkansas. Blair can be heard singing the song on *Not Far From Here . . . Traditional Tales and Songs Recorded in the Arkansas Ozarks*. Arkansas Traditions, no number. For another version of this song see H. M. Belden, *Ballads and Songs Collected by the Missouri Folk-Lore Society* (Columbia: University of Missouri Press, 1973; reprint of a work originally issued in 1940), 489.

2. Collected February 9, 1942, by Vance Randolph from Mrs. Maggie Morgan, Springdale, Arkansas. The text, with a melody line, is given in Vance Randolph, *Ozark Folksongs* (Columbia: University of Missouri Press, 1980; reprint and revision of a work originally issued 1946–1950), III, 104–05.

3. Collected January 6, 1941, by Dr. George E. Hastings, Fayetteville, Arkansas, from a student who lived in Long View, Arkansas. The text is given in Randolph, IV, 216.

4. Collected in 1972 by Leo Rainey from the Tommy Simmons Family, Mountain View, Arkansas. The text, with melody line, is given in Leo Rainey, Orilla and Olaf Pinkston, *Songs of the Ozark Folk* (Branson, Missouri: The Ozarks Mountaineer, 1981), 54–55.

5. Shenstone is quoted in volume III of *The Frank C. Brown Collection of North Carolina Folklore* (Durham: Duke University Press, 1952), 3.

6. For examples of such contradictory classifying, see Brown, III, 275 and Celeste P. Cambiaire, *East Tennessee and Western Virginia Mountain Ballads* (London: The Mitre Press, 1935), 37. Cambiaire lists a version of "Waggoner's Lad" as a ballad, while the editors of the Brown collection give it as a folksong.

7. Francis J. Child, *The English and Scottish Popular Ballads*, I (New York: Dover Publications, Inc., 1965; reprint of a work originally issued in 1882), vii.

8. Richard Chase, *American Folk Tales and Songs* (New York: The New American Library of World Literature, Inc., 1956), 229.

9. Collected February 12, 1942, by Vance Randolph from Mrs. Olga Trail, Farmington, Arkansas. The text with melody line is given in Randolph, I, 200–01.

10. Collected in April 1941 by Theodore R. Garrison from Mrs. Bertha Tuel, Marshall, Arkansas. The text with melody line is given on 39–41 of Garrison's unpublished M.A. thesis, "Forty-Five Folk Songs Collected From Searcy County, Arkansas," which was submitted to the English department at the University of Arkansas, Fayetteville, in 1944.

11. G. Malcolm Laws, Jr., *Native American Balladry: A Descriptive Study and a Bibliographical Syllabus* (Philadelphia: The American Folklore Society, 1964), 220.

12. Collected December 1979 by W. K. McNeil from Noble Cowden, Cushman, Arkansas. The text and melody line are given in W. K. McNeil, *Southern Folk Ballads* (Little Rock: August House, Inc., 1988), II, 53.

13. Collected in July 1942 by Theodore R. Garrison from Mrs. Martha Garrison, Marshall, Arkansas. A text is given on 126 of Garrison's M.A. thesis.

14. For an Arkansas version of "The Farmer's Curst Wife," see Randolph, I, 189–91. An Arkansas version of "Father Grumble" is given in Randolph, I, 321–23. Arkansas versions of "Devilish Mary" are given in Randolph, III, 187, 189–91. An Arkansas version of "The Young Man Who Wouldn't Hoe Corn" is given in McNeil, *Southern Folk Ballads*, I, 164–65.

15. Collected by Irene Jones Carlisle, June 29, 1951, from Lewis Bedingfield, Springdale, Arkansas.

16. Collected in July 1942 by Theodore R. Garrison from Mrs. Zona Baker, Zack, Arkansas.

17. Collected December 1979 by W. K. McNeil from Noble Cowden, Cushman, Arkansas.

18. Collected January 4, 1931, by Vance Randolph from Mrs. Emma L. Dusenbury, Mena, Arkansas. The text with melody line appears in Randolph, I, 67–68.

19. John Edward Hasse, *Ragtime: Its History, Composers, and Music* (New York: Schirmer Books, 1985), 2. The four main types of ragtime are instrumental rags, ragtime songs, ragtime waltzes, and "ragging" of classics and other pre-existing pieces.

20. John W. Work, *American Negro Songs and Spirituals* (New York: Bonanza Books, 1940), 32.

21. Quoted by Dorothy Scarborough in "The 'Blues' as Folksongs," *Coffee in the Gourd* (Austin: Texas Folklore Society, 1917), 53.

22. Johnson made the comment to Bruce Bastin in a conversation held October 22, 1972. It is reported in Bastin's *Red River Blues: The Blues Tradition in the Southeast* (Urbana and Chicago: University of Illinois Press, 1986), 5.

23. Bastin, 5.

24. Forten's remarks are quoted in Paul Oliver, *The Story of the Blues* (London: Barrie & Jenkins, 1969), 8.

25. Henry Goodman, ed., *The Selected Writings of Lafcadio Hearn* (New York: The Citadel Press, 1949), 224.

26. Daniels (1902–1947) made this recording for the Victor Talking Machine Company, October 24, 1927.

27. Liner notes for *Keep It To Yourself: Arkansas Blues Volume I: Solo Performances*. Rooster Blues R7605.

28. Liner notes for *Keep It To Yourself*.

29. Dena J. Epstein, *Sinful Tunes and Spirituals: Black Folk Music to the Civil War* (Urbana: University of Illinois Press, 1977), 30.

30. Epstein, 34.

31. See the discussion on 4–8 of L. Allen Smith, *A Catalogue of Pre-Revival Appalachian Dulcimers* (Columbia and London: University of Missouri Press, 1983).

32. I am indebted to George Lankford of Arkansas College, Batesville, for this information, which he acquired while doing research on the history of Marcella.

Notes to Talking Truth in Arkansas

1. Vance Randolph, *We Always Lie to Strangers* (New York: Columbia University Press, 1951).

2. See Leonard Williams, *Cavorting on Devil's Fork* (Memphis: Memphis State University Press, 1979).

3. See George E. Lankford, "The 'Arkansas Traveller:' The Making of a Frontier Icon," *Mid-America Folklore* 10, no. 1 (1982): 16–23.

4. For narrative, in addition to *We Always Lie*, see especially Vance Randolph's *Who Blowed Up the Church House?* (1952), *The Devil's Pretty Daughter* (1955), *The Talking Turtle* (1957), *Sticks in the Knapsack* (1958), all published by Columbia University Press. For fuller bibliography, see *For Love and for Money: the Writings of Vance Randolph*, Robert Cochran and Michael Luster, eds. (Batesville: Arkansas College Folklore Monograph Series No. 2, 1979).

5. See Linda Dégh, " 'The Belief Legend' in Modern Society: Form, Function, and Relationship to Other Genres," in *American Folk Legend: A Symposium*, Wayland D. Hand, ed. (Berkeley: University of California Press, 1971), 55–68, as well as the other articles in that volume.

6. Beulah Morain is a creative writer who lives in Tulsa, Oklahoma, but who travels a great deal in Arkansas. She reports: "I have reconstructed as much of my conversation as possible from my notes. This encounter took place in the fall of 1980. I visited with Hattie Mason again in the fall of 1981. She gave me a rather rambling account of her family history but nothing more of folklore interest. After the death of my husband, in March of 1982, it was several years before I returned to this area. When I stopped in the fall of 1985 I found that Hattie had died about a year before. She was buried near Mountain Home" (Beulah Morain, February 1988).

7. This recording of the legend of the belled buzzard does not stand alone. Vance Randolph noted it from newspapers in 1935 and 1938 and quoted an informant from Branson, Missouri, as saying that the story is "a tradition which

had its origin in the Ozark mountains." (*We Always Lie to Strangers*, 260f) Maybe so, but it is interesting to note that Irvin S. Cobb used the theme in a short story in 1913 in a setting completely removed from the Ozarks, suggesting that it is a migratory legend of much wider distribution. ("The Belled Buzzard," in *The Escape of Mr. Trimm*, [New York: George H. Dorman Co., 1913], 54–78.)

8. Melissa Calley was a historic preservation major at Arkansas College who wrote this account of her folklore collection in connection with a course in Ozark folklore.

9. Interview with Roland Calley, age forty-five, Gurdon, Arkansas, April 3, 1988. Recorded by Melissa Calley. Tape archived in Arkansas College Regional Culture Center.

10. John W. Roberts, "The 'Spook Light': A Missouri Parking Legend," *Mid-America Folklore* 7 (1979): 33.

11. Vance Randolph, *Ozark Magic and Folklore* (New York: Dover Publications, 1964), 233f.

12. Interview with Mildred Welch, April 1, 1988. Collected by Melissa Calley. Tape archived in Arkansas College Regional Culture Center.

13. Randolph, *Ozark Magic and Folklore*, 233.

14. Roberts, "The 'Spook Light,' " 31.

15. Calley interview.

16. Randolph, *Ozark Magic and Folklore*, 234.

17. Roberts, "The 'Spook Light,' " 31.

18. The motif is categorized as E530.1: *Ghost-like lights* in the *Type and Motif Index of the Folktales of England and North America*, Ernest W. Baughman, ed. (The Hague: Mouton & Co., 1966).

19. W. K. McNeil, *Ghost Stories from the American South* (Little Rock: August House, 1985).

20. Penney Wood is from Yellville, Arkansas. She was graduated in English from Arkansas College in 1988, just a month after writing this account of her collection for a class in Ozark folklore. Informant: William Earl Wood. Resident of Summit, Arkansas. Age: fifty-eight. Married, father of seven. Occupation: logger. Lifetime resident of Marion County. Interview: April 16, 1988. Tape archived in Regional Culture Center, Arkansas College.

21. This is E426: *Ghost as object*.

22. Randolph, *Ozark Magic and Folklore*, 229, 218, 219.

23. Two motifs involved here are E423: *Ghost in animal form* and E579*: *Ghost opens and closes doors*.

24. E422.1.1.3.1: *Headless ghost rides horse*.

25. Randolph, *Ozark Magic and Folklore*, 210.

26. Randolph, *Ozark Magic and Folklore*, 218.

27. This is E575: *Ghost as omen of impending calamity.*

28. Unpublished paper by Norma Barber of Batesville, Arkansas, a student at Arkansas College in 1988. The informant is anonymous and unrecorded. The motif is E291: *Ghosts protect hidden treasure.*

29. Lorrie Jenkins is from Newport, Arkansas, and a chemistry major at Arkansas College who recorded legends from several members of her family from several towns in the state for a course in Ozark folklore, 1988.

30. E2911.1: *Person killed to provide guardian ghost.*

31. Collected by Melissa Calley at Arkansas College (see her paper above). This is another example of E291: *Ghosts protect hidden treasure.*

32. See George Lankford, "Jayhawker Stories As Treasure Legends," *Kentucky Folklore Record* 32 (1986): 110–17.

33. See, for example, Jan Harold Brunvand, *The Vanishing Hitchhiker: American Urban Legends and Their Meaning* (New York: W. W. Norton, 1981).

34. See William M. Clements, "The Jonesboro Tornado: A Case Study in Folklore, Popular Religion, and Grass Roots History" in *The Charm is Broken,* W. K. McNeil, ed. (Little Rock: August House, 1984), 126–38.

Notes to Folk Architecture in Arkansas

1. This chapter is dedicated to Mrs. John Quincy Wolf, my first mentor. Two notable studies are: Jean Sizemore, "Vernacular Houses in the Arkansas Ozarks," Ph. D. diss., University of Iowa, 1990; and Diane Tebbetts, "Traditional Houses of Independence County, Arkansas," *Pioneer America* 10 (June 1978): 37–55. Useful information about folk architecture may be gleaned from such works as Vance Randolph, *The Ozarks: An American Survival of Primitive Society* (New York: Vangard Press, 1931) and Paul Faris, *Ozark Mountain Folks: The Way They Were* (Little Rock: Rose, 1983). Contemporary accounts by travelers such as Friedrich W. Gerstäcker, *Wild Sport in the Far West: The Narrative of a German Wanderer beyond the Mississippi, 1837–1843* (Durham, NC: Duke University Press, 1968) and George W. Featherstonhaugh, *Excursion Through the Slave States from Washington on the Potomac, to the Frontier of Mexico: With Sketches of Popular Manners and Geological Notes* (New York: Harper and Brothers, 1844) and personal reminiscences such as Samuel H. Chester, *Pioneer Days in Arkansas* (Richmond, VA: Presbyterian Committee of Publication, 1927) are also useful. In gathering information, I am indebted to Linda Joslin, Jeff Lewellen, Skip Stewart-Abernathy, Cy Sutherland, and Parker Westbrook. I am also indebted to Drew Beisswenger and Diane Tebbetts for their comments on early drafts, but most of all, to Jean Sizemore whose insights provided much stimulus. For assistance with the illustrations, I thank Barbara Lindsey-Allen of

the Arkansas Historic Preservation Program, Gail Brannen of Armtrong State College, Diane Tebbetts, and Paul E. Pyle, Jr.

2. Fred B. Kniffen, "Louisiana House Types," *Annals of the Association of American Geographers* 55 (December 1965): 549–77.

3. Such studies include: Henry Glassie, *Pattern in the Material Folk Culture in the Eastern United States* (Philadelphia: University of Pennsylvania Press, 1967); Terry G. Jordan, *Texas Log Building: A Folk Architecture* (Austin: University of Texas Press, 1978); Fred B. Kniffen, "Folk Housing: Key to Diffusion," *Annals of the Association of American Geographers* 55 (December 1965): 549–77; and Fred B. Kniffen and Henry Glassie, "Building in Wood in the Eastern United States: A Time-Place Perspective," *The Geographical Review* 56 (1966): 38–66.

4. For example, the largest log barn in Hempstead County, measuring thirty-six feet by seventy feet, is linked to barns in southern Appalachia. Built for Ben Phillips in 1917, the barn has two passages that run perpendicular to each other, dividing the barn into four sections. Each section, however, consists of two log cribs flanking a passage in the double-crib manner. Overall, its size, proportion, and function make it much like a transverse-crib barn. The barn also has a loft that projects three to four feet over the first floor on all four sides. Precedence for this feature may be found in the cantilever barns of the Tennessee-North Carolina borderland. They are particularly common in Sevier County, Tennessee, and usually consist of a traditional multi-crib plan with a log first floor with an overhanging frame loft supported by cantilevered beams. Ben Phillips, farm journal of 1917–18, Earl Steed, Blevins, Arkansas; and Marian Moffett and Lawrence Wodehouse, *The Cantilever Barn in East Tennessee* (Knoxville: The University of Tennessee, 1984), 7.

5. Ruth Polk Patterson, *The Seed of Sally Good'n: A Black Family of Arkansas, 1833–1953* (Lexington: University Press of Kentucky, 1985).

6. Amos Rapoport, *House Form and Culture* (Englewood Cliffs, NJ: Prentice-Hall, 1969), 2 and Fred Kniffen, "Folk Housing: Key to Diffusion," *Annals of the Association of American Geographers* 55 (December 1965): 549–50. Ultimately, houses and steads may be viewed within the context of all man-made structures and spaces upon the land, or of what is called the cultural landscape. Included in this context are divisions of land into lots and fields, and patterns of settlement, even those of entire cities. There are numerous articles and books on the cultural landscape. For basic definitions and overview see J. B. Jackson, *Discovering the Vernacular Landscape* (New Haven, CT: Yale University Press, 1984) and John R. Stilgoe, *Common Landscape of America, 1560–1845* (New Haven, CT: Yale University Press, 1982).

7. Leslie C. Stewart-Abernathy, "Urban Farmsteads: Household Responsibilities in the City," *Historical Archeology* 20 (1986): 5–15.

8. See Sarah Brown, "The Storm Cellar: A Compass on the Homesteads of Rural Arkansas," *Mid-America Folklore* 12 (Summer 1984): 1–16.

9. Sarah Brown, "Log Construction in the Washington Area of Southwest Arkansas," unpublished manuscript, Washington, Arkansas, 1986, 25–32. See also Donald R. Brown, "Stone County Multiple Resource Area Nomination to the National Register of Historic Places" (Little Rock: Arkansas Historic Preservation Program), 1985.

10. See Jan Harold Brunvand, *The Study of American Folklore: An Introduction*, 2d ed. (New York: W. W. Norton, 1978), 3–4 and 302–18; Henry Glassie, *Pattern in the Material Folk Culture in the Eastern United States* (Philadelphia: University of Pennsylvania Press, 1968), 1–17; and Warren E. Roberts, "Folk Architecture," in *Folklore and Folklife: An Introduction*, ed. Richard M. Dorson (Chicago and London: University of Chicago Press, 1972), 281–93 for definitions of folk, popular, and elite architecture. Folk and popular architecture are collectively termed vernacular. An excellent bibliographic essay on vernacular architecture scholarship is Dell Upton, "Ordinary Buildings: A Bibliographical Essay on American Vernacular Architecture," *American Studies International* 19 (Winter 1981): 57–75. For contributions to scholarship see current and forthcoming volumes of *Perspectives in Vernacular Architecture* (University of Missouri Press).

11. Talbot Hamlin, *Greek Revival Architecture in America: Being an Account of Important Trends in American Architecture and American Life Prior to The War Between The States* (New York: Dover Publications, 1944), 256.

12. Mr. and Mrs. Charley Baxter, "Matthews House Nomination to the National Register of Historic Places," (Little Rock: Arkansas Historic Preservation Program), 1983.

13. F. Hampton Roy and Ralph J. Megna, *Charles L. Thompson and Associates: Arkansas Architects, 1885–1938* (Little Rock: August House, 1982), 26 and 32; and Jean Sizemore, Sandra Taylor Smith, and Mary D. Thomas, "The Charles L. Thompson Thematic Nomination to the National Register of Historic Places" (Little Rock, Arkansas Historic Preservation Program, 1982).

14. Sarah Brown, "Evening Shade Multiple Resource Area Nomination to the National Register of Historic Places" (Little Rock, Arkansas Historic Preservation Program, 1981).

15. "Great Log House Under Construction," *Arkansas Gazette*, 23 December 1938.

16. Anthony S. Riddle and Dianna S. Kirk, "Lakeport Plantation Nomination to the National Register of Historic Places" (Little Rock: Arkansas Historic Preservation Program, 1974).

17. Thomas W. Hanchett, "The Four Square House Type in the United States," in Camille Wells, ed., *Perspectives in Vernacular Architecture* (Columbia: University of Missouri Press, 1987), 51.

18. Most popular, for quick identification of American architectural styles, is John S. Poppeliers, Allen Chambers, and Nancy B. Schwartz, *What Style Is It? A*

Guide to American Architecture (Washington, DC: The Preservation Press, 1986). Two standard American architectural histories are: James Marston Fitch, *American Building: The Historical Forces that Shaped It* (New York: Schocken Books, 1973) and Leland M. Roth, *A Concise History of American Building* (New York: Harper and Row, 1979). Works on Arkansas architectural history include Robert W. Duffy, *Beginnings: Historic Architecture in Arkansas* (Little Rock: Arkansas Historic Preservation Program, 1979), F. Hampton Roy, Charles Witsell, and Cheryl Griffith Nichols, *How We Lived: Little Rock as an American City* (Little Rock: August House, 1984) and the film series by Gordon Brooks, producer, *Arkansas: Its Architectural Heritage, 1800–1861* (1982), *Arkansas: Its Architectural Heritage, 1865–1917* (1984), and *Arkansas: Its Architectural Heritage, 1918–present* (1986), available through the Arkansas Endowment for the Humanities.

19. Dell Upton, "Traditional Timber Framing," in *Material Culture of the Wooden Age*, ed. Brooke Hindle (Tarrytown, NY: Sleepy Hollow Press, 1981), 35.

20. The debate about which Old World immigrant group is responsible for bringing log construction to America has been between proponents of Scandinavian and German origin. A Swedish origin was supported early by Harold R. Shurtleff in *The Log Cabin Myth*. There is little question that the seventeenth-century settlers of New Sweden were the first to make extensive use of log construction. More recently, however, scholars, including Kniffen and Glassie, have stated that because of their comparatively few numbers, the Swedes did not transfer log building technology to the greater population. These scholars give credit to the German immigrants of the early eighteenth century. Harold R. Shurtleff, *The Log Cabin Myth* (Cambridge, MA: Harvard University Press, 1939). Kniffen and Glassie, "Building in Wood," 58–59.

21. Dell Upton, ed. *America's Architectural Roots: Ethnic Groups that Built America* (Washington, DC: The Preservation Press, 1986), 13.

22. Kniffen, "Folk Housing," 558.

23. Diane Tebbetts and Sarah Brown, "Independence County House May be Architectural Link to Colonial America" *Arkansas Preservation* 3 (Summer 1984): 5–6.

24. Upton, "Traditional Timber Framing," 59–60.

25. Fitch, *American Building*, 121; Roth, *A Concise History of American Architecture*, 121–22; and Upton, "Traditional Timber Framing," 88–90.

26. Steve Mitchell, Donald R. Brown, and Michael L. Swanda, "Board Shanty: Box Construction in White county, Arkansas," *Pioneer America Society Transactions* 10 (1987): 9–11 and Diane Tebbetts, "Traditional Houses of Independence County, Arkansas," *Pioneer America* 10 (June 1978): 43–44. Historic structures surveyors have developed a quick test for identifying box-

frame houses: if the structure sways under the force of a hearty shove, then it is probably of box-frame construction.

27. See Harley J. McKee, *Introduction to Early American Masonry: Stone, Brick, Mortar, and Plaster* (Washington, DC: The National Trust for Historic Preservation and Columbia University, 1973).

28. Henry Glassie states that "Perhaps the only place in the New World where the catted chimney remains common is in the Ouachita Mountains of Arkansas." Although Glassie may be correct about the relative prevalence of the Arkansas mud-cat chimney, he is mistaken about its general location. It is not the Ouachita Mountains where the mud-cat chimney is common, but the Gulf Coastal Plain of southern Arkansas. Glassie, *Pattern in Material Folk Culture*, 113. Amos McBride recalls the repair in 1913 or 1914 of the mud-cat chimney on the log Westmoreland house built in the 1890s near Prescott, Nevada County. According to Mr. McBride, mud-cat chimneys were common in the area when he was growing up because "you couldn't get no brick for nothin'." To repair the chimney, long (two to three-foot) bundles of crab-grass were dried in the sun. Then, mud was put into a barrel, inside which was a paddle. The paddle was turned by a circulating mule. This mechanism was much like that used to make sorghum molasses. As the mule walked and turned the paddle, the mud was worked to a smooth pliable consistency. Then, the long bundles of dried grass were rolled in the mud on a table. These grass and mud bundles were called cats. Making the cats, according to Mr. McBride, was the easy part. The hard part was the actual repair of the chimney. "You had to have an awfully strong fellow to throw those cats up to another fellow who would catch them and wrap them around the wood frame of the chimney." Interview with Amos McBride, near Prescott, Arkansas, 1981.

29. Upton, "Traditional Timber Framing," 61.

30. Frazier D. Neiman, *The "Manor House" Before Stratford: Discovering the Clifts Plantation* (Stratford, VA: Robert E. Lee Memorial Foundation, 1980), 31 and 38; and Dell Upton, "The Origins of Chesapeake Architecture," in *Three Centuries of Maryland Architecture*, ed. The Maryland Historic Trust (Annapolis, MD: The Maryland Historic Trust and the Society for the Preservation of Maryland Antiquities), 45–46.

31. For a discussion of the Georgian mind-set reflected in American architecture and material culture see James Deetz, *In Small Things Forgotten: The Archeology of Early American Life* (Garden City, NY: Anchor Books, 1977) and Henry Glassie, *Folk Housing in Middle Virginia: A Structural Analysis of Historic Artifacts* (Knoxville: University of Tennessee Press, 1975).

32. Washington, Arkansas, Southwest Arkansas Regional Archives, SMF 323.

33. Sizemore, "Vernacular Houses in the Arkansas Ozarks," 36–37.

34. Michael Southern, "The I-House as a Carrier of Style in Three Counties

of the Northeastern Piedmont," in *Carolina Dwelling*, ed. Doug Swaim (North Carolina State University, 1978), 70–83 discusses how one traditional house form built throughout the nineteenth century "carries" the successive wave of high architectural style.

35. Jay Edwards, "French," in *America's Architectural Roots: Ethnic Groups that Built America*, ed. Dell Upton (Washington, DC; The Preservation Press, 1986), 63–64.

36. Edwards, 63–65.

37. Edwards, 63–65.

38. John Vlach, "Afro-Americans," in *America's Architectural Roots*, ed. Upton, 42–45.

39. Edwards, "French," 64.

40. Pierce Lewis states that a single county in east-central New York probably had more true Greek Revival houses than the entire state of Alabama. Pierce Lewis, "Common Houses, Cultural Spoor," *Landscape* 19 (1974): 14.

41. Dell Upton, "Pattern Books and Professionalism: Aspects of the Transformation of Domestic Architecture in America, 1800–1860," *Winterthur Portfolio* 19 (Summer/Autumn 1984): 144–49.

42. Sizemore, "Vernacular Houses in the Arkansas Ozarks," 304–05.

Notes to Customs and Beliefs

1. The New Orleans *Picayune* March 19, 1837, headlined an article about Arkansas LIFE IN THE FAR WEST.

2. Richard A. Barrett, *Culture and Conduct: an Excursion in Anthropology.* (Belmont, CA: Wadsworth Publishing Company, 1984), 113

3. Maurie Sacks, "Computing Community at Purim Among Suburban Orthodox Jews," American Folklore Society Society Annual Meeting, 21 October 1987, 2.

4. Ernst Cassirer, *Language and Myth*, trans. Susanne K. Langer (New York: Dover Publications Inc. 1946), 33, 92.

5. Deidre LaPin, et al. *Hogs in the Bottom: Family Folklore in Arkansas* (Little Rock: August House, Inc., 1982).

6. Keith Sutton, "How 'bout Them Hogs," *Arkansas Game and Fish*, (January/February 1986): 29.

7. Patrick K. Ford, trans. and ed., *Mabinogi and Other Medieval Welsh Tales* (Los Angeles: University of California Press, 1977), 119ff.

8. Charlene Smith, personal interview, 23 November 1987.

9. Tad Tuleja, "The Turkey," *American Wildlife in Symbol and Story*, Angus

K. Gillespie and Jay Mechling, eds. (Knoxville: University of Tennessee Press, 1987), 26–27.

10. Edythe Simpson Hobson, personal interview, 20 May 1987.

11. Mildred Johnson Smith, director, Museum of Black History, Old Washington, Arkansas, personal interviews, 12 July 1987, 3 February 1989.

12. Mildred Smith.

13. Mildred Smith.

14. Terri Hines, "The Ways," research paper, University of Arkansas at Little Rock, 1987.

15. Margaret Ann Millar, "Mary Jane Clark: Family Tradition Bearer," research paper, University of Arkansas at Little Rock, 1986.

16. Jerry Dean, "The Lovely Ghost of Lorance Creek Can Still Raise Hackles at Halloween," *Arkansas Gazette*, 26 Oct. 1986.

17. Alan Henry, personal interview, April 1986.

18. William A. Wilson, "The Deeper Necessity: Folklore and the Humanities," *Journal of American Folklore* 104 (1988): 166.

19. Peggy Huffman, "Witching for Water," *Rural Arkansas* (May 1981): 4.

20. Vance Randolph, *Ozark Magic and Folklore* (New York: Dover Publications, 1964), 85.

21. Mikhail Bakhtin, *Rabelais and His World*, trans. Helene Iswolsky (Bloomington: Indiana University Press, 1984), 91.

22. Averell Tate, "Arkansas Superstitions," research paper, University of Arkansas at Little Rock, 1985.

23. Nancy McDonough, *Garden Sass: A Catalog of Arkansas Folkways* (New York: Coward, McCann & Geoghegan, 1975), 271.

24. Lollie Miller, *Full Moon: Letters and Diaries* ed. Mary Meadearis (Old Washington, AR: Southwest Arkansas Regional Archives, 1987).

25. Randolph, 204.

26. W. C. Cunningham, personal interview, 3 June 1987.

27. Richard M. Dorson, *Bloodstoppers & Bearwalkers: Folk Traditions of the Upper Peninsula* (Cambridge, MA: Harvard University Press, 1952), 155; Randolph, 122ff.

28. Cheryl Anderson, "Stoppin' Blood," research paper, University of Arkansas at Little Rock, 1987.

29. Anderson.

30. Roberta Miller, personal interview, 9 April 1988.

31. Otto Rayburn, *Otto Rayburn's Folk Encyclopedia* Vol. C-16, Special Collections Department, David W. Mullins Library, University of Arkansas, Fayetteville.

32. Mildred Smith.

33. Mildred Smith.

34. Polly Robertson, personal interview, 13 October 1986.

35. Verona Goodwin, "Homing," research paper, University of Arkansas at Little Rock, 1986.

36. Marilyn Hambrick Sickel, personal interview, 5 December 1988.

37. Cassirer, 92.

38. Hobson.

39. Eugene D. Genovese, *Roll, Jordan, Roll: The World the Slaves Made* (New York: Pantheon Books, 1974), 200.

40. Hines.

41. Goodwin.

42. Willa Howard, personal interview, 6 August 1987.

43. Goodwin.

44. Mary Webb, personal interviews, 18 May, 6 August 1987.

45. Sacks, 2.

46. Patricia Washington McGraw, personal interview, 29 November 1988.

47. Cunningham.

48. Leo Ryles, personal interview, 27 May 1987.

49. Mrs. R. C. Childress, personal interview, 7 July 1987.

50. Queen Ester Smith, personal interview, 18 May 1987.

51. Jack Santino, "Occupational Ghostlore: Social Context and the Expression of Belief," *Journal of American Folklore* 101 (1988): 217.

Notes to Traditional Arkansas Foodways

1. Fred W. Allsopp, *Folklore of Romantic Arkansas*, Vol. 2 (New York: Grolier Society, 1931), 51.

2. In B. A. Botkin, ed. *Lay My Burden Down: A Folk History of Slavery* (Chicago: University of Chicago Press, 1945), 10.

3. Henry Morton Stanley, *The Autobiography of Sir Henry Morton Stanley*, ed. Dorothy Stanley (New York: Greenwood Press, 1969; orig. published, 1909), 146–47.

4. Orville W. Taylor, *Negro Slavery in Arkansas* (Durham, NC: Duke University Press, 1958), 137–38.

5. Taylor, 134.

6. Milton D. Rafferty, *The Ozarks: Land and Life* (Norman: University of Oklahoma Press, 1980), 148.

7. In Deirdre LaPin, Louis Guida, and Lois Patillo, *Hogs in the Bottom: Family Folklore in Arkansas* (Little Rock: August House, 1982), 104.

8. In Taylor, 132.

9. Nancy McDonough, *Garden Sass: A Catalog of Arkansas Folkways* (New York: Coward, McCann, & Geoghegan, 1975), 67–68.

10. Emmett Adams, "Wild Hoggin' in the Ozarks," *The Ozarks Mountaineer* (April 1981): 44.

11. Charles Arrowood, "There's a Geography of Humorous Anecdotes," in B. A. Botkin, ed., *A Treasury of Southern Folklore: Stories, Ballads, Traditions, and Folkways of the People of the South* (New York: Crown, 1949), 130.

12. Adams, 45.

13. Vance Randolph, *The Ozarks: An American Survival of Primitive Society* (New York: The Vanguard Press, 1931), 31–32.

14. Margaret [Jones] Bolsterli, "The Origins of Southern Taste," *Arkansas Times* (January 1986): 57.

15. Bolsterli, "Origins," 57.

16. Tate C. Page, *The Voices of Moccasin Creek*, N.p.: n.p., n.d., Tomlinson Library, Arkansas Tech University, Russellville, AR, 976.71/P145v2, c. 6, 246.

17. Page, 241.

18. Bolsterli, "Origins," 58.

19. McDonough, 73.

20. Friedrich Gerstäcker, *Wild Sports in the Far West*, trans. (New York: John W. Lovell, n.d.), 214–15.

21. In McDonough, 72.

22. Nannie Stillwell Jackson, *Vinegar Pie and Chicken Bread: A Woman's Diary of Life in the Rural South, 1890–1891*, ed. Margaret Jones Bolsterli (Fayetteville : University of Arkansas Press, 1982), 54.

23. Jackson, 34.

24. Allsop, 76–77.

25. In McDonough, 279.

26. In Charles W. Joyner, "Soul Food and the Sambo Stereotype: Foodlore from the Slave Narrative Collection," *Keystone Folklore Quarterly* 16 (1971): 175.

27. Scott Bond, *Life of Scott Bond* in Taylor, 134–35.

28. Fred Berry and John Novak, *The History of Arkansas* (Little Rock: Rose Publishing, 1987), 42.

29. Rafferty, 149.

30. Allsopp, 75–76.

31. Henry R. Schoolcraft, *Schoolcraft in the Ozarks*, Hugh Park, ed., Arkansas Historical Series 3 (Van Buren, AR: Press-Argus Printers, 1955), 95. Reprint of *Journal of a Tour into the Interior of Missouri and Arkansas in 1818 and 1819* (London: 1821).

32. Hallie Jabine-Sayle, "The Early Days of Arkansas," *Arkansas Pioneers* (January 1913). Reprinted in *Reminiscences of Arkansas Pioneers: Pages from the Arkansas Pioneers Magazine 1912–1916*, by Pulaski County Assn. of Arkansas Pioneers (Little Rock: n.p., 1986), 27.

33. Taylor, 135–36.

34. Gerstäcker, 154.

35. Vance Randolph, *We Always Lie to Strangers: Tall Tales from the Ozarks* (New York: Columbia University Press, 1951), 77.

36. McDonough, 88.

37. Margaret Jones Bolsterli, "The Very Food We Eat: A Speculation on the Nature of Southern Culture," *Southern Humanities Review* 16 (1982): 123–24.

38. Taylor, 137.

39. In McDonough, 158.

40. McDonough, 165.

41. McDonough, 162.

42. Jewell Kirby Fitzhugh, "Sorghum Time Meant Hard Work, Good Cookery," *The Ozarks Mountaineer* (October 1986): 65.

43. In McDonough, 168.

44. Gerstäcker, 278.

45. Jewell Kirby Fitzhugh, "Mama Knew Her Greens," *The Ozarks Mountaineer* (April 1981): 19.

46. McDonough, 9.

47. Pam Bristow, "Folk Food," unpublished paper, 1980, 15–16.

48. Thomas Nuttall, *A Journal of Travels into the Arkansas Territory During the Year 1819*, ed. Savoie Lottinville, American Exploration and Travel Series 66 (Norman: University of Oklahoma Press, 1980), 127.

49. Nancy Cooper Holoman Guinn, "Rural Arkansas in the '20's," *Arkansas Pioneers* (January 1913). Reprinted in *Reminiscences of Arkansas Pioneers: Pages from the Arkansas Pioneers Magazine 1912–1916*, by Pulaski County Assn. of Arkansas Pioneers (Little Rock: n.p., 1986), 33.

50. Sam Bowers Hilliard, *Hog Meat and Hoecake: Food Supply in the Old South, 1840–1860* (Carbondale: Southern Illinois University Press, 1972), 50.

51. Hilliard, 50.

52. Jewell Kirby Fitzhugh, "Light Bread Tops Favorite Recipes of Past," *Arkansas Democrat* (Little Rock), Sunday Magazine, 23 July 1967, 11.

53. Fitzhugh, "Light Bread."

54. McDonough, 74.

55. Bristow, 3.

56. In McDonough, 75–76.

57. In Bristow, 7–8.

58. Jewell Kirby Fitzhugh, "Vinegar: Household Product of Many Uses," *The Ozarks Mountaineer* (September 1974): 38.

59. Taylor, 138n. 40.

60. Maya Angelou, *I Know Why the Caged Bird Sings* (New York: Bantam, 1971), 19.

61. Allsop, 103–04.

62. In McDonough, 121.

63. In McDonough, 122.

64. In Bristow, 11.

65. In McDonough, 140–41.

66. Lucy Dietrich, personal interview, 9 April 1983.

67. Gerstäcker, 221–22.

68. Gerstäcker, 265–66.

69. Angelou, 115–16.

70. John Gould Fletcher, "Polk County Possum Club," *Arkansas Gazette*, 5 Jan. 1941, Sunday Magazine, 3.

71. Stephen Steed, "43rd Annual Coon Supper a Success at Gillette," *Arkansas Gazette*, 12 Jan. 1986.

72. In Allsopp, 127.

73. Vance Randolph, *Ozark Magic and Folklore* (New York: Dover, 1964), 53–71. Reprint of *Ozark Superstitions* (New York: Columbia University Press, 1947).

74. Patrick Dunahoo, *Cotton, Cornbread, and Cape Jasmines: Early Life on the Plantations of the Arkansas River Delta* (Benton, AR: privately printed, 1985), 82–83.

75. Louise Harms, personal interview, 7 March 1983.

76. Margaret [Jones] Bolsterli, ed., Introduction, *Vinegar Pie and Chicken Bread: A Woman's Diary of Life in the Rural South, 1890–1891*, by Nannie Stillwell Jackson (Fayetteville: University of Arkansas Press, 1982), 16.

77. Bolsterli, Introduction, 27–35.

78. John Gould Fletcher, *Arkansas* (Chapel Hill: University of North Carolina Press, 1947), 375.

79. Dietrich.

80. Berry and Novak, 142.

81. In Allsopp, 279–81.

Notes to Folk Festivals and Celebrations

1. See *Sing Out! The Folk Song Magazine* 33, no. 3 (Spring 1988), for a list—by no means exhaustive—of 177 folk festivals. See also Joseph T. Wilson and Lee Udall, *Folk Festivals: A Handbook for Organization and Management* (Knoxville: University of Tennessee Press, 1982).

2. For information of the public sector roles of folklorists, see Burt Feintuch, ed., *The Conservation of Culture: Folklorists and the Public Sector* (Lexington: University Press of Kentucky, 1988).

3. Basic sources on folkloristic approaches to the study of festivals are Jan Harold Brunvand, *The Study of American Folklore, An Introduction*, 3d ed. (New York: W. W. Norton & Co., Inc., 1986), 328–49; Robert J. Smith, "Festivals and Celebrations," in *Folklore and Folklife, An Introduction*, ed. Richard M. Dorson (Chicago: University of Chicago Press, 1972), 159–72; and Beverly J. Stoeltje, "Festival in America," in *Handbook of American Folklore*, ed. Richard M. Dorson with Inta Gale Carpenter (Bloomington: Indiana University Press, 1983), 239–46. An important collection of theoretical essays on festival by folklorists and other students of culture is Victor Turner, ed., *Celebration: Studies in Festivity and Ritual* (Washington: Smithsonian Institution Press, 1982).

4. Arnold Van Gennep, *The Rites of Passage*, Monika B. Vizedom and Gabrielle and L. Caffee, trans. (Chicago: University of Chicago Press, 1961).

5. "We'd give a forty-year service pin, too," said Earlene Baker, assistant vice-chancellor for Finance and Administration, "but I've never heard of anyone making it that far. The pins are all the same, except for the different numbers." Telephone interview, Fayetteville, Arkansas, August 1, 1988. I also learned about University of Arkansas retirement policies from Koda Vanderlip, accounting supervisor in Personnel Services, in a telephone interview on July 26, 1988.

6. Mick McKinnis, taped interview, Fayetteville, Arkansas, August 8, 1983. Subsequent citations attributed to McKinnis are to this interview.

7. John Abbott, taped interview, Fayetteville, Arkansas, September 8, 1983. Subsequent citations attributed to Abbott are to this interview.

8. Head Motherfucker in Charge. Asked if Al Jamison had ever so described himself, McKinnis said, "Hell, no! I used to call myself that, sometimes."

9. See I Kings 1:1–4.

10. References to *King Lear* are to Act I, scene 1, line 40 and line 138.

11. Under the title "The Hopes of Heaven our Support under Trials on Earth," this hymn by Isaac Watts (1674–1748) first appeared in *Hymns and Spiritual Songs* (1707). The melody to which it is usually sung today first appeared in print in Ananias Davisson's *Kentucky Harmony* (1817) but almost certainly predates that publication.

12. The data for this description of a typical gospel anniversary were gathered during a survey project conducted for the Texarkana Historical Museum in the summer of 1984 and during work on a documentary video in collaboration with Deborah Nolan Luster in the fall of 1987. The latter project was funded in part by the Arkansas Arts Council. For a view of a different aspect of gospel performance, see Anthony Heilbut, *The Gospel Sound: Good News and Bad Times*, rev. ed. (New York: Limelight, 1985); and Kip Lornell, *"Happy in the Service of the Lord": Afro-American Gospel Quartets in Memphis* (Urbana: University of Illinois Press, 1988). The Center for the Study of Southern Culture at the University of Mississippi recently started publishing *Rejoice: The Magazine of Gospel Music* on a quarterly basis.

Index